DO YOU Read ME?

ROBIN PEEL

BLACKWELL
EDUCATION

CONTENTS

TO USERS OF *DO YOU READ ME?*

Do You Read Me? and the National Curriculum

Do You Read Me? has been developed from experience of devising, teaching and examining English and English Literature courses.

The activities, assignments and resource material in *Do You Read Me?* satisfy the requirements of the Attainment Targets and Programmes of Study for Key Stage 4 in the National Curriculum. Students undertake varied, stimulating and stretching tasks, which provide opportunities to practise and develop the skills that will be assessed at the end of Key Stage 4, currently through GCSE.

The Teacher's Book for *Do You Read Me?* gives a complete correlation of Units to the Attainment Targets and Programmes of Study for English.

The chart below shows how *Do You Read Me?* fits with the levels of English in the National Curriculum.

PROFILE COMPONENTS

	SPEAKING AND LISTENING (AT 1)	READING (AT 2)	WRITING (ATs 3 and 4/5)
	Do You Read Me? sources, activities and assignments develop students' capacity to express themselves effectively in a variety of speaking and listening activities, matching style and response to audience and purpose. The units in this column are those where source material or assignments relate to a Level.	*Do You Read Me?* encourages students to read widely, across genres and across time. The organisation of the book encourages students to read, understand and respond to all types of writing. The units in this column are those where source material or assignments relate to a Level.	*Do You Read Me?* sources, activities and assignments develop the ability to construct and convey meaning in written language, matching style to audience and purpose. The units in this column are those where source material or assignments relate to a Level.
Level 5	How to use this book, 1.1, 1.2, 1.3, 1.5, 2.1, 2.3, 2.6, 2.7, 2.9, 2.12, 2.13, 3.1, 3.2, 3.8, 3.12, 4.3, 4.4, 4.7, 4.8, 4.9, 5.1, 5.2	How to use this book, 1.1, 1.2, 1.3, 1.4, 2.1, 2.5, 2.6, 2.7, 2.8, 2.9, 2.10, 2.12, 3.1, 3.2, 3.4, 3.7, 3.9, 3.10, 3.11, 3.12, 4.1, 4.2, 4.3, 4.4, 4.5, 5.1, 5.2	How to use this book, 1.1, 1.2, 1.3, 2.1, 2.3, 2.4, 2.6, 2.7, 2.9, 2.12, 3.1, 3.2, 3.3, 3.4, 3.7, 3.8, 4.1, 4.2, 4.4, 4.8, 5.1, 5.2
Level 6	1.1, 1.3, 1.5, 2.1, 2.3, 2.4, 2.6, 2.7, 2.8, 2.9, 2.10, 2.12, 2.13, 3.1, 3.2, 3.8, 3.12, 4.3, 4.4, 4.5, 4.7, 4.8, 4.9, 5.1, 5.2	How to use this book, Introduction to Genre, 1.1, 1.2, 1.3, 1.4, 2.1, 2.3, 2.4, 2.5, 2.6, 2.7, 2.8, 2.9, 2.10, 2.11, 2.12, 3.1, 3.2, 3.3, 3.4, 3.6, 3.7, 3.8, 3.9, 3.10, 3.11, 3.12, 4.1, 4.2, 4.3, 4.5, 4.7, 4.8, 5.1, 5.2	How to use this book, 1.1, 1.2, 1.3, 2.1, 2.3, 2.4, 2.6, 2.7, 2.9, 2.10, 2.12, 3.1, 3.2, 3.3, 3.4, 3.5, 3.7, 3.8, 3.12, 4.1, 4.2, 4.3, 4.4, 4.7, 4.8, 5.1, 5.2
Level 7	1.2, 1.3, 1.5, 2.2, 2.3, 2.4, 2.6, 2.7, 2.8, 2.9, 2.10, 2.12, 2.13, 3.1, 3.6, 3.8, 3.9, 3.10, 3.12, 4.1, 4.2, 4.3, 4.4, 4.5, 4.7, 4.8, 4.9, 5.1, 5.2	1.2, 1.4, 2.2, 2.3, 2.5, 2.6, 2.7, 2.8, 2.9, 2.10, 2.11, 2.12, 2.13, 3.1, 3.3, 3.4, 3.5, 3.6, 3.7, 3.8, 3.10, 3.11, 3.12, 4.1, 4.2, 4.3, 4.4, 4.5, 4.6, 4.7, 4.8, 5.1, 5.2	1.1, 1.5, 2.3, 2.4, 2.6, 2.7, 2.9, 2.10, 2.11, 2.12, 3.1, 3.3, 3.5, 3.7, 3.8, 3.9, 3.10, 3.11, 3.12, 4.1, 4.2, 4.3, 4.4, 4.5, 4.8, 5.1, 5.2
Level 8	1.1, 1.5, 2.1, 2.2, 2.3, 2.4, 2.6, 2.9, 2.10, 2.11, 2.12, 2.13, 3.1, 3.6, 3.8, 3.9, 3.10, 3.12, 4.1, 4.2, 4.3, 4.4, 4.5, 4.6, 4.7, 4.8, 4.9, 5.1, 5.2	2.2, 2.3, 2.5, 2.6, 2.7, 2.8, 2.9, 2.10, 2.11, 2.12, 2.13, 3.1, 3.3, 3.4, 3.5, 3.6, 3.8, 3.9, 3.10, 4.1, 4.2, 4.3, 4.4, 4.5, 4.6, 4.7, 4.8, 5.1, 5.2	1.5, 2.3, 2.6, 2.9, 2.10, 2.11, 2.12, 3.1, 3.3, 3.4, 3.5, 3.7, 3.8, 3.9, 3.10, 3.11, 3.12, 4.1, 4.2, 4.3, 4.4, 4.5, 4.6, 4.8, 5.1
Level 9	2.2, 2.6, 2.9, 2.10, 2.11, 2.12, 2.13, 3.1, 3.6, 3.8, 3.9, 3.12, 4.1, 4.2, 4.3, 4.4, 4.5, 4.6, 4.7, 4.8, 4.9, 5.1, 5.2	2.2, 2.3, 2.6, 2.9, 2.10, 2.11, 2.12, 2.13, 3.1, 3.3, 3.4, 3.5, 3.6, 3.7, 3.9, 4.1, 4.2, 4.3, 4.5, 4.6, 4.7, 4.8, 5.1	2.2, 2.3, 2.9, 2.10, 2.11, 2.12, 3.1, 3.3, 3.4, 3.5, 3.7, 3.8, 3.9, 3.10, 3.11, 3.12, 4.1, 4.2, 4.3, 4.4, 4.5, 4.6, 5.1
Level 10	2.2, 2.6, 2.9, 2.10, 2.11, 2.12, 2.13, 3.1, 3.6, 3.8, 3.12, 4.1, 4.2, 4.3, 4.4, 4.7, 4.8, 4.9, 5.1, 5.2	2.2, 2.3, 2.9, 2.10, 2.11, 2.12, 2.13, 3.1, 3.4, 3.5, 3.6, 3.7, 3.9, 4.1, 4.2, 4.6, 4.7, 4.8, 5.1	2.2, 2.3, 2.10, 2.11, 2.12, 3.1, 3.3, 3.4, 3.5, 3.7, 3.8, 3.9, 3.10, 3.11, 3.12, 4.1, 4.2, 4.3, 4.5, 4.6, 5.1
All levels	Teacher's Book	Teacher's Book	Teacher's Book

HOW TO USE THIS BOOK

Do You Read Me? is a book which can be used in a number of ways.

- It can be used for Individual Study. It is possible to work through the book on your own, selecting the activities which you feel you can do well.

- It can be used by Groups working on separate units, with the teacher circulating. At various points the teacher may wish to stop the work and ask one group or another to comment on the point of the unit they have been working on, and report to the class on what they have understood and learnt.

- It can be used by the whole class working on the same unit and then either progressing to the same activity or to separate activities.

Whether a single approach is adopted, or, as is more likely, a combination of approaches, the work will result in the production of a wide range of coursework, opportunities for discussion, and examination practice, thus preparing you for a wide range of syllabuses. All you need to know are the exact requirements of the syllabus you are following. You will get that information from your teacher, or the relevant examination boards.

Coursework

Coursework Requirements

If you are following a straightforward GCSE English course you will probably have to submit between five and ten units of coursework in a folder, depending on the Board and the syllabus. Each coursework unit should be about 500 words in length.

If you are following a GCSE (Mature) syllabus the coursework requirements may be more substantial. For instance, the LEAG (Mature) syllabus (100% coursework) requires you to submit four single units of work, but each unit should normally be between 1,000 and 1,200 words in length.

If you are following a GCSE course within CPVE or TVEI then you may be able to use some of your project work as GCSE coursework units.

Building up Coursework

Although coursework requirements vary from Examining Board to Examining Board, you will normally be asked to submit between five and ten pieces, demonstrating a variety of work, including imaginative, transactional, argumentative and personal response writing. You should try to develop a sense of audience and structure, and achieve a high standard of presentation and mechanical accuracy. Each piece of coursework should be around 500 words in length, or, alternatively, could be made up of several smaller pieces – for example, two letters and a report which are related in some way, each consisting of 160 words. (See Teachers' Book).

Ideally, the pieces should be fronted by a cover sheet giving details of the talk, source material and conditions (home or classroom?). You (and your teacher) will choose the best pieces and put them in a folder. Present the work attractively, with clear and legible handwriting.

At least one piece of coursework usually has to be done in classroom conditions. The others can be done at home or in the library. You are encouraged to do a draft version, discuss that with a teacher, and then write out an improved version.

Some boards require that one piece should be a response to literature. If you are following a mature syllabus the literary element may be in the examination, and your coursework pieces may be much longer (around 1,000 words) but fewer in number.

Remember that during your course you will do far more pieces of writing than you can include in your folder when it is finally submitted, but this will allow you to select the best pieces. Of course you must ensure that your folder includes the required range of work, which usually means it must contain at least three of the following:

Checklist: Types of Writing	Examples
Personal Response to Literature	Poem, Prose, Drama or Videotext
Informative Writing	Letters, Reports, Instructions
Imaginative Writing	Stories, Personal Experience Writing, Descriptive Prose or Poetry
Opinion or Discursive Writing	Arguing a case, or presenting the pros and cons of a position before offering a view

Before You Begin

Marking Strategy: What is good writing?

Before you begin, talk about what you would like to see rewarded in your work. Agree about what constitutes good English. Can written work be 'good' without being:

◆ Clear?
◆ Spelt accurately?
◆ Paragraphed appropriately?
◆ Interesting?
◆ In clear handwriting?
◆ Punctuated properly?

Put these qualities in order of importance.

Self-Assessment: Questionnaire

We all have some problems with English, and the purpose of this questionnaire is to discover the pattern of your problem. The results will be kept confidential, so try to be frank in your assessment of your strengths and weaknesses. Make a copy of the questionnaire below. (There is a photocopiable master in the *Do You Read Me?* Activity Book if your teacher has a copy.) For each of the items, ring one of the numbers 1 to 7. 1 means that the subject causes you no problem whatsoever, 7 indicates that it causes you considerable difficulty, while 4 means that it is neither particularly easy nor difficult.

Using a copy of this questionnaire, assess your own strengths and weaknesses.

Spelling		1 2 3 4 5 6 7
Punctuation	Full stops	1 2 3 4 5 6 7
	Commas	1 2 3 4 5 6 7
	Speech Marks	1 2 3 4 5 6 7
	Apostrophes	1 2 3 4 5 6 7
	Colon/Semicolon/Dash	1 2 3 4 5 6 7
	Capital Letters	1 2 3 4 5 6 7
Vocabulary	Understanding the words you meet	1 2 3 4 5 6 7
	Finding the words you want	1 2 3 4 5 6 7
Handwriting		1 2 3 4 5 6 7
Essays	Thinking of ideas	1 2 3 4 5 6 7
	Starting	1 2 3 4 5 6 7
	Ending	1 2 3 4 5 6 7
	Paragraphing	1 2 3 4 5 6 7
	Writing too much	1 2 3 4 5 6 7
	Writing too little	1 2 3 4 5 6 7
Writing	Stories	1 2 3 4 5 6 7
	Your opinions	1 2 3 4 5 6 7
	Descriptions	1 2 3 4 5 6 7
	Technical Descriptions	1 2 3 4 5 6 7
Understanding	Understanding the passage	1 2 3 4 5 6 7
	Understanding the questions	1 2 3 4 5 6 7
	Writing what you mean	1 2 3 4 5 6 7
Working too slowly		1 2 3 4 5 6 7
Examination timing		1 2 3 4 5 6 7
Writing notes	for yourself	1 2 3 4 5 6 7
	for others	1 2 3 4 5 6 7
Letters	Layout — personal	1 2 3 4 5 6 7
	Layout — formal	1 2 3 4 5 6 7
	Getting the content right	1 2 3 4 5 6 7
	Getting the right tone/style	1 2 3 4 5 6 7
Writing reports		1 2 3 4 5 6 7
Thinking clearly		1 2 3 4 5 6 7
Answering questions in class		1 2 3 4 5 6 7
Asking questions in class		1 2 3 4 5 6 7
Using a library for reference purposes		1 2 3 4 5 6 7
Talking in a small group		1 2 3 4 5 6 7
Giving a talk		1 2 3 4 5 6 7

You may wish to keep a personal record of your progress by making a much bigger copy of the following table. Fill it in each week.

WEEK COMMENCING:			
Day	Describe what you have learnt each day	Describe the methods you have used	Coursework completed
Monday			
Tuesday			
Wednesday			
Thursday			
Friday			
Saturday			

Alternatively, you may wish to keep a log or journal describing each day's work. This log or journal can be handed in at the end of the course as a piece of coursework.

Drafting and Editing

The draft version of a piece of writing should consist of notes, a rough outline and a loosely written version. Only after completing a draft version should you do your final, carefully written version. Here is a sample draft version of a well-known story.

NOTES

Egg
Wall
Crash
King's Horses
King's Men

OUTLINE

Humpty Dumpty – egg – sits on wall – falls off – smashes –
King's Horses – King's Men – arrive – fail to put him back together

LOOSELY WRITTEN VERSION

Humpty Dumpty sat on a wall and fell all the way to the ground,
where – being an egg – he was smashed to pieces.
King's Horses and King's Men arrived but could not reassemble
Humpty Dumpty.

Get into the habit of writing an initial draft version which you then go on to discuss with someone. Then write an improved version. The finished unit of work may represent the fruits of three or four separate drafts, spread over several weeks.

For example, try improving the third version of the Humpty Dumpty story by incorporating some of the following suggestions:

- What did he look like?
- When did the accident happen?
- What was he thinking?
- What words were spoken?
- What were the feelings of the King's Men?

Opening Up: Reading Books

We are all users of language. We speak, we fill in forms, but we do not all read books. Yet we all like stories. That is partly why we go to the cinema and watch television. It seems that the older children get, the less they read the books that provide stories. Why should this be? Here is a newspaper article aimed at adults, that considers this question.

If you were given a book or a book token for a present would you be pleased or disappointed?

Coming to the End of a Chapter

Richard Bourne

from
The Guardian.

*Is there?
Discuss*

Are these the reasons teenagers do not read much?

*What does this mean?
Is it true?*

Why is it that there is often a decline in the amount of a child's reading at around the age of 14? A whole lot of problems, from poor performance in public exams at 16 to regression to semi-literacy among adults, could be tackled more effectively if we had the answer.

Pauline Heather, at the Centre for Research on User Studies at Sheffield University, has just completed a detailed study of the leisure reading of 60 youngsters aged 13 to 15. Using a series of interviews and the diaries they kept themselves, she shows that for around 40 per cent of them, the book reading habit is almost non-existent; fewer than half spent over two hours a week reading any book, non-fiction or fiction, for their own pleasure.

It is not as though the children who do not read books are necessarily living circumscribed or TV orientated lives, or never see a book in their own home. Many who do not read books are still avid readers of teenage magazines. Helen, one of the girls in the study who did not read books, went to the local leisure centre with friends most evenings, to the youth club once a week, and watched an hour of television each night as well as doing an hour's homework. Phillip, who was reading both car books and Enid Blyton, was at one point claiming that he spent 10 hours a week reading, but had virtually stopped altogether by the end of the 18 month study.

Many of the reasons that the children themselves gave for not reading, or reducing their reading of books, were justifications rather than explanations. They talked about the pressures of exams, the summer holidays, family commitments and a difficulty in finding suitable books to read. However those who read more, also referred to the time available in the school holidays, and said they had found better books to read.

Pauline Heather accepts that school holidays create a disruption in children's reading habits, for better or worse, but does not consider that either television, homework or leisure activities correlate well with leisure reading. However she does find that, as teenagers grow older, there is a move from more solitary to more gregarious activities.

The main reason she is sceptical about the explanation of lack of time, the effect of increased homework and so on, is the heavy reading of magazines she reports. "There is no marked decline in magazine reading during the study, and the majority of the pupils read magazines. As some pupils read more than one magazine this must take up quite a lot of their time. The most popular magazines were those covering Airfix modelling, football, motor bikes, and World War II. The most popular teenage magazines were Jackie, Patches and My Guy.

The study confirms that there is a tailing off of book reading at this time in a young person's life, but the author considers that the roots lie in earlier habits and experience.

Do you see your parents reading— often? rarely? never?

Those who were ceasing to be book readers were more likely to have a father in a manual occupation, or one or more parents who did not read books themselves. Schools which did not have class libraries, library lessons, and silent reading periods, a qualified librarian, a school bookshop, or school book club were also more likely to have non-readers of books.

One of the clearest conclusions is the importance of buying and owning books in developing a youngster's private reading: 68 per cent of the sample bought books and this was the biggest source of books they read, slightly ahead of both the public library and borrowings from friends and family. Each of these sources was more than twice as important as the school library.

This may help to still the anxieties of English teachers who have often felt instinctively that choosing and buying your own book is one of the best supports for leisure reading, but who have felt uncomfortable at becoming an arm of the commercial book trade. The report suggests that schools should have some arrangement for selling books, as well as collections available for borrowing and use in work and leisure areas outside the library.

How important are book jackets?

In school libraries, books should be displayed so that pupils can see the jacket. Magazines should be available and books should be displayed by type – science fiction, horror, mystery, and so on. "Pupils would probably be more likely to use school libraries if more books based on television programmes and films were stocked".

Have you read any books as a result of seeing a film or television programme?

The teenage sections in public libraries were popular, although pupils of this age would never go into a children's section. Pauline Heather believes that public libraries could do more to provide suggested reading lists, perhaps on a national basis, of books on particular themes; these could combine fiction and non-fiction. In general she feels that a lot of young people are unaware of new fiction for teenagers and English teachers as well could do more to read from and discuss it.

How many of you belong to a public library?

The actual books which happened to be read by the Sheffield and Derbyshire children during the study included many by Isaac Asimov, Agatha Christie, Enid Blyton, Catherine Cookson, Ian Fleming, James Herriott and Douglas Reeman. There were also a number by authors who had made a hit with this particular age group – Willard Price, E. E. Smith and J. R. R. Tolkien. The non-fiction had a strong bias to war, machinery, and sport, as though this was being defined to a large extent in terms of boys' interest. Not much of this literature could be described as improving in the Victorian sense, but it was greatly enjoyed by the readers.

Do you recognise these authors?

Opening Up: Reading Magazines

Here is another newspaper article, this time about reading magazines.

Who is the article aimed at?

*Do you agree?
Are teenagers influenced by comics or magazines*

Do you think the girls and boys at your school or college have equal opportunities?

Is Your Daughter being Brainwashed?

from the
Daily Mirror

What kind of paper is the Daily Mirror? Why is it called 'the Mirror'? (Think of other newspaper names.)

Jackie, Britain's top teenage girls' magazine, celebrated its 1,000th issue this week. Almost every young girl reads it at some time, and one in three have bought it over two decades. That makes it very influential indeed.

"Twenty Years On and Still at the Top" blares the Press handout. But what has happened to Jackie readers? Twenty years on they're still at the bottom.

Girls, even in 1989, are lagging behind in almost every field at school and work despite attempts on their behalf to be more enlightened about education and provide equal opportunities.

Times have changed, but girls' images of themselves haven't. And where do they get those from? You've guessed it ...

Comics have an enormous influence on children. A survey has shown that a staggering 47 per cent of Britain's youngsters choose them as their favourite reading matter. And naturally they are affected by the contents.

In Jackie they learn that trendy girls don't do their homework. They're too busy dreaming about boys. But the fun really starts when the prey is caught. Jackie advises: ''If he still fusses about wanting to play darts with the lads when you've insisted he takes you to the disco, deal with him firmly. This is best done by bursting into tears ...''

Picture stories follow the same line. They usually start with a pretty girl dropping her shopping or losing her pet dog in the hope that some handsome boy will come to the rescue. It's the traditional image of girls in a nutshell: pretty, helpless, petulant and dumb.

How many girls in the class have read Jackie? How many boys?

'No wonder girls never get anywhere when they continually see themselves in this role,' says Rosemary Stones, a researcher at the Children's Rights Workshop. 'The teenage comics are the very worst. They took off in the Sixties with Romeo and Valentine and were full of handsome men with chiselled chins and girls with luxurious curls and six-inch eyelashes. Boys go from Hornet and Hotspur to DIY or car magazines, or even Playboy, I suppose. Girls are left in a soppy, romantic dreamland, where their one interest in life is to get – and keep – a man. Boys are taught teamwork, to stand together. Girls are told implicitly that other girls are spiteful, not to be trusted.'

In a quick survey of girls' comics like Judy, Debbie and Mandy, we found typical stories like Wee Slavey, about a cruelly abused servant girl from the 18th century, and Educated Edith, the tale of a talented girl who has to skimp on her schoolwork to look after her poor, sick father. But it isn't only girls who get a stereotyped image.

How many people in the class would agree that comics are their favourite reading matter?

Working-class kids are loud, scruffy and insolent. Middle-class kids are creepy and wet. Upper-class kids are snobbish and brutal. Nicholas Tucker, a psychologist who specialises in children's literature, says: 'Images in comics help children to back up the judgments and prejudices they see around them. The whole world of comics needs shaking up and bringing up to date.'

What attitude to these magazines does the writer have?

Jackie is looking forward to another steady twenty years' sales. By that time there might be a few more bright young girls around. And maybe, just maybe, they'll stop buying it.

You may like to compare the language used in this article with the language from the *Guardian* article on the previous page.

Opening Up: Writing

A Reading Log

A piece of coursework you could start straight away is a reading log or journal. Every time you read a newspaper article, magazine, short story, novel, poem or play, write a description of the piece and your response to it. Over the term this will build up into a record of your reading autobiography.

Autobiography

Or, you could write the first chapter of your own autobiography. Call it 'Self Portrait' or 'My Early Life'. Include, if you can:

+ information about where your grandparents came from,
+ information about where your parents came from and where they met,
+ information about your childhood.

PART 1: INTRODUCTION TO GENRE

Genre (pronounced 'johnrer') means 'type' or 'sort'. It is a word worth introducing very early because most English courses encourage you to become aware of different kinds of writing, and when it is suitable to use them.

In this book we will look at the various types and forms of writing that you will be asked to read or write, and in so doing we will distinguish between the demands and conventions of practical (sometimes called 'transactional') writing, as opposed to imaginative writing (stories, poems, etc.). Linked to this is the idea of purpose (why was the writing done?), readership (who was it intended for?) and expectation (what do we expect from each of the different types of writing?). We could list these a little more clearly as follows:

PURPOSE   What is the writer's purpose? What is the writer trying to achieve by using a particular genre?

READERSHIP   Does the writer have a particular readership in mind? Is he/she, for example, writing for children, for teenagers, for computer buffs?

EXPECTATION   As readers, what do we expect from this type of writing? For example, what would you expect from an AA Book or AIDS leaflet? How would this differ from what you expect from a short story?

As writers of letters or reports or discussion pieces we would be wise to satisfy the reader's expectations that we write clearly, accurately, and stick to the subject. But as writers of poems and stories we can afford to defy the reader's expectation and spring some surprises, as Benjamin Zephaniah does in the following poem:

According to my Mood

Benjamin Zephaniah

I have poetic licence, i WriTe thE
way i waNt.i drop my full stops where i
like... MY CAPITAL LeteRs go where i
liKE.
i order from MY PeN, i verse the
    way i like (i do my spelling write)
Acording to My MOod.
i HAve poetic licence,
i put my commers where i like ,,((()).
(((my brackets are write((
I REPEAT WHen i likE.
i can't go rong,
i look and i.c.
It's rite.
i REpeat when i liKe. i have
poetic licence!
don't question me????

The poet is using poetic licence to deviate from the usual rules of spelling and punctuation. You can play around with language in a poem. If this was meant to be a letter of application for a job it would be a disaster!

Finally, if you look at the contents page of this book you will see just how many different types of text we shall be considering: comics, magazines, TV programmes, films, pop lyrics, information writing, descriptions, anecdotes and others. But before we look at these, let us begin by focusing on the three genres of writing – prose, poetry and drama – with which English is primarily concerned.

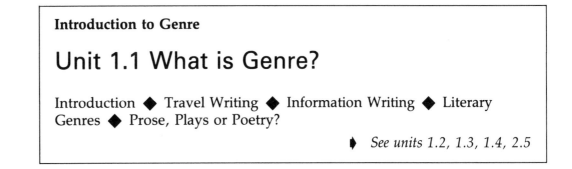

Introduction to Genre

Unit 1.1 What is Genre?

Introduction ◆ Travel Writing ◆ Information Writing ◆ Literary Genres ◆ Prose, Plays or Poetry?

◗ *See units 1.2, 1.3, 1.4, 2.5*

Introduction

One way of understanding the idea of genre is to think about the different types of films there are. We talk about thrillers, disaster movies, science fiction movies and murder mysteries, amongst others: these are all genres.

Another way of looking at it would be to consider the different types of music. Here are a few, shown in a diagram:

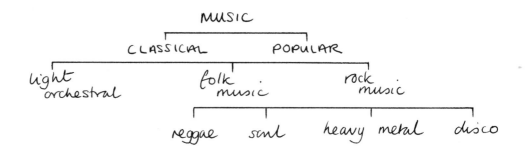

Draw your own diagram. See how much further you can go and how many different types of music you can identify. For instance, could you think of different types of Reggae, Soul or Disco to continue this 'family tree'? In groups compare your diagrams.

Now draw a similar diagram identifying different types of writing, starting with 'Text'.

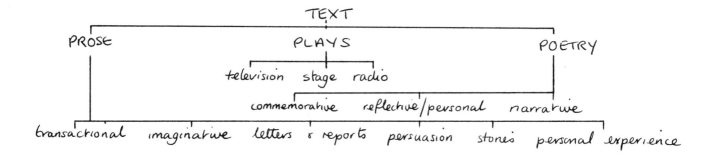

What is the point of classifying writing like this? A simple answer is that in all forms of English we are concerned with what things *mean*. A change in the shape or form of a piece of writing can change the meaning.

Travel Writing

Travel writing is a well-established form, and as the name suggests, is about the people, situations and scenery encountered in travel – at home or abroad. Here is a short piece of travel writing. It starts with a scene observed on someone's travels, leading to reflection:

One Less Octopus at Paxos

Russell Hoban

From *Granta 9* Penguin

We were at our regular swimming-place which is partly pebbly beach and partly big flat rocks when there came along in the shallows among the rocks by the shore a stocky young woman in a hooded wet-suit top with a diving mask and a snorkel and flippers and a speargun and a big sheath-knife strapped to her right leg. She was nosing among the underwater rocks in an ardent and serious way like a dog at a rabbit hole. She fired the speargun, then held up the spear with an octopus writhing on it. It was a mottled pinky-brown and its head was about as big as two clasped hands.

She slid it off the spear, grabbed it by a couple of tentacles, and beat it again and again on a flat rock, spattering briny drops each time. The octopus clung to the rock with its free tentacles; they came away with sounds like kisses as she peeled it off the rock and put it into a plastic bag.

She had pushed up her mask and pushed back her hood. She had a dark face, a serious look and a heavy frown. She had a short dark curling hair. She had a squeeze-bottle of detergent; a bystander explained that she'd squirted it into the octopus's hiding-place in the rocks to make it come out (not being able to breathe) and be speared by her.

Later I found myself imagining that young woman's preparations for her trip to Paxos. I saw her at the windows of travel agents, I saw her turning the pages of brochures, I saw her looking at octopus pictures in books. I saw her marking off days on a calendar. I saw her at the supermarket, picking up bottles of detergent and reading their labels. I saw her packing her wet-suit, her mask and snorkel, her flippers, her speargun, her knife, her bottle of detergent. I saw her in the underground, sitting up straight with a serious face, going to Victoria. Her luggage was a rucksack and a diver's bag made of heavy PVC. I saw her on the train to Gatwick. I saw her checking in at the airline counter. I saw her on the plane to Corfu eating breakfast with a serious face, perhaps reading a diving magazine.

I saw her on the boat from Corfu to Paxos looking steadfastly at the sun-points on the water and watching for the shape of the island.

I saw her in her room unpacking the wet-suit, the mask and snorkel, the flippers, the speargun, the knife, the bottle of detergent. I saw her sitting on the bed looking down at her naked feet.

Questions

1. What do we learn about
   a the octopus?
   b the girl?
2. The passage falls into two parts – descriptive and imaginative. Imagine you are the writer, Russell Hoban. Your editor has told you that the piece ought to finish with the description at the end of the third paragraph. What argument could you put forward to support the inclusion of the second half of the article?

Activity

Jot down the places you have travelled to – either on holiday or to stay with friends or relatives. Write about a person, a place or an incident that sticks in your mind from a time when you were away from home. Write the account for publication in a travel magazine and follow your piece with a letter offering it for publication.

Information Writing

Animal Welfare

Animal Squad

This is Sid Jenkins (centre), a chief inspector with the RSPCA. In 1986 a BBC TV camera crew followed him around as he investigated cases of animal abuse. The programmes that followed shocked the nation. Across the country some 40 other chief inspectors are also engaged in similar work. They are supported by 210 inspectors and other staff. The workers in the field also need back-up from specialist departments based at the RSPCA's headquarters in West Sussex. These include Legal, Overseas, Parliamentary, Education, European, Research Animals, Animal Homes, Veterinary, Farm Animals, Wildlife and Special Investigations and Operations. The investigatory department officers are involved in undercover work on illegal activities such as dog fighting.

Facts and Figures

In 1986 over 83,000 complaints were investigated by RSPCA officers. That compared with 64,500 in 1985. 1986 saw 925 cases of cruelty to dogs and 190 cases of cruelty to cats. A total of 1911 convictions for cruelty to animals were obtained in 1986, and the number of cautions issued by inspectors as a result of complaints rose to 6800 from 4228 in 1985! Why is it, then, that more and more people are complaining about cruelty to animals? Is the public growing more cruel, or are people becoming increasingly concerned and reporting cases they see earlier and more often than before?

Punched, beaten, whipped – and all because it was hungry!

The young alsatian was hungry. When food arrived, the dog dashed across and started to gobble it down.

Its master was furious. He grabbed the poor animal and punched it. Then he beat it with a slipper, lashed at it with a riding crop and finally threw it bodily against a wall. The man's friends were horrified. The local RSPCA inspector was called and the culprit was convicted of cruelty. Happily the dog made a complete recovery and was given a good home with a caring owner. One of the RSPCA's important roles is to help educate people in knowing how to care for their animals properly so that incidents like this do not occur.

Things to notice
- The personal element is missing. The writer is giving us information, rather than revealing feelings and thoughts.
- The writing is packed with facts and figures.
- The writing is not impartial – it assumes that the RSPCA does good work.
- The sentences are short; the writing seems to be aimed at the general reader. It is not continuous; it is broken up into sections, making it easier to read.

Activities
1. Imagine you are Sid Jenkins: write a report of the young alsatian case. Begin 'I was called out to 25 Sherwood Way'.
2. Write a letter to your local RSPCA office, inviting an officer either to talk to the whole class or be interviewed by two members of the class.
3. 'People first, animals second.' Interview twenty people and ask them how they feel about dogs in towns. Are dogs a nuisance? Write up your findings.

Literary Genres

In this book we will be looking at many different types of text, including not only writing but also films and television. However, you would expect an English book to focus on written texts – literature – so let us start by looking at the three basic literary genres:

GENRE

Poetry

Mother's Nerves
My Mother said: if just once more
I hear you slam that old screen door
I'll tear my hair out
I'll dive in the stove
I gave it a bang
And in she dove.

Collected Poems
X. J. Kennedy

Prose

DEATH SPEAKS: There was a merchant in Baghdad who sent his servant to market to buy provisions and in a little while the servant came back, white and trembling, and said, Master, just now when I was in the marketplace I was jostled by a woman in the crowd and when I turned saw it was Death that jostled me. She looked at me and made a threatening gesture; now, lend me your horse, and I will ride away from this city and avoid my fate. I will go to Samarra and there Death will not find me. The merchant lent him his horse, and the servant mounted it, and he dug his spurs in its flanks and as fast as the horse could gallop he went. Then the merchant went down to the market-place and he saw me standing in the crowd and he came to me and said, Why did you make a threatening gesture to my servant when you saw him this morning? That was not a threatening gesture, I said, it was only a start of surprise. I was astonished to see him in Baghdad, for I had an appointment with him tonight in Samarra.

Collected Stories
Somerset Maugham

Plays

MEG:	Is that you, Petey?
	Pause
	Petey, is that you?
	Pause
	Petey?
PETEY:	What?
MEG:	Is that you?
PETEY:	Yes, it's me.
MEG:	What? (*her face appears at the hatch*) Are you back?
PETEY:	Yes.
MEG:	I've got your cornflakes ready. (*she disappears and reappears*) Here's your cornflakes. (*he rises and takes the plate from her, sits at the table, props up the paper and begins to eat. Meg enters by the kitchen door.*) Are they nice?
PETEY:	Very nice.
MEG:	I thought they'd be nice. (*she sits at the table*) You got your paper?
PETEY:	Yes.
MEG:	Is it good?
PETEY:	Not bad.
MEG:	What does it say?
PETEY:	Nothing much.
MEG:	You read me out some nice bits yesterday.
PETEY:	Yes, well, I haven't finished this one yet.
MEG:	Will you tell me when you come to something good?
PETEY:	Yes.
	Pause
MEG:	Have you been working hard this morning?
PETEY:	No. Just stacked a few of the old chairs. Cleaned up a bit.
MEG:	Is it nice out?
PETEY:	Very nice.
	Pause
MEG:	Is Stanley up yet?
PETEY:	I don't know. Is he?
MEG:	I don't know. I haven't seen him down yet.
PETEY:	Well, then, he can't be up.
MEG:	Haven't you seen him down?
PETEY:	I've only just come in.
MEG:	He must be still asleep.

The Birthday Party
Harold Pinter

Questions

1. What differences do you notice in the way these examples of genres are set out on the page?
2. Imagine that you cannot read English. What do you notice about the patterns of the words in each extract?
3. Consider the point of the Somerset Maugham story. Think about who is telling the story: titles often carry an important message.

Activities

1. Look again at the poem called 'Mother's Nerves', and then write about 400 words on the things that get on *your* nerves and the things that you do that might get on *other people's* nerves.
2. Write the Somerset Maugham story as a poem. Call it *Death Speaks*. Here are your first two lines:

   > Trembling and shaking the servant returned.
   > He has seen me in the Baghdad market.

3. Look again at the extract from the play and then write a five minute breakfast, tea time or Sunday lunchtime conversation that might take place in your home.

Prose, Plays or Poetry?

Look at these six extracts and decide whether they are taken from prose, plays or poetry. Give your reasons, after looking at the examples on the previous page.

1. In my childhood trees were green
   And there was plenty to be seen.

2. Stubbs: Him! . . .
   (There is a pause. Then Stubbs says)
   . . . All right, Humpty? Up you go. Get Pete's frisbee back for him.

3. On the day of the explosion
   Shadows pointed towards the pithead:
   In the sun the slagheap slept.

4. As he turned to go on, he spat speculatively. There was a sharp, explosive crackle that startled him. He spat again. And again, in the air, before it could fall to the snow, the spittle crackled. He knew that at fifty below spittle crackled on the snow, but this spittle had crackled in the air.

5. LECTRIC What's he on about?
   ADRIAN I don't know
   BILLY   An historical figure, called David Bowie . . .
   LECTRIC Who's he?

6. The tramp was big and squarely built, and he walked with the rolling stride of the long road, his steps too big for the little streets of the little town.

Warning

> Books will not always fit conveniently into the slots we make for them. Verse plays (plays written in verse) are both poetry and plays! Russell Hoban's *One Less Octopus at Paxos* could just as easily be called personal writing as information writing. On the other hand *Mother's Nerves* is definitely poetry and not prose.

Introduction to Genre

Unit 1.2 Genre: Prose

Introduction ◆ Dog Fight 1: non-fiction ◆ Dog Fight 2: fiction ◆ Fact or fiction? ◆ Prose or Poetry?

◗ *See units 2.6, 2.11, 3.4, 3.6, 3.7*

Introduction

Prose is the straightforward form in which most of us write. When we are not making something up we write non-fictional prose, often to persuade or argue. A large part of the writing you do in examination courses will be in the form of letters, essays, reviews and reports, all of which are non-fictional. But you will also write stories in prose.

Dog Fight 1: Non-fiction

The following article appeared in a newspaper. It is an account of a recent trial in which some men were accused of arranging dog fights, which are illegal. The article is non-fiction because it deals with facts; nothing has been made up or imagined here.

Dog Fight 1

Eleven men charged with offences connected with dog fighting appeared in court, at Cheshunt, Hertfordshire, yesterday in the first case of its kind in this century.

The prosecution said the alleged fight was in the opinion of an RSPCA inspector, "the most barbaric act of deliberate cruelty" he had ever dealt with.

The case featured a video recording allegedly made by the defendants which showed two bull terriers savaging each other for over 40 minutes, urged on by cheering men.

One of the dogs was so badly injured that despite three operations she had to be destroyed.

The prosecution said the fight was broken up when RSPCA investigators and police raided an old barn off Coopers Lane Road, Enfield, north London, on May 11.

Mr. David Waters, prosecuting, said that a dog-fighting ring had been fashioned out of old doors, which were stained with blood. Most of the gamblers and spectators had fled across the fields but were chased and caught or arrested later.

Mr. Waters said the fight was raided in a joint police and RSPCA operation. Two bull terriers were in the ring. A number of vehicles had been parked on the land to block entry to the area.

He said an outstanding feature of the case was that the spectators came from different parts of England to the fight. There would be considerable evidence that gambling was taking place.

When the officers surrounded the barn and entered a video camera was running. This recording was shown to the court yesterday.

The public were warned that it contained very upsetting scenes. A number of people left the court room during the showing, visibly upset.

The colour video allegedly showed two of the men accused of arranging the dog fight, Wilcoxson and Hossell.

The bull terriers, a Staffordshire bitch called Spice and a dog called King, clashed immediately the men holding them let go. One dog bit deeply into the other's head.

There were screams of pain as the animals mutilated each other and flashes from spectators' cameras lit up the ring. "It's a bit darker here than it was last time" said a voice.

The dogs were urged on by the men. The dog who appeared to be the stronger dragged the other animal around the ring, shaking it like a flimsy toy, "Look, his teeth are coming out," said an excited voice as the camera zoomed in then panned across the carpeted floor, which was now spotted in dark red blood.

After the fight, the bitch alleged to belong to Wilcoxson was examined by a vet who reported that the entire skin and muscle covering the lower jaw bone was ripped off, exposing the lower jaw-bone. The left lower canine tooth had been ripped out. The right upper canine tooth had been pulled out of its socket and the bridge of the animal's nose was badly bitten and its jaw flap extensively mauled.

The bitch had to be destroyed. The hearing continues.

We use the word fiction to describe that which is imagined or invented. Here is an example taken from a novel.

Dog Fight 2: Fiction

White Fang – half-dog, half-wolf and a great fighter – has finally met his match in the bulldog, Cherokee. They have been matched in a dog fight on which bets have been placed.

Dog Fight 2

from
White Fang
Jack London

And still the bull-dog, with grim certitude, toiled after him. Sooner or later he would accomplish his purpose, get the grip that would win the battle. In the meantime he accepted all the punishment the other could deal him. His tufts of ears had become tassels, his neck and shoulders were slashed in a score of places, and his very lips were cut and bleeding – all from those lightning snaps that were beyond his foreseeing and guarding.

Time and again White Fang had attempted to knock Cherokee off his feet; but the difference in their height was too great. Cherokee was too squat, too close to the ground. White Fang tried the trick once too often. The change came in one of his quick doublings and counter-circlings. He caught Cherokee with head turned away as he whirled more slowly. His shoulder exposed. White Fang drove in upon it; but his own shoulder was high above, while he struck with such force that his momentum carried him on across over the other's body. For the first time in his fighting history, men saw White Fang lose his footing. His body turned a half-somersault in the air, and he would have landed on his back had he not twisted, catlike, still in the air, in the effort to bring his feet to the earth. As it was, he struck heavily on his side. The next instant he was on his feet, but in that instant Cherokee's teeth closed on his throat.

It was not a good grip, being too low down toward the chest; but Cherokee held on. White Fang sprang to his feet and tore wildly around, trying to shake off the bull-dog's body. It made him frantic, this clinging, dragging weight. It bound his movements, restricted his freedom. It was like the trap, and all his instinct resented it and revolted against it. It was a mad revolt. For several minutes he was to all intents insane. The basic life that was in him took charge of him. The will to exist of his body surged over him. He was dominated by this mere flesh-love of life. All intelligence was gone. It was as though he had no brain. His reason was unseated by the blind yearning of the flesh to exist and move, at all hazards to move, to continue to move, for movement was the expression of its existence.

Round and round he went, whirling and turning and reversing, trying to shake off the fifty-pound weight that dragged at his throat. The bull-dog did little but keep his grip. Sometimes, and rarely, he managed to get his feet to the earth and for a moment to brace himself against White Fang. But the next moment his footing would be lost, and he would be dragging around in the whirl of one of White Fang's mad gyrations. Cherokee identified himself with his instinct. He knew that he was doing the right thing by holding on, and there came to him certain blissful thrills of satisfaction. At such moments he even closed his eyes and allowed his body to be hurled hither and thither, willy-nilly, careless of any hurt that might thereby come to it. That did not count. The grip was the thing, and the grip he kept.

White Fang ceased only when he had tired himself out. He could do nothing, and he could not understand. Never in all his fighting, had this thing happened. The dogs he had fought with did not fight that way. With them it was snap and slash and get away, snap and slash and get away. He lay partly on his side, panting for breath. Cherokee still holding his grip, urged against him, trying to get him over entirely on his side. White Fang resisted, and he could feel the jaws shifting their grip, slightly relaxing and coming together again in a chewing movement. Each shift brought the grip closer in to his throat. The bull-dog's method was to hold what he had, and when opportunity favoured to work in for more. Opportunity favoured when White Fang remained quiet. When White Fang struggled, Cherokee was content merely to hold on.

The bulging back of Cherokee's neck was the only portion of his body that White Fang's teeth could reach. He got hold toward the base, where the neck comes out from the shoulders; but he did not know the chewing method of fighting, nor were his jaws adapted to it. He spasmodically ripped and tore with his fangs for a space. Then a change in their position diverted him. The bull-dog had managed to roll him over on his back, and still hanging on to his throat was on top of him.

Questions

Working in small groups consider the following:

1. What differences in language are there between the two extracts? How can you tell one comes from a newspaper and the other from a novel? Find some sentences in the second extract (fiction) of the kind you would not expect to find in a newspaper article like the first extract (non-fiction).
2. Which of the two passages interested you more? Give your reasons.

Activities

1. Imagine that you are a reporter watching the White Fang v Cherokee fight. The rest of the spectators do not realise you are a reporter. Write an article describing this illegal fight.
2. Write an ending for the Jack London story, then, in groups, talk about the various endings you have written. See if you can find out how Jack London ended the story.
3. From the first extract pick out the evidence which is likely to persuade the judge either to acquit or convict the men.
4. In addition to dog-fighting, cock-fighting and bear-baiting are sports which have been very popular in the past but are now illegal. Are there any other sports involving animals which you think should be outlawed? Think of fox-hunting, fishing, horse-racing and bull-fighting, for example. What arguments are put forward to defend them?

Fact or Fiction?

Sometimes the reader does not know whether he/she is reading fact or fiction because they look alike and sometimes sound alike. In a famous radio broadcast, Orson Welles made fiction – a Martian invasion – sound like fact. There were realistic news bulletins announcing the arrival of the spaceships and many Americans really believed they were being invaded.

Prose or Poetry?

Here is an extract from a description of a pig farm, followed by a poem on the same subject:

Most of the bacon that we pick up on supermarket shelves and that ends up on our breakfast plates comes from pigs reared in factory farms. Large sheds, made of corrugated asbestos or steel, house rows of pigs kept in clean concrete pens. The pigs are well fed, healthy and grow rapidly. Although they never see the light of day, nor have the freedom to trot around a field, that is the price we are willing to make them pay so that we can have cheap rashers with our fried eggs.

Pig Farm Supreme

Wes Magee

Sunday p.m. and we're up at the 'big house'
with its shorn lawns and Union Jack streaming
from a white flagpole. The porch is porticoed.
The place seems to grow out of the countryside.

Behind the house the farm spreads across Ireland.
No rusting tractor, lame hen, or pile of tyres.
No stinking dunghill steaming in the sunshine.
In Magee tweeds the manager shakes my hand.

He leads us through cathedral barns, down steep steps,
underground to the long gallery of pigs.
Here we troop past tier upon tier of cages,
each with its squash of porkers waiting the chop.

The lights are never out; nights tacked on to days.
The food, balanced to the gram, jets through tube chutes
and all the snouts go down, snuffling and snaffling.
The noise, the heat, the stink of meat beats your head.

Its *then* you see the cage floors. No straw in sight,
just iron slats through which crud pours to shower
the cells beneath. Twice daily the beasts are hosed.
The scrubbed-up pigs glow as candyfloss.

Back at the house we're served tea and wheaten bread
by girls with skin like ice and eyes brown as bark.
Sun burnishes the wall-length windows. The floor's
polished just enough to let you break your back.

And far, far below the pigs swell in their cells,
their lives worked out in weights and water, blood near
boiling, their endless days filled tight with screaming.
Knives are ground on stones. And it's going on now.

Questions

1. What information is in the prose extract which is not in the poem?
2. We can assume that the poem is concerned with more than just information. Unlike the prose extract it possibly contains a deeper meaning. Read the poem again and consider the ways in which it affects you.

See units 2.5, 2.10, 3.6, 4.8

Introduction to Genre

Unit 1.3 Genre: Poetry

Introduction ◆ Poetry ◆ Responding to Poetry

Introduction

Popular songs often have regular verses, so we are very familiar with the form of verse or poetry. But when verse is printed on the page, as poetry, with the music in the words, people begin to get worried. We are more used to talking and listening, than we are to reading and writing. In this unit we will take a brief look at poetry to see what it is we mean by 'poetry'. In Unit 4.8, we will look at poetry in more detail.

Poetry

What is distinctive about poetry? Read these two examples aloud and try to pick up the music – the rhythm – of the verse.

Nooligan

Roger McGough

I'm a nooligan
dont give a toss
in our class
I'm the boss
(well, one of them)

I'm a nooligan
got a nard 'ead
step out of line
and youre dead
(well, bleedin)

I'm a nooligan
I spray me name
all over town
footballs me game
(well, watchin)

I'm a nooligan
violence is fun
gonna be a nassassin
or a nired gun
(well, a soldier)

Dumb Insolence

Adrian Mitchell

I'm big for ten years old
Maybe that's why they get at me
Teachers, parents, cops
always getting at me
When they get at me
I don't hit em
They can do you for that
I don't swear at em
They can do you for that
I stick my hands in my pockets
And stare at them
And while I stare at them
I think about sick
They call it dumb insolence
They don't like it
But they can't do you for it
I've been done before
They say if I get done again
They'll put me in a home
So I do dumb insolence

Things to notice

- First of all the imagination is at work. These poems were not written by a hooligan or by a ten year old. That is one thing to notice.

- Another is the shape of the poems. Words have been arranged together in clusters (lines) to make blocks (verses).

Questions

1. What do the two poems have in common? Look at the words in particular.
2. What differences are there between the two poems?
3. Who do you think the author expects to read them?
4. What are the poets telling us?

Activities

1. Compare the two poems using these headings which should be copied into your book. To start you off a couple of boxes have been filled in already.

	NOOLIGAN	DUMB INSOLENCE
Content: what is the poem about?		
Shape		
Words	'Nooligan' is a made-up word. 'A hooligan' might speak like this (and drop the 'h'). Other examples are . . .	
Feeling		
Point	The last line is important because . . .	

2. Divide into pairs and role-play a situation in which a character (played by you) meets the other person (played by your partner). You could be:

Bully   Timid Person

Truant   Truancy Officer

Failure   Successful Person

Try to get inside the character you have chosen. Imagine how he/she would react in the presence of a person who is very different from him/her, or his/her opposite.

3. Write a poem called 'Bully', 'Truant', or 'Failure' as if you are that person.
4. Take any poem from this book, or an anthology, and write a short appreciation using the following plan:

Para. No.	Questions to ask yourself
1	How has the poem affected you?
2	What is the poem about?
3	What do you think of the shape and words of the poem?
4	What is the feeling and point of the poem?

Responding to Poetry

When you respond to a poem, you are saying what its exact effect is on you, the reader. Ask yourself:

* What it makes you hear (think about the sounds in the poem)
* What it makes you see (look at the images – the pictures – in the poem)
* What it makes you feel (look at the emotions and the atmosphere of the poem)
* What it makes you think (what are the themes of the poem?)

To discover how a poem has a particular effect on the reader, you may need to look very closely at the words, the rhythm and the structure of the poem. But before examining the component parts of the poem, you must *experience* the poem; it is no good trying to analyse a poem before you have *felt* it. So always read a poem slowly, several times, hearing its sounds in your head. You will probably find as you do this that pictures, feelings and ideas begin to form in your mind. At this stage you could jot down everything you can about these pictures, feeling and ideas. Only then will it be time to start thinking about a more formal, ordered response to the poem. (In Unit 2.5 we will look more closely at how to analyse poems.)

Here is a short poem by Elizabeth Jennings.

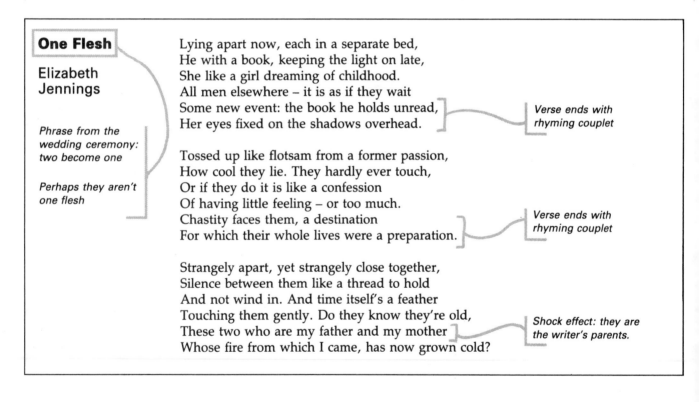

One Flesh

Elizabeth Jennings

Phrase from the wedding ceremony: two become one

Perhaps they aren't one flesh

Lying apart now, each in a separate bed,
He with a book, keeping the light on late,
She like a girl dreaming of childhood.
All men elsewhere – it is as if they wait
Some new event: the book he holds unread,
Her eyes fixed on the shadows overhead.

Verse ends with rhyming couplet

Tossed up like flotsam from a former passion,
How cool they lie. They hardly ever touch,
Or if they do it is like a confession
Of having little feeling – or too much.
Chastity faces them, a destination
For which their whole lives were a preparation.

Verse ends with rhyming couplet

Strangely apart, yet strangely close together,
Silence between them like a thread to hold
And not wind in. And time itself's a feather
Touching them gently. Do they know they're old,
These two who are my father and my mother
Whose fire from which I came, has now grown cold?

Shock effect: they are the writer's parents.

Commentary

A response to this poem might start like this:

This is a short, sad poem, which shocks. The narrator withholds from us the information that the two people are her parents, so that when she says 'These two who are my father and mother', we suddenly realise that she is not talking about two old people observed from afar, but her own flesh and blood. It is a poem about growing old and growing apart.

Activities

1. Try responding to the following poem using the commentary on the Elizabeth Jennings poem as a model. You may also find it useful to ask yourself the questions listed above the Jennings poem.

The Old Couple

F. Pratt Green

The old couple in the brand-new bungalow,
Drugged with the milk of municipal kindness,
Fumble their way to bed. Oldness at odds
With newness, they nag each other to show
Nothing is altered, despite the strangeness
Of being divorced in sleep by twin-beds,
Side by side like the Departed, above them
The grass-green of candlewick bedspreads.

In a dead neighbourhood, where it is rare
For hooligans to shout or dogs to bark,
A footfall in the quiet air is crisper
Than home-made bread; and the budgerigar
Bats an eyelid, as sensitive to disturbance
As a distant needle is to an earthquake
In the Great Deep, then balances in sleep.
It is silence keeps the old couple awake.

Too old for loving now, but not for love,
The old couple lie, several feet apart,
Their chesty breathing like a muted duet
On wind instruments, trying to think of
Things to hang on to, such as the tinkle
That a budgerigar makes when it shifts
Its feather weight from one leg to another,
The way, on windy nights, linoleum lifts.

2. This unit began by talking about the verses in pop songs. Here is a challenge. Write a new verse for a song that is in the charts. (Make sure it fits the tune!) First, copy down the words of the first verse and then put your new verse, or verses, underneath. (The words of current chart hits are often printed in *Smash Hits*.)

Introduction to Genre

Unit 1.4 Genre: Plays

Introduction ◆ Setting out plays: Macbeth and The Crucible

◗ *See units 2.3, 3.6, 3.11, 3.12, 4.7*

Introduction

Plays appear as a form of writing but are meant to be performed in some way. A performance can be in a theatre, on radio, or as a film or video for cinema or TV. The term 'drama' is generally used to describe the performance; the term 'text' or 'script' is used to describe the written form. A performance does not have to involve physical action; a group reading can be a performance.

Setting out Plays: *Macbeth* and *The Crucible*

In a book the text of a play will look like this:

Macbeth		*(Thunder and lightning. Enter three witches)*	*How will they enter? How will they be dressed?*
William Shakespeare	1 Witch:	When shall we three meet again? In thunder, lightning or in rain?	
	2 Witch:	When the hurly-burly's done, When the battle's lost and won.	*What will they be doing?*
	3 Witch:	That will be ere the set of sun.	
	1 Witch:	Where the place?	
	2 Witch:	Upon the heath.	
	3 Witch:	There to meet with Macbeth.	
	1 Witch:	I come, Graymalkin!	*Graymalkin = a cat*
	2 Witch:	Paddock calls.	*Paddock = a toad*
	3 Witch:	Anon!	
	All:	Fair is foul, and foul is fair: Hover through the fog and filthy air.	
		(Exeunt.)	*How will they leave?*

Here is a play written more recently, although it actually deals with the Salem witch trials in the 1600s, in which innocent men and women were accused of witchcraft by a group of children. Tituba is a servant. Here she is being interrogated by Parris, Hale and Putnam, three ministers.

The Crucible	TITUBA:	*(frightened by the coming process)* Mister Reverend, I do believe somebody else be witchin' these children.
Arthur Miller	HALE:	Who?
	TITUBA:	I don't know sir, but the Devil got him numerous witches.
	HALE:	Does he! *(It is a clue)*. Tituba, look into my eyes. Come look into me.
		(She raises her eyelids fearfully)
	PARRIS:	Who came with him?
	PUTNAM:	Sarah Good? Did you ever see Sarah Good with him? Or Osburn?
	PARRIS:	Was it man or woman came with him?
	TITUBA:	Man or woman. Was-was woman.
	PARRIS:	What woman? A woman you said. What woman?
	TITUBA:	It was black dark, and I –
	PARRIS:	You could see him, why could you not see her?
	TITUBA:	Well, they was always talking; they was always running round and carryin' on –
	PARRIS:	You mean out of Salem? Salem witches?

Questions

1. Pick out the words from *Macbeth* that reinforce the idea that the witches are actually supernatural.
2. What evidence is there in *The Crucible* that the three ministers *want* to believe in witches?

Activities

1. In small groups read these two extracts, or the full scenes from which they come, then decide:

   a how you would dress the characters
   b what kind of setting you would have
   c what would the characters be doing in this scene?

   They would not just be standing about. If there is room in the classroom mark out a stage on the floor and experiment with different positions for the characters. Alternatively you could use chessmen or felt tip pens for the characters and a piece of paper for the stage.

2. Write a ten-minute scene (set it out like the extract from *The Crucible*, but include instructions about how the words are spoken and what actions the characters should perform). Imagine that four teenagers come face to face with an old woman whom they have been tormenting.

   • In the first part of the scene the teenagers argue about what they have done to her.
   • In the second part she is introduced to them and slowly and awkwardly they begin to get to know her.
   • In the third part they learn something surprising about her, something that makes them respect her.

Introduction to Genre

Unit 1.5 Summary Unit

Coursework Assignments 1–5

▶ *See units To the student, 1.1*

Coursework Assignment 1:

Choose a theme such as love, freedom, America, nuclear war or animal rights. Then look at a number of poems or song lyrics (from *Smash Hits*, perhaps) that deal with this theme. Next, make a final selection of your favourites from this group. Copy out the poems and song lyrics you have chosen, arrange them in an order (it could be according to writer, or in chronological order), write a brief commentary on each and then an introduction for the whole section. You now have produced an anthology of songs and lyrics on your chosen theme. You now need to compile an index and design a cover for it. The title of the anthology can be the theme itself. You should aim to have between ten and twenty pieces in your anthology.

Coursework Assignment 2:

Divide into groups and discuss what items have been in the news recently. Write down four or five of them. Choose one item (it might be a kidnap, a disaster or a terrorist bombing) and write about it in the form of: **a** a script; **b** a poem; **c** a journalist's report.

Aim to use these different forms of writing (genres!) to communicate different types of information. The journalist's report should be factual and informative, whereas the poem could convey the emotions of the people involved.

Coursework Assignment 3:

Save this assignment for the end of term. Consider the texts – stories, plays, poems – that you have read in full. What would be gained and what would be lost if a poem was written out as prose, and a play such as *Macbeth* was written as a novel? Think of five books you have read, and consider whether they could be easily turned into: (a) plays, (b) films. Or you could compare the film or TV version of a novel (such as *1984* or *A Passage to India*) with the book itself.

Coursework Assignment 4:

Unit 1 showed how each of the three main genres can be further divided into different types of prose, drama and verse. Make your own giant diagram on the wall or on a piece of wallpaper. Underneath each type or sub-type of writing place examples of the genre. You could do this as a whole class, or in groups or pairs.

Coursework Assignment 5: Choosing the Appropriate Genre

If you have something you want to write about, does it matter which genre you choose? The answer is, yes it does! You should choose the form which is appropriate for the message you want to communicate and appropriate to the expectations of the reader.

For instance, you would not normally write a poem when applying for a job with a bank. That may seem obvious. But choosing the appropriate genre is not always straightforward. Below are six potential subjects for writing, together with a choice of forms in which you could write about them. Match the subjects with the form you think would be most appropriate: poem, report, play, short story, prose essay or prose letter.

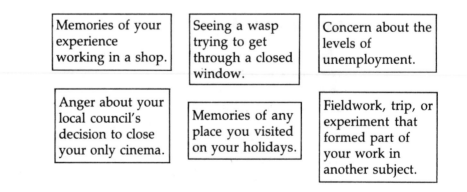

| Memories of your experience working in a shop. | Seeing a wasp trying to get through a closed window. | Concern about the levels of unemployment. |
| Anger about your local council's decision to close your only cinema. | Memories of any place you visited on your holidays. | Fieldwork, trip, or experiment that formed part of your work in another subject. |

Select one of the subjects and write about it in your chosen form. At the end add a note explaining why you chose that particular form.

PART 2: READING DIFFERENT TYPES OF TEXTS

Although reading, writing, listening and speaking are all related activities in any English course, part 2 of the book encourages you to think about the process of reading in particular.

It starts by considering visual texts (comics, and film and television programmes). These forms supply us with the pictures. Then we move on to texts which have no pictures, where we, the readers, must imagine the pictures for ourselves.

Before we begin it is worth remembering that whenever we read, we read with a purpose in mind. We may read for pleasure, or to extract information, for example. If we wish to extract information from a telephone directory, we will be very selective in what we read, whereas when reading a novel we will read from the first page to the last.

Reading Different Types of Texts

Unit 2.1 Reading Comics and Magazines

Introduction ◆ Reviews ◆ Changes in Comics ◆ Plot Sequencing ◆ Prediction ◆ Gender Roles in Comics and Magazines

◗ *See units 2.9, 2.11, 3.4, 3.5, 3.11*

Introduction

Comic characters like Superman, Batman, Wonderwoman, Spiderman and Charlie Brown appeared in comic strips long before they appeared in films and television programmes. Most of us, whether or not we like reading, spend some of our time looking at comics or comic strips. As infants we learnt to read from picture books, by matching words to pictures. One thing that all of these – films, television programmes, picture books, comics and teenage magazines – have in common, is that they tell stories, step by step. Wherever there have been people there have been stories, ever since the earliest times. The fascination of the story lies in wondering how it will end.

If we take a careful look at comics we can begin to see how the stories are being told, and how we all have certain expectations about how they should proceed. But first, some reading leading to discussion.

Reviews

A review is a careful critical look at something. The *Observer* magazine gave some teenagers a collection of comic annuals to review, and here are their responses. Read the reviews, noting the informal or 'colloquial' language. Would a more formal response have been more informative? Is it a real review or something more personal? What does it tell you about the reviewers? What are they trying to do?

Get into the habit of writing annotations like those opposite. It is a way of carrying on a dialogue with the text.

Activities

1. Jot down the names of all the comics and teenage magazines that you have read or seen. Then in pairs give the comics a star rating, as shown in the example. Give reasons for the stars you award.
2. Now write brief reviews of the comics and magazines:
   i in the kind of language used in the example – aimed at young teenagers;
   ii in the kind of language you would use if doing the survey for a company planning to bring out a new comic.

Annual Report

What does the reviewer really think? Can you write this in non-slang English and get over the "feeling"?

Find other examples of informal English

THE SMASH HITS YEARBOOK (EMAP)***

This is called a 'yearbook' which sounds much cooler than 'annual'. The 'No. 1 Year Book' is almost identical, but they are both well-designed and look classier than the other annuals. There are lots of 'groovy pics' of your 'fave popsters' and pages and pages of their smart Alec remarks. Nicely produced, not much in it.

Why do you think these teenagers gave Rupert five stars?
Are they joking?

RUPERT (Express Newspapers)*****

This is the 51st 'Rupert' annual and Rupert freaks will be glad to see that the little bear has not taken to wearing Nike training shoes or Levi's 501s. But who needs casual cred if you're the star of an annual that already contains six amusing new stories. As essential as Christmas pudding.

MY GUY ANNUAL (IPC Magazines)**

How much of this reviews the annual?

What does this mean?

A Madonna record or any record?

The title says it all. This is about getting 'guys', getting over them and getting them back again. It features some dazzlingly awful photo-stories. Of all the 'girls' annuals' this is easily the most vomit-inducing. Most of them are very old-fashioned, although this year's *Jackie* annual has broken new ground with a daring feature on men's underwear. 'My Guy' sticks to a very simple and sexist view of the world. A feature entitled 'Secrets of a Superstud' tells of the hard life led by one teenage Casanova. This story is followed by a moral warning – girls shouldn't lead on boys, who are poor, fragile creatures. Elsewhere, there's a quote from a teenage girl who says, 'You can only be just good friends with grotty-looking boys.' Riveting stuff.

An example of IRONY

JUDGE DREDD ANNUAL (IPC Magazine)***

Are these real ratings?

Could these annuals have been reviewed any other way?

The cult figure from the cult comic 2000 AD dashes around the pages like a second-rate Darth Vadar, saying, 'Sometimes you have to fight dirty to catch the real scum.' Very subtle, this one. Good pictures, artwork far ahead of the rest.

DENNIS THE MENACE (D. C. Thomson)****

Dennis devotees will want 'The Beano Book' as well as this one. Unlike most of the annuals we read, this will take longer than 10 minutes to get through. After a couple of liqueur chocolates you are guaranteed a few laughs to liven up the two most boring days of the year.

EASTENDERS SPECIAL (Grandreams, published by arrangement with the BBC)**

Frighteningly uninteresting. While struggling to stay conscious you too can learn that Anita Dobson is 'lovely', Leslie Grantham is one of our 'leading heart-throbs' and Letitia Dean's nickname is Tisha. Don't give this to your 93-year-old granny – the excitement could kill her.

MADONNA SPECIAL (Grandreams)**

Tacky. Tacky. Tacky. A lot of out-of-date photos, so fuzzily reproduced you need a pair of binoculars to make sure they are of Madonna. The man who wrote the Madonna annual has penned similar opuses on Paul Young and A-Ha. Trying to write something interesting about Paul Young can't have been easy and with the Madonna annual, the strain is beginning to tell. Under the heading of 'Dislikes' we are informed, 'Certain unisex fashions don't appeal to her.' Buy a record instead.

RAMBO ANNUAL (World International Publishing)*

This annual plumbs new depths of mediocrity. The worst drawings in the history of illustration. Unpleasant stories about guerillas with silly names like Sergeant Havoc. Avoid at all costs.

*****   Worth switching off the TV for
****   More exciting than charades
***   As thrilling as the Queen's Speech
**   Better gags in a cracker
*   A genuine Xmas turkey

Changes in Comics

This article appeared in *The News on Sunday*.

Little Phony bashes the Beano

News on Sunday

TUT TUT. There's no accounting for girls these days.

When I was young we had standards and we stuck to them. We knew a proper comic when we saw one.

Minnie the Minx was our One True Heroine. She expressed the anarchist delinquent that lurked, however deeply, in all our hearts.

Now I fear she is losing her grip.

She and her Beano pals are said to be hanging by their fingertips to market supremacy. And who is up there stamping on those filthy fingernails with manicured hoof?

Sinister

Why, it is the new best-selling magazine, My Little Pony.

Peachy and Twinkles would never dream of wrestling with authority. Nor would any of their sickening, softie stablemates. They wouldn't dare.

My Little Pony is a mega-buck industry.

There's no escaping it. I worry for the future.

If young minds are force-fed from this sinister tub of saccharine, can the noble spirit of the Minx survive?

Questions

1. Why were the words 'Phony' and 'bashes' used in the headline?
2. Why does the writer like *Minnie the Minx?*
3. Why doesn't the writer like *My Little Pony?*
4. Much of the article is written in a chatty, conversational style. Find two examples of this.
5. Sometimes the writer uses more difficult language. What do these words mean: 'anarchist', 'manicured', 'saccharine', 'sinister'? What do these expressions mean: 'market supremacy', 'mega-buck industry'?
6. What do you notice about these two expressions: 'filthy fingernails', 'sickening softie stablemates'?

Activities

1. Do cartoon and comic book heroes and heroines influence the way we behave?
2. What is meant by 'authority'? Have certain people the right to be 'in authority'? Should authority be challenged? Sometimes? Never?

Plot Sequencing

Does the order in which the parts of a story are told really matter? Usually we expect one event to cause, and be followed by, another. If we tell Jack and Jill backwards, the story becomes rather puzzling:

Jill came tumbling down after Jack who had cracked his head open.
They climbed a hill to fetch a pail of water. Jack fell down.

Where do you need to put the word 'Earlier' to make sense of this?

Some novels deliberately do not describe the events in the order in which they happen. (*Wuthering Heights*, for example, actually opens with the end of the story!) Describing a later event before other events that precede it chronologically can be an effective way of making a story more interesting. You may like to experiment with this when you next write a story. But telling the bits of a story in a random order can be very confusing for the reader. Here is a comic strip which shows this. Can you work out which order the pictures ought to appear in?

Activity

For this activity you will need a page from a comic strip or a photo-story magazine and a pair of scissors. Cut out the individual pictures, then shuffle them. Working in pairs give the jumbled pictures to your partner and see if he/she can put them in the appropriate order.

Prediction

Look at the following. They are the opening frames of a comic book story. Where do you think the story is set?

Activity

Predict what is going to happen next. You will need to find clues in the story so far to help you to do this. Continue the story as a written narrative. You may find it helpful to ask yourself these questions:

- What kind of story is it so far?
- What kind of story is it going to be (serious, comic, romantic, supernatural)?
- What is the setting?
- Will you have the same setting?
- Who are the characters? What are their names? What are they like?
- What is on the back of the truck in the truck-stop?
- Where is the story going? How will it end?

(Turn to page 246 for the next few frames of this story.)

Gender Roles in Comics and Magazines

Some comics and magazines are aimed at one sex; they are targeted at those they see as the average or conventional boy or girl.

JUST 17   Aimed at girls

SEPTEMBER 23   NUMBER 171

CONTENTS

SMASH HITS   Aimed at both sexes

contents

Activities

1. Compare and contrast the two contents pages
   - What do you find in *Just 17* but not in *Smash Hits*?
   - What appears in both?
   - What differences are there in the language?
   - How do you account for these differences?
2. Think about and discuss the following in groups or as a class:
   - **a** What are these magazines trying to do? Do you think they aim to inform, to entertain, or to do both?
   - **b** Do you think people read magazines like these selectively, a bit at a time, or from cover to cover?
   - **c** Do you think the words or the pictures are the most important thing in these magazines? Why do you think photographs are used to tell stories in girls' magazines, whereas drawings tend to be used in boys' magazines?

> **Reading Different Types of Texts**
>
> # Unit 2.2 Reading Television Programmes
>
> Television Programmes ◆ Brookside: A TV Soap with a
> Difference ◆ What is News?
>
> ◗ *See units 3.3–3.5, 3.9–3.12, 4.6, 4.7*

Television Programmes

We do not usually talk about reading television programmes. But television, no
less than comic books, has its own language or code and, if we step back, we can
begin to recognise some of the familiar signs. By doing this we are reading the
programme.

But you may say, quite reasonably, that anyone can understand what they see
on television. Why on earth do you need to 'read' it? There are two reasons:

1. Everything you see on television is someone's version of events and reflects
    someone's view of the world. We take that for granted when we read a
    book, but we tend to forget it when we watch television. Television somehow
    seems more 'real' than books which have a named author. But all television
    programmes, including the news, have an author or authors.
2. The way you present something changes the way people see or read it. Look
    at photograph A, taken from a television advertisement. What seems to be
    happening?

A

B

In fact the skinhead is saving the man from a falling stack of bricks, as picture B
in the advertisement shows! Without that picture, we would 'read' the scene
very differently.

Of the many different kinds of programmes on television, we will concentrate in
this unit on a form of television drama (soap operas), and news programmes.
But let us begin by trying to identify types of programmes according to the BBC's
Charter, which requires it to EDUCATE, ENTERTAIN and INFORM.

Activities

1. In pairs or groups, using a copy of the TV Times or Radio Times, try to continue this table by adding programmes under the appropriate headings.

EDUCATE	ENTERTAIN	INFORM	OTHER
Tomorrow's World Horizon	Eastenders Dallas	News Panorama	

Exchange lists and see which list is longest: Educate, Inform, or Entertain? What does this tell you about TV's role as seen by television programme planners?

2. Write down your top 20 programmes. Compare your list with the top 20 of the rest of the class and with the top 20 in the published ratings. Are there any programmes in your list which did not make it into other people's lists or the published ratings? What does your list say about you?

3. Write about 500 words on 'What I love and hate about television'. First plan your essay by writing a list of the programmes on TV that you love or hate, giving reasons for your feelings. You could draw up a table as below:

LOVES	Reasons	Examples	HATES	Reasons	Examples
NEWS	Always changing. Lots of stories. Real.	9 o'clock News Channel 4 News	GAME SHOWS	Stupid questions. Smarmy Presenters	The Price is Right
COP SHOWS	Real issues		SOAPS	Really stupid plots	

Brookside: A TV Soap with a Difference

No Pub in Brookside Close

Stuart Doughty

Producer

Brookside which is now in its fourth year and is consistently the most watched programme on Channel 4, is proud to have a number of features which make it unique among British soaps.

The 'Rovers Return' (in Coronation Street), the 'Queen Victoria' (in Eastenders) and the Motel (in Crossroads) all provide a central meeting place for characters. Here they can exchange news and gossip, new characters can quickly introduce themselves and communal celebrations can be held. For the programme makers the convenience of such a device is obvious.

But this 'meeting place' device can quickly become unrealistic: how many streets are there where everybody goes to the same pub – every day? Judging by their patronage of the 'Rover's' most of the regulars of Coronation Street should be bankrupt alcoholics.

The jovial togetherness that is rampant in many soap opera pubs reflects a blitz-like community spirit that does not exist any longer in our cities, even if it ever did.

Brookside wanted to be more realistic and reflect life as it is now. A new estate of nondescript architecture like Brookside Close does not have much sense of community. (Nor much sense of place – visually **Brookside** could be anywhere in the country.) Instead the characters living on the Close were set up to provide a clash of opinion and life style – almost an anti-community feeling.

And recently a new family, the Corkhills, have moved in to add a third side to the management/union debate represented by the Collins and Grant families. One could never imagine all the diverse **Brookside** characters using the same pub.

By rejecting the easy comfort (for writers) of a central meeting place, we have made **Brookside** look more realistic – and in rejecting the 'street community' ethic, we have also made it more modern.

(Interestingly, Eastenders has placed itself in the cosy, 'old-fashioned' community spirit of a Victorian East End square rather than the bleaker suburban environment.)

Without a pub or cafe there is far less opportunity for characters to meet. Writers have to work harder to get characters into conversation – and it is even harder with characters like divorcee Heather who lives alone: one is limited as to how much she can talk to her answer machine!

The only concession we have made to the 'meeting place' idea is to install a post box at the end of the Close. It is probably highly unrealistic for the Post office to put one in such a position in a cul-de-sac, but it does provide us with a focal point, albeit a very small one, round which our characters may occasionally gather.

Questions

1. In what ways is *Brookside* different from other soaps, according to the article?
2. What evidence is there that the writer is closely connected with the programme and biased in favour of it?

Activity

1. Write a brief description of *Brookside* (no more than 250 words). You have to explain the serial to American TV companies who are thinking of buying it for the US market. Use only the information in the passage.
2. Select a TV soap opera or crime drama that you have seen recently but do not normally watch. Then, write an essay of about 500 words that looks critically at the programme. The following diagram may give you an idea of the areas you should concentrate on in your essay.

The Characters

Does the programme have stock characters (stereotypes)
For instance is there:
an obvious hero a good but unlucky person
a villain   a scheming man or woman
Do the characters seem more complex and less clear-cut? How realistic are they?
What types of people don't appear?
Children   Rich people
Poor people   Black people

Language

Do the characters speak in the way you speak?
Do they speak British English, American English or even Australian English?
Do the characters have regional accents?
Does the dialogue sound natural?

NAME OF PROGRAMME

Setting

● British or foreign?
● Which precise area (city, country or suburb?)
● Indoors or outdoors?
● Studio or location?

Soundtrack/Music

● Does the programme have a memorable theme tune?
● How else is music used in the programme? For atmosphere? or to fill in gaps in dialogue?

Plot

● Believable or far-fetched?
● How many stories are going on at the same time?

What is News?

What is news? Is the Princess of Wales's hemline news? Are the plots of soap operas news? Should the news always end with a funny or 'royal' item to cheer us up? What is the main purpose of television news? Is it meant to inform, educate or entertain? List these three possible functions of television news in what you consider to be their order of importance.

Activities

1. Watch the same day's evening news broadcasts on all four TV channels. Then answer these questions:
   a What was the lead story on each news programme?
   b Were there differences in the way the same news items were treated in different broadcasts? Did the broadcasts use studio commentaries, interviews with experts, film reports, or all three?
   c What was the point of the chosen treatment? Was it intended to educate, inform or entertain?
   d How much 'home' and 'foreign' news was there in each broadcast? Was the foreign news given a link with Britain? (For instance, a car crash in France in which a British holidaymaker is killed is both foreign and home news; a cyclone in Bangladesh that kills 20,000 people is purely foreign news.)
   e How many minutes of the news broadcasts you monitored were about events in (a) Britain, (b) America, (c) Europe, (d) the rest of the world?
   f Which news story that you monitored is likely to be still in the news in a week's time? (Check your hunch in a week's time.)
2. On the hour, during the day, BBC Television provides a five minute news bulletin. Here are 12 news stories. In groups, decide which stories you will include in your news bulletin (you can have no more than eight), how long you will give to each story (minimum 15 seconds) and the order in which you would include them.

   Write the script for this news bulletin. Make sure it lasts exactly five minutes when you read it.

Eight hurt in blast

● TWO policemen and six civilians have been injured in an IRA bomb attack on a Royal Ulster Constabulary Land-Rover in Londonderry. Two blast bombs hit the vehicle in Shipquay Street, close to the city centre last night.

Tourists still face delays

● THERE was good news and bad news for sun-seeking British holidaymakers as they flew out to Spanish tourist resorts today. Spanish air traffic controllers have called off today's threatened 24-hour strike over pay. But anyone flying from the UK could still face delays because of an overtime ban and work-to-rule by engineers who service Britain's air traffic control computers.

Gunman keeps police at bay

● A MAN armed with a shotgun was keeping police at bay early today after holding his ex-wife hostage for more than three hours. Armed police have sealed off the area, and trained negotiators were talking with the man, believed to be in his 40s. The siege in Penistone, South Yorkshire, began at 6.10 last night when someone heard a shot and alerted the police.

Athlete freed on bail

● BRITISH Olympic athlete David Jenkins, alleged mastermind of a £44-million-a-year black market in body-building anabolic steroids, was released from jail yesterday on bail of almost £500,000. Jenkins' American wife was waiting when the 35-year-old former 400-metre runner left the jail where he had spent four months.

Another ship attacked

● IRAQ said its warplanes today attacked another "large naval target" – the term used for a tanker or merchant ship – in the Gulf. The new strike, so far unconfirmed by independent shipping sources, is the 14th claimed by Iraq since it resumed strikes on Iranian oil installations and tankers last Saturday.

Britons hurt in train crash

● TWO passenger trains crashed in the popular Algarve resort of Olhao, killing up to five people and injuring 29 others, including four Britons, officials said. Three Britons were released from hospital after treatment for minor injuries. A fourth, Mr. Charles Coleman, 74, was still in hospital today.

25 killed in raids

● THREE waves of Israeli jets pounded targets in Palestinian camps near Sidon today, killing 25 people and wounding 40, police said. The 10-minute blitz left black smoke billowing into the sky as ambulances and fire engines raced through the port city 25 miles south of Beirut, witnesses said.

Gas cloud mystery

● A MYSTERIOUS gas cloud which put 15 people in hospital has vanished as quickly as it came. The black mass swept in from the sea off Kent, yesterday, causing sore throats and streaming eyes across the county from Ramsgate to the Isles of Sheppey and Thanet.

New anti-AIDS fight

● THE GOVERNMENT today launched a £5 million campaign against drug abuse and AIDS – amid warnings that in some parts of Britain one in two addicts is infected with the deadly virus. Social Services Secretary Mr John Moore said: "The threat is not only to the drug users themselves but to the unborn babies of infected mothers, to the sexual partners of drug abusers and, from them, to the general population."

16-hour Gulf blitz

● IRAN ambushed five ships in a 16-hour blitz in the Gulf overnight while Iraq, maintaining relentless pressure against Tehran's oil exports, reported its 10th raid on Iranian tankers in five days. Gulf-based shipping sources said it was the most explosive night in the six years of the tanker war.

Unhappy end for SDP

● SDP delegates meet today to pay their last respects to the party they formed six years ago to break the mould of British politics. Last night many of the delegates made it plain they were disillusioned and disheartened by the bitter merger row that had divided the party.

Full steam ahead for John

● THE world's oldest man was today rediscovering the magic of steam trains. Just a little more than a week after a hectic birthday visit to London, 110-year-old John Evans was going on another British Rail outing. The former Welsh miner, who spent 60 years in the pits, was joining passengers on a special 31-mile trip between Swansea and Carmarthen.

Reading Different Types of Texts

Unit 2.3 Reading Films

Introduction ◆ Gregory's Girl: Film and Book ◆ A Film Review

◗ *See units* 2.2, 2.8, 2.10, 3.4, 3.10–3.12, 4.3, 4.4, 4.6, 4.7

Introduction

We read films. Not simply by watching them, but by recognising the conventions, the titles and the different types of films – the *genres*.

We read films:

- **by recognising the kinds of films**

HORROR   WESTERN   DETECTIVE   COMEDY   SCIENCE FICTION

SPACE FANTASY   LOVE STORY

- **by recognising stock situations**

GIRL IS CHASED BY A MONSTER AND FALLS OVER

HERO/HEROINE IS TRAPPED AS DANGER APPROACHES

TRAPPED STRANGERS FALL IN LOVE

CAR CHASE

TOM, IN PURSUIT OF JERRY, RUNS INTO A BRICK WALL/DOOR/FENCE

- **by recognising stock characters**

DUMB BLONDE

POWER-MAD VILLAIN

COOL DETECTIVE

ACCIDENT-PRONE INNOCENT

- **by noticing the tricks and techniques of camerawork**

CLOSE UP   LONG SHOT   FADE   HAND-HELD CAMERA SHOT

SOFT FILTER   ZOOM IN/OUT

- **by noticing the use of special effects**

SPACECRAFT   METAMORPHOSIS e.g. from man to werewolf

FLASHBACK

- **and by considering how films are different from books**

LENGTH   STORY IS TOLD IN PICTURES

USUALLY 'READ' AT ONE SITTING

COMPLEX CHARACTERS ARE DEVELOPED THROUGH SPEECH

Gregory's Girl: Film and Book

We can see this by looking at *Gregory's Girl*, a story of a Scottish fifth-former who becomes infatuated with Dorothy, a girl who has replaced him in the school football team. Here is an extract from the novel compared with a school shooting script adapted from the acting version. Madeline is Gregory's 11 year old sister.

Scene 9 In the Café. Madeline and Gregory are sitting at a table in a cubicle.

Gregory's Girl

Actor's script

MADELINE   You need some new trousers. These baggy ones are awful. I'll see Mum about it. Blue ones, Italian. If you're going to start falling in love you'll have to start taking care of yourself, how you look ...

CAMERA 1
C/u Gregory
looking depressed

GREGORY   Are Italians good dressers?

MADELINE   They have lots of style. And they make nice trousers. Steve's sister was telling me about Dorothy. She's very attractive... I knew you would fall for that type. She wears nice things... she's got style.

Cut back to m/s

GREGORY   She's quarter Italian.

C/u Madeline

MADELINE   Don't get too serious about her, if you can help it. Have you asked her out? I can tell you things... You were good to me when other boys *hated* their sisters. [*There is a pause.*] Those sweaters in Mr Manly. What colour did you like?

Gregory's Girl

The Novel

'You need some new trousers,' she told him matter-of-factly as they slipped behind Woolworth's and emerged into the main thoroughfare of the precinct. It was bustling and crowded, late shoppers merging with idling homegoers. 'Those baggy ones are awful,' Madeline grimaced. 'I'll see Mum about it. Blue ones would be nice – Italian. If you're going to start falling in love you'll have to start taking care of yourself ...'

'Are Italians good dressers?' Gregory asked glumly; he was thinking of Renaldo.

'They have lots of style,' said Madeline. 'And they make nice trousers.' She paused to glance in a shop window. Gregory waited. 'Richard's sister was telling me about Dorothy; she's very attractive,' Madeline resumed. 'I knew you would fall for that type. She wears nice things; she's got style.'

'She's quarter Italian,' said Gregory. His emotional state was improving marginally; if all these other people were

Back to m/s

GREGORY   The brown.

MADELINE   Brown! That's you... grey, black... *brown*! You don't *think* about colours, do you?... If you don't take an interest in yourself, how can you expect other people to be interested in you?... Talk to Dorothy... ask her out... she won't say no, I'll bet you... but don't treat her too special... if you're too romantic it could scare a girl off.

GREGORY   What kind of things should I say?

CAMERA 2
L/S
Through café
window

MADELINE   Good Heavens! Don't plan it, don't *think* about it... *do it*! You need new shoes as well.
[*Another pause.*]

GREGORY   So I should think less about love and think more about colours.

MADELINE   You've got it.
[*The WAITRESS comes up for their order.*]

WAITRESS   What would you like?

MADELINE   A ginger beer, please, with some vanilla ice cream and some lime juice, but don't stir it please.

GREGORY   Coffee please.

WAITRESS   What colour.

GREGORY   Brown please. [*Pause.*] They don't do blue coffees here, Madeline, this isn't Italy. No style here at all.

MADELINE   [*Gets bit serious.*] Do you dream about her, when you're sleeping I mean?

GREGORY   Yes.

MADELINE   That means you love her. It's the one you have the dreams about that counts.
[*A pause.*]

GREGORY   What do you dream about?

MADELINE   I just dream about ginger beer and ice cream, I'm still a little girl, remember?
[*By now the drinks have arrived. Toying with her drink*] The nicest part is just before you taste it. My mouth goes all tingly. But that can't go on forever...

taking such an apparent interest in his infatuation perhaps it wasn't such a dead loss after all.

'Don't get too serious about her, if you can help it,' Madeline warned. 'Have you asked her out?'

Gregory shook his head; he still felt too leaden to go into lengthy excuses.

'I can help you,' Madeline went on. 'I'm a girl. I can tell you things. You were good to me when other boys hated their sisters.' Gregory grinned faintly at that; it made him feel quite good inside. There really wasn't that much wrong with Madeline. He started to think positively.

They paused again outside a menswear shop. It was having a sale of all wool sweaters. 'Which colour do you like?' asked Madeline.

'The brown,' said Gregory unhesitatingly; he liked brown – dark colours seemed safe to him.

'Brown,' said Madeline scornfully. 'That's you all over – grey, black, brown! You don't think about colours, do you?'

Gregory shrugged; he hadn't thought about it before. They moved on.

'If you don't take an interest in yourself, how can you expect other people to be interested in you? You've got to talk to Dorothy, you've got to ask her out. She won't say no. I bet you. But don't treat her too special. If you're too romantic it could scare a girl off.'

Gregory listened, rapt. Even if she was a bit young, it could be quite useful having a sister – a kind of mole in the opposition camp. 'What kind of things should I say?' he asked seriously.

'Good heavens!' exploded Madeline, sounding at least thirty years older than she was. 'Don't plan it, don't think about it – do it!' She glanced down at his moccasins. 'You need new shoes too. And buy me a drink.'

They were outside a brightly lit café with tables that had yellow plastic tops and green tubular legs. They sat down next to the window.

'A ginger beer, please, with some vanilla ice-cream and some lime juice,' said Madeline in one breath. 'But don't stir it please!' Suddenly she was ten years old again.

The waitress looked at Gregory.

'Coffee please,' he said.

'What colour?' asked the waitress.

Gregory glanced at Madeline; it was

GREGORY   Be careful with those. I put down my chronic acne to over indulging in ginger beer and ice cream at a formative age.

MADELINE   You might be right, but medically speaking boys are more likely to get acne than girls.

clear he was under test. 'Brown please,' he said.

Madeline sighed theatrically. The waitress went away.

'They don't do blue coffees here, Madeline,' Gregory whispered. 'This isn't Italy. No style here at all.'

She stuck her tongue out at him. They relaxed and stared out of the window.

'Do you dream about her, when you're sleeping I mean?' Madeline asked suddenly.

Gregory thought about it. 'Yes,' he decided.

Madeline nodded. 'That means you love her. It's the one you have the dreams about that counts.'

The waitress returned and left the drinks.

'Who do you dream about?' Gregory asked.

'I just dream about ginger beer and ice-cream. I'm still a little girl, remember?' Madeline chided. She was stirring her drink slowly with a straw, watching the colours mix. She smiled secretly. 'The nicest part is just before you taste it. My mouth goes all tingly.' She sighed. 'But that can't go on for ever.' And sucked fiercely on the straw. That was his problem, thought Gregory instantly. Anticipating the moment too much, relishing his own indecision. He must act – now while the iron was hot.

Film scripts are shorter than novels because films can show things visually which novels have to describe in words.

Questions

1. What is in the first paragraph of the novel extract that is not in the script?
2. After Gregory's question 'Are Italians good dressers?' the novel has a sentence. Why doesn't the sentence appear in the script?
3. Find another example of something that appears in the novel which does not appear in the script. Suggest why there is this difference.
4. The script has one scene in the café. How many scenes does the novel have?
5. What would you have the camera do during the first pause? (If you are stuck for an answer, look at the novel!)
6. What would the camera do during the second pause?
7. What do we learn about (a) Madeline, (b) Gregory? What sort of relationship do they have?

Activities

1. Write about 400 words about a brother or sister or cousin, concentrating on how they treat you and how you treat them. Write your piece as a diary entry.
2. Write a story called 'The Première' or 'Film Dreams', or 'Close up', or 'The Forgotten Star'. The story does not have to be about the cinema, but imagine you are writing it for a film magazine article called 'Going to the Pictures'.

A Film Review

Spend ten minutes reading the following review of the film, *Gregory's Girl*.

An exhilarating view of teenage fantasy life

Gregory's Girl (A)

Screen on the Green, Islington

As writer and director of *That Sinking Feeling* and *Gregory's Girl*, Bill Forsyth instantly establishes himself as a comic author of singular gifts. In any other country this – and the fact that singlehanded Forsyth has demonstrated the possibility of a native Scottish feature cinema – would have been proudly proclaimed long ago. In Britain we are still so diffident about the possibility of a national cinema that eighteen months and six months, respectively, have gone by since *That Sinking Feeling* and *Gregory's Girl* were premiered at successive London Film Festivals; and it has taken until now for the films to be publicly shown in London.

Better late than never: *That Sinking Feeling* opens at the ICA this week, and *Gregory's Girl* at the Screen on the Green next, and I can only exhort anyone and everyone to see these hugely enjoyable pictures.

While *That Sinking Feeling* soars into fairy tale, *Gregory's Girl* sticks closer to realistic possibilities, or at least contains itself within the fantasy view of life of teenage schoolchildren. Gregory (Gordon John Sinclair, who, like most of the rest of the cast, also appears in *That Sinking Feeling*) is a great silly streak of a boy with the absorbed obsessiveness that frequently afflicts the adolescent male, and who attributes his dizziness to growing too fast. He cannot remember to switch off electric toothbrushes, and jay-walks to school, jumping around fending off imaginary assailants.

He is no odder, for all that, than the rest of his schoolmates, every one of them thrown off-centre by some odd obsessive interest. (One is a passionate photographer, another a pastrycook, a third a factophile). The only thing they have in common and which slightly sharpens their focus on life is a growing curiosity about girls.

The girls, for their part, are a lot more knowing and self-possessed, and tolerant, in a patronizing, testy, maternal way, of their infantile male companions. Gregory falls foolishly in love with a girl football player who replaces him in the forward line; but, when her mind proves to be inextricably stuck into the game, he finds his affections adapt quite easily.

Forsyth's best comedy comes out of his delight in other people's introversion and preoccupation, the amiable, blind pursuit, in grown-ups as well as the kids, of private strange concerns. There is a fine inconsequent moment when the acidulous headmaster is caught happily tinkering out a ragtime tune during break, absently dismissing the small boys who have come to watch.

Forsyth is not only a prodigal inventor of comedy, but he has the gift of turning all his cast into richly accomplished comic actors. Gordon John Sinclair is in real life an apprentice electrician; but under Forsyth's direction he is a comedian of the first rank, never mistiming a gesture, a line or a grimace of his amiable, wide-eyed pixie face. The supporting cast are as expert, and the greatest test is Forsyth's ability to blend a tried professional into the ensemble: the comedian Chic Murray plays the headmaster who, besides his musical interlude, grows indecently gluttonous over the products of the cookery class.

The film is packed with treats and treasures: Gregory's sweet reliance on the mature protection and advice of his little sister; Gregory teaching "horizontal dancing" to a newly discovered girlfriend; lovely throwaway inventions of mise-en-scene such as a conversation shot on a playground roundabout.

Above all these two films are the clearest demonstration that talent is not bought with money. Forsyth (whether as a thrifty Scot or a film-maker who knows what he is doing) brought in *Gregory's Girl* below his budget of £200,000. (That means, just by rule of thumb, that you might finance seventy or eighty such films for the price of one *Raise the Titanic*.) *That Sinking Feeling*, he says, cost nothing at all apart from the film stock: everyone invested his services on a cooperative basis. Yet these two films are as lively in look as any you can currently find in London, and a lot more entertaining.

Questions

1. What do we learn from the review about Gregory and the actor who plays him?
2. Which paragraphs are mainly about the director of the film and which are about the film itself?
3. Which sentences show that the reviewer really likes the film?

Activities

1. Rewrite the part of the review that deals with the characters other than Gregory. You could start 'Apart from Gregory there are many entertaining and interesting characters . . .'.
2. Imagine that you are a member of a school or college film society. You have not seen the film yet but have to write a preview to appear in your college or school magazine. Concentrating on the section of the review that deals with the film itself, extract the appropriate information and write the preview. Begin '*Gregory's Girl* is next month's film. It is about . . .'.
3. Choose two films that you have seen recently. If possible choose two films that have something in common (two films about Vietnam? two horror films? two 'teen' movies?). Review and compare them. Before starting this activity, you may wish to read the section which follows.
4. Next time you watch a film – at the cinema or on TV – write a 400 word review of it for your local paper immediately afterwards, while it's still fresh in your mind. This is how newspaper reviewers have to work to meet their deadlines. Think about the following when you write your review:
   - What kind (genre) of film is it?
   - Is it like any other film?
   - Where and when is it set?
   - Who are the main characters, and which actors or actresses play them?
   - Are the characters believable? Do you care about what happens to the characters?
   - Is the film itself believable?
   - How is the setting used? Is the place where the film is set important to the story?
   - What was the music like? Was it appropriate to the subject and atmosphere of the film?
   - Did you enjoy the film? What sort of people should go to see it?
5. A video shop commissions you to do some research into the types of films people watch. Your sources of information are this week's *TV Times* and *Radio Times*, and this week's best-selling video list in a music paper, such as *NME*. Write a report for the shop, concentrating on the following questions:
   - How many films are being shown on each TV channel this week?
   - What kinds of films are being shown on TV this week? Make a list of the number of different types (e.g. thrillers, comedies, and so on).
   - How old are the films shown on TV?
   - When are films broadcast on TV? Are particular types of film shown at certain times? Can you detect a pattern?
   - Which are the best-selling videos this week?

Reading Different Types of Texts

Unit 2.4 Words and Pop Music

Introduction ◆ Pop Music and Advertising ◆ The Words of Pop ◆ Reading Covers and Lyrics

◗ *See units 1.3, 2.11*

Introduction

Most pop songs have words – 'lyrics' – although sometimes they are less important than others. One early rock and roll song started with these words: A WopBopaLooBopBawopBamBoom. A writer called Nik Cohn used this as the title for a book about pop music. Here is how it begins.

Roots

Nik Cohn

Modern pop began with rock 'n' roll in the middle fifties and, basically, it was a mixture of two traditions – Negro rhythm 'n' blues and white romantic crooning, coloured beat and white sentiment.

What was new about it was its aggression, its sexuality, its sheer noise and most of this came from its beat. This was bigger and louder than any beat before it, simply because it was amplified. Mostly, pop boiled down to electric guitars.

Of course, electric guitars were nothing new in themselves – they had been around for years in jazz and R&B and had even been featured on some white hits, notably those by Les Paul, but they had never been used as bedrock, as the basis of a whole music. Crude, powerful, infinitely loud, they came on like space-age musical monsters and, immediately, they wiped out all of the politeness that had gone before.

Pre-pop, from the thirties on, dance music had got bogged down in the palais age – the golden era of the big bands, when everything was soft, warm, sentimental, when everything was make-believe.

It's one of the clichéd laws of showbiz that entertainment gets sloppy when times get tough and, what with the depression, the war and its aftermath, times had gotten very tough indeed. Hemmed in by their lives, people needed to cling tight in the dark of dancehalls, to be reassured, to feel safe again. Reality they could very well do without.

Always, that's the kind of situation that Tin Pan Alley thrives on and songs about moonlight, stardust, roses and bleeding hearts were duly churned out by the truckload. Then along came rock and roll.

This is a piece of writing giving us information, but in an informal, relaxed way. The audience – one which wants to read about pop music – will not object to the informality.

Questions

1. When was big band music popular, and when was it replaced by rock and roll?
2. How was rock and roll different from earlier music?
3. Why was romantic music so popular before rock and roll?

4. Some of the words used in the passage are special words taken from the world of music. Choose two of the following and explain what they mean. Use a dictionary if necessary.

   Crooning   Jazz   R & B   Tin Pan Alley

5. Nik Cohn calls dance music soft, warm, sentimental. What is his equivalent description of rock and roll?

6. The language Nik Cohn uses is not as simple as it may appear. What do these words mean?

   Sentiment   Aftermath   Clichéd

7. Does the definition of rock and roll in the first three paragraphs apply to pop music today? Give reasons for your answer.

Activity

Imagine you work for a publisher who is bringing out a book about a singer or a band. You have been asked to write a piece outlining their history and achievements to appear on the back cover of the book. Write a brief description of the singer/band, using the following example as a model:

> The Rogues are rough, rebellious and raunchy. They mix and match traditional Irish music, late '70's punk and '80's pub rock. It all fuses into a powerful cocktail, but these gap-toothed tinkers would be unwelcome party gatecrashers. No smart haircuts, no pretty boy looks or robot dancing. The six members are all from Dublin, and play instruments ranging from penny whistles and tea trays to electric guitars. They are set to blow away U2 and become the band of the '90's . . .

Pop Music and Advertising

Pop songs are often used as advertising jingles, and an advertisement can often lead to the re-release of the song and a return to the charts. Can you think of any examples? Why do you think advertisers use pop songs to sell things? What qualities might pop songs have that make them good material for advertisements?

Activity

Think of a product – it could be Coca Cola, potato crisps, a car or a bank – and choose an appropriate pop song to use in an advertisement for that product Briefly describe the advertisement, and say why the song 'fits' the product.

The Words of Pop

These can be meaningless, witty, thoughtful, political, daft, memorable or in some cases, as the next unit suggests, possess real poetic qualities. But pop lyrics are best at revealing the interests and values of the generation that produced them. Here is a lyric made famous by Elvis Presley (though written by Carl Perkins) from the period in which rock and roll was born – the mid fifties:

Blue Suede Shoes
 	
Carl Perkins
	You can burn my house
	Steal my car
	Drink my liquor from an old fruit jar
	Do anything
	You want to do
	But ah-ha-honey
	Lay off my shoes
	And don't you, don't you tread on my
	    blue suede shoes.
	You can do anything, but lay off my blue
	    suede shoes.
		Ordinary things
		do not matter
		
		Style matters
		most

What do you think people value nowadays? What valued items would (a) you, (b) your parents, (c) your friends, be most upset about if they were damaged in some way?

Activity

Divide into pairs. One of you is the interviewer, the other the guest on a radio programme called *My Life and Music*. The guest selects six records that he/she would take to a desert island. While the guest chooses, the interviewer prepares questions to ask him/her about his/her life. It is a well-known format. Now create a programme in which the interviewer asks the guest the questions about his/her life, pausing at intervals to play the records. Make a tape-recording of the interview, listen to it and write out a transcript.

Reading Covers and Lyrics

Just as there are different types of television programmes there are also different types of music. We all have a kind of music that we like best, whether it is Heavy Metal, Soul, Jazz, Classical or the music that is loosely called Pop. These and other kinds of music are all marketed and packaged in the form of albums, cassettes or compact discs. They all have covers with pictures and words that have been carefully selected and assembled.

To prepare for the following activity you will need some record sleeves or cassette covers.

Activities

1. Look at a record cover or its cassette or compact disc equivalent and use the following questions as the stimulus for a piece of writing.
    a Describe the picture or pictures on the cover. Why do you think this picture or design was chosen? What are your first impressions of the sleeve/cover?
    b What words appear on the cover? Are any of the words in very big letters? If so, explain why they are so prominent.
    c How much information are we given on the cover? Is it too much, too little, or just about right? What information are we given?
    d What type of music is on this record/tape? Describe it to someone who has not heard the album before.

2. Listen to a recording of a song from the charts and copy down the lyrics. Then, in groups, discuss the song, considering the following questions in particular:

   a What is the song about? Is it easy to understand? Give reasons for your answer.

   b Are the words important or is it just the sound and the music that matter? Or are both equally important?

   c What kind of audience do you think the singer or group had in mind when they made this record? Would it appeal to people of all ages?

3. Write a letter to a record company asking for more information about a musician, a singer or a band. (Companies issue press releases.)

   a Write a letter asking for an interview with a singer in a band of your choice.

   b Devise twenty questions to ask the singer in the interview.

   c Write a transcript of the interview as you would imagine it.

Reading Different Types of Texts

Unit 2.5 Reading Poetry

Introduction ◆ Beezley Street ◆ How to Read a Poem ◆ Problems in Reading Poems

◗ *See units 1.3, 2.10, 3.6, 4.8*

Introduction

Poetry is a kind of writing that makes powerful use of the imagination. Poets like playing games with words and it is fascinating how a word or a line can suggest different things to different people.

Beezley Street

You may think that poetry is something you have to search out, that it is less a part of your daily lives than comics, television or pop. But good pop songs have things in common with poetry, particularly in their imaginative language, and use of rhyme and strong rhythm. Here is part of a pop poem by John Cooper Clarke about a street in Liverpool called Beezley Street. It was originally released as a record, with a backing track.

Beezley Street

John Cooper Clarke

cars collide colours clash   *Repeated 'c' sound*
disaster movie stuff
for the man with the fu manchu moustache
revenge is not enough

there's a dead canary on a swivel seat
there's a rainbow in the road
meanwhile on beezley street
silence is the mode   *Separate stanzas*

in the kingdom of the blind
where the one-eyed man is king
beauty problems are redefined
the doorbells do not ring
light bulbs pop like blisters
the only form of heat
where a fellow sells his sister
down the river on beezley street

the boys are on the wagon
the girls are on the shelf
their common problem
is that they're not someone else
the dirt blows out
the dust blows in
you can't keep it neat
it's a fully furnished dustbin
16 beezley street

vince the ageing savage
betrays no kind of life   *Rhyme*
but the smell of yesterday's cabbage
and the ghost of last year's wife   *Rhyme*
through a constant haze
of deodorant sprays
he says retreat
alsatians dog the dirty days
down the middle of beezley street

eyes dead as viscous fish
look around for laughs
if i could have just one wish
i would be a photograph
on this permanent monday morning
get lost or fall asleep
when the yellow cats are yawning
round the back of beezley street

people turn to poison quick
as lager turns to piss
sweethearts are physically sick
every time they kiss
it's a sociologist's paradise
each day repeats
uneasy cheesy greasy queasy beastly beezley street   *Repeated 'e' sounds*

Activities

1. Read *Beezley Street* again and use the words in the poem to describe the kind of place Beezley Street is.
2. Read the poem again and jot down your reactions to it on a sheet of paper. Then listen to the recorded version of *Beezley Street* looking at the lyrics as you do so. What is the effect of the music in the recorded version? Jot down your reactions.

How to Read a Poem

Read the poem silently to yourself, jotting down your immediate reactions to it, and noting, in particular, the emotions it arouses in you and the pictures that form in your mind as you read it.

Ask yourself questions about the poem:
• Does the title give you a clue to what the poem is about, or is it misleading?
• What do you think is the point of the poem?
• What do you notice about the words used in the poem? Do they describe abstract things – such as feelings – or physical objects? Does the writer use any images or striking comparisons? What use does the poem make of rhyme?
• What do you notice about the rhythm of the poem?
• Why is it written as a poem?

Find a partner, read the poem out loud to one another and then discuss the ideas you have about it.

Write the poem out for yourself, breaking it up into units of meaning that appear to concentrate on particular themes, emotions or images. You could use highlighter pens or written annotations to identify the different sections.

Activity

Choose a poem from the end of Unit 2.10 and read it following the procedure described above.

Problems in Reading Poems

It can be difficult to understand some poems because:

a The words are difficult – they are from an earlier century, or are in non-standard English;
b you don't understand the references;
c the ideas are complex;
d there's not meant to be a simple meaning – a single explanation;
e the lines are broken up in strange ways;
f the words are meant to make you *feel*, rather than think.

Don't expect to understand a poem straight away. A poem is like a fossil in a rock. You have to dig out the meaning. Read it twice, three times – jot down your thoughts and responses on a separate piece of paper, or if you have a copy of the poem, on that.

Wha happen black girl is a powerful poem which you might initially find difficult. The annotations will help you to focus on its difficult points and understand the poem better.

Wha happen black girl

Angela Mars

Wha happen black girl
You know here about family planning
how you just ah' breed so

Who is the poet talking to here?

And you Mr so call black brother
Me know you believe in spreading the seed
but what life can you offer to the girl that
you just breed

And here?

Poverty and misery
Huh' but nourished with fools love
you think that you can support even the lord
above

What do you notice about the words and the punctuation?

And when the children grow up
Ma what you gonna tell them
Dem papa was a sailor
He was more like a tailor
You know see him sew up your life good
and proper.

Do the short, punchy lines hammer the message home more powerfully than prose would?

Before you read the next poem, *Poem for my Sister*, think about your own brothers and sisters. Do you get on well with them? Do they annoy you? Do you confide in them?

Poem for my Sister

Liz Lochhead

My sister likes to try my shoes,
to strut in them,
admire her spindle-thin twelve-year-old legs
in this season's styles.
She says they fit her perfectly,
but wobbles
on their high heels, they're
hard to balance

I like to watch my little sister
playing hopscotch, admire the neat hops-and-skips of her,
their quick peck,
never-missing their mark, not
over-stepping the line.
She is competent at hopscotch

I try to warn my little sister
about unsuitable shoes,
point out my own distorted feet, the callouses,
odd patches of hard skin.
I should not like to see her
in my shoes.

What lies behind this?

I wish she would stay
sure footed,
        sensibly shod.

Questions

1. Why is the poem in three sections?
2. How old do you imagine the speaker of the poem to be?
3. What sort of woman is the narrator of the poem?
4. Write headings for each of the three sections.
5. What is the little sister good at?

Activity

1. Write the younger sister's reply, in verse, or a 'Poem for my Brother' (or cousin).
2. We started with *Beezley Street* by John Cooper Clarke. Try writing a poem about your road, or a road you know well. Before you start, look at this poem, *Amy Road*, written by a student. It is about the street he grew up in. The poem describes his memories of the road.

Amy Road	Street lamp on the corner
	Soft night-time pool of snow and light
Michael	The Sainsbury's lorry's crushed my sledge
Pattison	And I'm left with bits of firewood
	Near the woodyard wall
	Whose brickyard pillars made perfect wickets
	Last summer, but mind the cars.
	I ran down the road, then cycled.
	Then Vespa'd in a Parka
	Then drove my Dad's Austin
	It's choc-a-block with cars now
	Beatrice, Ellis, Amy
	Three daughters, three roads
	I don't visit anymore.
	Farewell old friends.

Here are some of the images and memories the writer brings into the poem:

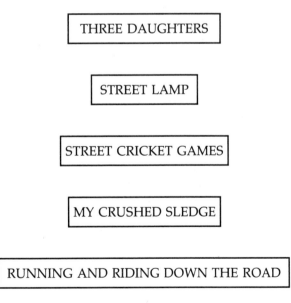

THREE DAUGHTERS

STREET LAMP

STREET CRICKET GAMES

MY CRUSHED SLEDGE

RUNNING AND RIDING DOWN THE ROAD

Think about the street you live (or lived) in and pick out similar images and memories that form in your mind as you do so. Use these images as the basis of your poem. Do not worry if they seem too ordinary – they may well be all the more effective for that.

Reading Different Types of Texts

Unit 2.6 Reading Information

Varieties of Language, Audience and Information ◆ Information in Symbols ◆ Reading Forms ◆ Reading Statistical Information ◆ Statistics and Information Writing ◆ Public Information

◗ *See units 1.2, 2.11, 3.7*

Varieties of Language, Audience and Information

Popular newspapers and television news broadcasts present information about a variety of subjects – such as the economy, Parliament and sport – using language that people can understand, even if they do not know very much about the subject. You do not need specialist knowledge to understand a newspaper headline.

Each of the following is an example of writing directed towards a particular kind of reader, and assumes that the reader understands certain specialised words or phrases. (These are usually known as *jargon*.) The extracts assume that the readers will be receptive to the information in this form.

The left-hander was 36 after he had played defensively at the first two deliveries. Five balls later, he was 56 and most of the 55,000 crowd were standing to applaud his pugnacity.

The first hint of the onslaught came from the third ball, a well-fighted off-break which was greeted with flashing bat and feet, and driven high to bounce a couple of feet inside the fence at deep mid-on. Then Greig pitched short, Hookes, on one knee, swung him fine to the boundary. The next was a classical cover-drive, past the ubiquitous Randall to the fence. Showing his versatility, Hookes took the next ball off his toes through the vacant mid-wicket area to reach his 50 in only 66 balls with eight fours. It also signalled the 50 partnership.

Trouble up the Volga

White: Portisch
Black: Timman

1	Nf3 g6	25	Bc6 Red8
2	e4 Bg7	26	Qc5 d3
3	d4 d6	27	Nb4 d2
4	c4 Bg4	28	Nd3 Qb3
5	Be2 Nc6	29	Nf2 Qa4
6	Be3 e5	30	g3 a6
7	d5 Bxf3	31	b6 Rdc8
8	Bxf3 Nd4	32	b7 Rxc6
9	Bxd4 exd4	33	Qa7 Rxb7
10	Na3 Ne7	34	Qxb7 Rc1
11	0-0 c6	35	Qf3 Qd4
12	Rb1 0-0	36	Kg2 Re1
13	Nc2 c5	37	Nd1 Bf8
14	b4 Nc8	38	Qf2 Qd5
15	Qd3 Qc7	39	Kg1 Rxf1 +
16	Be2 Re8	40	Kxf1 f6
17	bxc5 dxc5	41	exf6 Bxd6
18	f4 b5	42	Qe3 Kf7
19	Rxb5 Nd6	43	Ke2 Bc5
20	e5 Nxb5	44	Qc3 Qe4 +
21	cxb5 Qa5	45	Kf1 Qh1 +
22	d6 Qxa2	46	Ke2 Qxh2
23	Qc4 Qb2	47	Kfl Qh1 +
24	Bf3 Rab8		White resigns

WILLIAM HARTSTON

DIVIDE FOR BACK OPENING

Next row: k. 37(40,43,47), cast off 4. k. to end. Cont. on first 37(40,43,47) sts only until work meas. 53(53,55,55) cm from beg. ending on RS.

Shape Shoulder

Cast off 11(13,14,16) sts. at beg. of next row (12(13,15,16) sts. at next alt. row. Work 1 row, cast off. Rejoin yarn to rem. sts. and rep. as for other side reversing shaping.

FRONT

As Back until work meas. 10cm from beg. ending on WS. Using a separate ball of C colour for each motif, work from graph omitting 2nd C colour, at random all over front (we worked 11 motifs), at same time shape Armholes when work meas. 32(32,33,33) cm by casting off 8 sts. at beg. of next 2 rows 78(84,90,96) sts. Cont. straight until work meas. 47(47,48,48)cm from beg. ending on WS.

DIVIDE FOR NECK

Next row: k. 39(42,45,48), turn and p. to end. First row: k. to last 2 sts. K.2 tog. Second row: p.2 tog. p. to end. Rep. these 2 rows until 23(26,29,32) sts. rem. ending on WS.

Shape Shoulder

Cast off 11(13,14,16) sts. at next row. 12(13,15,16) sts. at next alt. row. Rejoin yarn to rem. sts. and complete to match reversing all shapings.

SLEEVES

Using 3¼mm needles and MC cast on 76(76,78,78) sts. and work 4 rows st.st. k. 2 rows. Cont. in st.st. for 4 more rows. Change to 3rd C and work 2 rows st.st. Cont. in MC, inc. one st. at each end of . . .

THIS WEEK'S release of Rock Against Racism's debut LP, 'RAR's Great Hits', marks an uneasy truce in a battle of ideas that has been raging within RAR for the past several months.

The debate, about questions of political direction, centred around the formation of a limited company, RAR Ltd., to handle the album finances. Four members of RAR's ten-strong central committee resigned, including the three chief 'Temporary Hoarding' workers Ruther Gregory, Syd Shelton and Dave Widgery, after protesting that RAR was becoming too business-minded and claiming that other committee members had acted undemocratically.

The crux of this accusation was that the prospective company was not accountable to RAR members and that details of its formation had been withheld from delegates at RAR's last annual conference at the behest of managing-director John Dennis.

These questions were thrashed out at RAR'S latest quarterly gathering, where it was agreed that only in officio committee members – who're elected annually – could serve as directors of the company.

New committee members were elected to replace the resignees, who reaffirmed their belief in RAR's ideals and intend to continue work at branch level. But with 'Temporary Hoarding' in temporary disarray, the conference decided to put the paper in abeyance and plans are now afoot to replace it with a series of Chinese-style wall-posters, specifically geared to local issues.

Although the dispute has left an inevitable residue of personal acrimony, all 'sides' worked together on the new album and RAR plans to be back on the frontline this autumn with an extensive Rock Against Thatcher campaign to rout the Tories.

YOU CAN HELP PEOPLE ALONG THE ROAD TO SURVIVAL.

To survive, you must reach a road. Walk for days, struggle over mountainous terrain – but for many in Ethiopia today, you must reach a road to survive. This single strip can mean the difference between life and death for millions of people. Dotted along its narrow potholed route, food distribution centres ensure that the people in the drought-affected areas of Ethiopia have the hope as well as the food to sustain their fragile hold on life.

Currently Oxfam is providing emergency relief not only in Ethiopia, but Mozambique, Kampuchea and many other countries around the world. Your gift will be used wherever the need is greatest.

Spectroscopist

Beecham Pharmaceuticals is a large British-owned international company with an outstanding track record for developing and marketing new medicines from our extensive research programmes. We have six research sites in the South East of England employing around 1800 staff and an on-going expansion programme is under way.

Due to internal promotion a Spectroscopist is required to work within a laboratory which provides NMR, MS and IR services for research and development chemists and biochemists at our Chemotherapeutic Research Centre, which is based in the countryside near Dorking, Surrey.

The laboratory is equipped with modern spectroscopic instrumentation which includes Bruker 250 and 400MHz NMR spectrometers and VG 70/70, VG ZAB and Finnigan TSQ70 mass spectrometers. The successful applicant will work closely with other spectroscopists. He or she will be involved primarily in obtaining NMR spectra and reporting results to research and development chemists and biochemists.

Candidates should be qualified to degree or PhD level and have enthusiasm for spectroscopic structure elucidation. Awareness of modern NMR spectroscopy would be particularly advantageous.

To the right candidate we will offer a highly competitive salary together with the fringe benefits associated with a large successful company. Relocation expenses will be paid if appropriate.

To apply, please send your CV, together with an indication of current salary, to the Personnel Manager, Beecham Pharmaceuticals Research Division, Brockham Park, Betchworth, Surrey RH3 7AJ.

Beecham
Pharmaceuticals

Activities

1. First read all six extracts, then in groups, see if you can identify:
   a What the extract is about;
   b The audience for whom the writing is intended;
   c Where the passage is likely to have appeared.
2. Write out a title for each extract.
3. Select one of the titles and write about the same subject, either in prose for a general audience, or in verse.

Information in Symbols

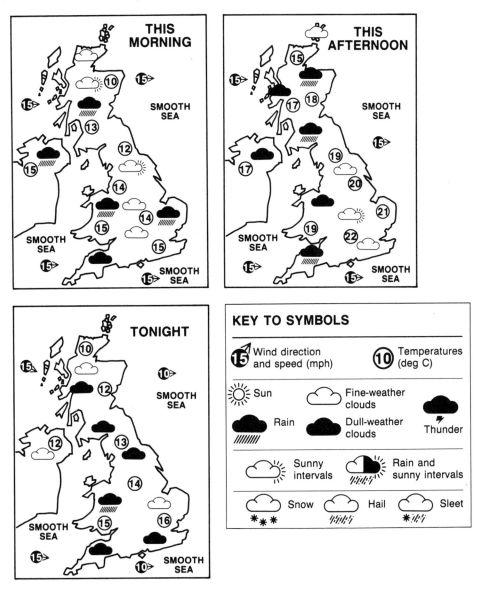

Activities

Activities

1. Study the three weather maps and then write a weather forecast to be read out by a television weather man. You could read your forecast out loud to the class if you wish.
2. How much information is presented here? How much would you need to know beforehand to make sense of this? How clear are the symbols? What do they mean?
3. Why do the British talk about the weather so much?
4. Write a piece about the kind of weather you like, calling it 'Favourite Weather'. Here are some of the different kinds of weather you might write about:

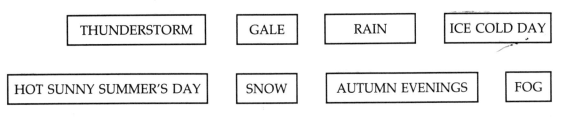

THUNDERSTORM   GALE   RAIN   ICE COLD DAY

HOT SUNNY SUMMER'S DAY   SNOW   AUTUMN EVENINGS   FOG

Describe how this weather affects you, other people and the landscape.

Reading Forms

Camp America is an organisation which recruits young people to work on summer camps in the USA. Read the following application form for Camp America and the notes which go with it.

Activities

1. Make a copy of the form and fill it in. Write a letter of application to go with it.
2. Visit your local post office. Choose three forms (such as a TV licence form, a driving licence form or an application form for a passport) and try filling them in. Then write a report on how clear they are, and how easy to fill in.

Reading Statistical Information

1 Leisure activities by sex, 1973 Great Britain

	Persons engaging in activity frequently[1]			Persons engaging in activity rarely[2]				Persons engaging in activity frequently[1]			Persons engaging in activity rarely[2]		
	Men	Women		Men	Women			Men	Women		Men	Women	
		in full-time employment	Other		In full-time employment	Other			in full-time employment	Other		In full-time employment	Other
Activities at home:							**Activities not at home:**						
Watching television	92	87	92	3	9	5	Visiting friends, family	69	75	73	11	11	9
Reading papers	84	63	80	4	9	8	Going to pub, etc.	62	62	31	29	29	54
Relaxing	73	62	73	17	27	19	Going out for a meal	35	36	21	26	19	35
Listening to music	57	66	69	13	13	15	Club societies	25	19	18	56	75	74
Reading books	37	39	41	39	38	43	Taking part in sport	32	13	7	63	81	91
							Watching sport	31	8	5	52	77	80
							Cinema, theatre, etc.	18	24	9	51	37	54
							Going to bingo	7	13	13	90	86	84

1. Respondents engaging in activities at home for an hour a day or more; for activities outside the home, 'frequently' means two or three times a month or more.
2. Respondents engaging in activities at home for less than an hour a month; for activities outside home, 'rarely' means less than once a year.

2 Leisure activities: League football attendances England and Wales

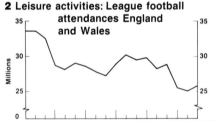

1957/58 1960/61 1963/64 1966/67 1969/70 1972/73 1974/75

3 Leisure activities: Cinemas and television

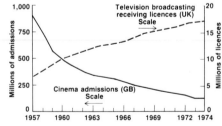

Television broadcasting receiving licences (UK) Scale

Cinema admissions (GB) Scale

1957   1960   1963   1966   1969   1972 1974

4 Holidays

	1964	1969	1974[1]
Holiday[2] visits abroad by UK residents			
Austria	4.7	4.0	3.3
Belgium/Luxembourg	5.3	3.4	2.6
France	12.2	11.2	18.0
Irish Republic	24.0	18.2	7.7
Italy	12.2	8.4	7.4
Netherlands	3.3	3.5	2.8
Spain	14.9	26.7	30.9
Switzerland	6.0	3.8	2.3
Western Germany	4.5	3.5	2.6
Rest of Western Europe	5.7	6.8	9.6
Other countries[3]	7.2	10.5	12.8
Total visits (thousands = 100%)[3]	4,590	5,346	6,662
Holidays[4] taken in Great Britain by residents of Great Britain (millions)	31.0	30.5	40.5

1. Provisional.
2. Holiday as defined by the respondent in the International Passenger Survey.
3. Includes holidays on cruise ships not assigned to particular areas.
4. Defined in the British National Travel Survey as trips of four or more nights away from home, considered to be holidays by the travellers.

Activity

Choose one of tables 1-4 and:

a Write a paragraph explaining what the statistics in the table reveal.

b Write another paragraph describing your personal response to these statistics. Do they surprise you? Have things changed since these statistics were recorded? (As further research you might visit the reference section of your local library and compare the above tables with some more recent government statistics relating to these areas.)

CAMP AMERICA Application Form

Membership No. ______

A
SURNAME/FAMILY NAME ______
FIRST NAME ______ MIDDLE INITIALS ______
CORRESPONDENCE ADDRESS ______
POSTCODE/COUNTRY ______
TELEPHONE ______
PARENTS TELEPHONE ______
PASSPORT NO. ______

B
MALE/FEMALE Weight? ______ Height? ______
Married? Yes ☐ No ☐ Spouse Applying? Yes ☐ No ☐
Nationality ______ Your Occupation ______
Tick if your are the following:
Nurse ☐ Qualified Teacher ☐ University/College Graduate ☐
College/Employer ______ Course content ______
Drivers Licence? Yes ☐ No ☐ Do you smoke? Yes ☐ No ☐
Birth Date ______ (in words) / ______ / ______
Month Day Year

AGE ON JUNE 1st ______

C **DATE OF AVAILABILITY**
JUNE ______

D **DATE DUE HOME** ______

E
Please indicate to which ONE programme you are applying. (tick box)
Make this preference immediately known to your interviewer.
Counsellor ☐ Campower ☐ Family Companion ☐
Would you also like to be considered for a Family Companion position?
Yes ☐ No ☐

F
Do you have experience with American camp programmes?
Yes ☐ No ☐
If yes, in which years? ______
Name of Camp ______
As Camper or Counsellor? ______

PLEASE STAPLE 3 OF THE 4 REQUIRED PASSPORT SIZED PHOTOGRAPHS HERE
USE ATTRACTIVE PHOTOGRAPHS ONLY!
WRITE YOUR NAME ON THE BACK OF EACH PHOTOGRAPH
PUT THE BEST PHOTO ON TOP

G
What is your active religion? ______

H
Would you be willing to work in a Scout Camp? (equivalent to Guide or Pioneer).
Yes ☐ No ☐
Scout/Guide/Ranger experience?
Yes ☐ No ☐
Level ______

I
Would you accept placement at a camp for the learning disabled? ie with children who may be difficult, maladjusted or with emotional problems etc.
Yes ☐ No ☐

J **CAMPOWER APPLICANTS COMPLETE SECTION P**

AREA A - SPORTS

Activity	No	1 or 2
Archery	AA	
Fencing	AB	
Golf	AC	
Basketball	AD	
Judo	AE	
Karate	AF	
Tennis	AG	
Riding	AH	
Riflery	AI	
Soccer	AJ	
Track/field athletics	AK	
Volleyball	AL	
Floor Gymnastics	AM	
Uneven parallel bars	AN	
Balance beam	AO	
Cycling	AP	
Other ______		

AREA B - WATERFRONT

Activity	No	1 or 2
Diving (board)	BA	
Diving (scuba)	BB	
Water-skiing	BC	
Sailing	BD	
Canoeing	BE	
Kayaking	BF	
Motorboat Driving	BG	
Windsurfing	BH	
Other ______		

AREA C - SWIMMING

Activity	No	1 or 2
Swimming	CA	
Life Saving	CB	
Competitive Swim	CC	

AREA D - SCIENCE & OTHERS

Activity	No	1 or 2
Electronics	DA	
Ham Radio	DB	
Astronomy	DC	
Go-Carts	DD	

AREA D - SCIENCE & OTHERS (contd)

Activity	No	1 or 2
Computers	DE	
Radio Broadcast	DF	
Other ______		

AREA E - RELIGION

Activity	No	1 or 2
Bible Study	EA	
Religious Education	EB	
Other ______		

AREA F - CRAFTS

Activity	No	1 or 2
Woodwork	FA	
Metal Work	FB	
Pottery	FC	
Ceramics	FD	
Wheel	FE	
Kiln	FF	
Puppetry	FG	
Leatherwork	FH	
Jewellery	FI	
Weaving	FJ	
Sewing	FK	
Nature Crafts	FL	
Rocketry	FM	
Model Making	FN	
Macrame	FO	
Stained Glass	FP	
Silkscreen	FQ	
Batik	FR	
Other ______		

AREA G - FINE ARTS

Activity	No	1 or 2
Painting	GA	
Sketching	GB	
Sculpturing	GC	
Other ______		

AREA H - VISUAL ARTS

Activity	No	1 or 2
Photography	HA	
Video	HB	
Other ______		

AREA I - PIONEERING

Activity	No	1 or 2
Hiking	IA	
Outdoor Cooking	IB	
Overnight Camping	IC	
Campcraft	ID	
Rock Climbing	IE	
Ropes Course	IF	
Canoe Tripping	IG	

AREA J - NATURE

Activity	No	1 or 2
Forestry	JA	
Ecology	JB	
Botany	JC	
Wildlife	JD	
Farm Animal Care	JE	

AREA K - PERFORMING ARTS

Activity	No	1 or 2
Acting	KA	
Directing	KB	
Stage Management	KC	
Scenery	KD	
Costuming	KE	
Dance: Ballet	KF	
Modern	KG	
Folk	KH	
Aerobics	KI	
Jazz	KJ	

AREA L - MUSIC

Activity	No	1 or 2
Piano: Popular	LA	
Accompany	LB	
Classical	LC	
Show/Musical	LD	
Sight Read	LE	
Transpose	LF	
Guitar: Folk	LG	
Classical	LH	
Rock	LI	
Popular	LJ	
Instruments	LK	
Other ______		

K
Are you experienced and willing to accept placement at camps for the following:—
Mentally handicapped campers?
Yes ☐ No ☐
Physically handicapped campers?
Yes ☐ No ☐
If Yes, ask your interviewer for a supplementary insert.

L
Best activities — List your best 3 activities from Section J.
Note, these will not be considered preferences, and your application may be chosen, based on any of your skills.

Activity	Alpha Code (as listed in J)
1st	
2nd	
3rd	

M
Do you hold Swimming Instruction or Life Saving Certificates?
Yes ☐ No ☐
If Yes — specify certificates ______
Other certificates (eg RSM, LTA, RYA, FA etc.) ______
Other activities not listed in J ______

FOR OFFICE USE

FEE CATEGORY

REFER TO THESE NOTES AS YOU COMPLETE THE FRONT OF THE APPLICATION FORM

SECTION A

1. Complete with your name — as shown on your passport.
2. Ensure you include your postcode and if outside the U.K. your country.
3. Include your telephone area code followed by the number.
4. Check that your passport is valid until at least October/November. If you do not currently possess a valid passport you must apply for one IMMEDIATELY — enter the date of your passport application in the number area.

SECTION B

1. Delete MALE/FEMALE as appropriate.
2. Please convert weight from stones to pounds (2.2 lbs = 1 kilo) ie 1 stone = 14 pounds therefore 9st 4lbs would be entered as 130 lbs.
3. Height should be entered in feet and inches (2½ cms = 1 inch).
4. Enter your current marital status and whether your spouse is applying.
5. Enter your nationality — that is the country from which your passport is issued.
6. State your current occupation. If you have just finished studies or may begin them in the following year enter Student. You can not enter unemployed as an occupation — please call our London office for advice in this instance.
7. Enter the name of your college or employer (company name).
8. Detail the subjects of your course of study if a student.
9. If you hold a current full drivers licence enter a tick for YES. It is a great advantage to possess a full licence particularly for Family Companion Applicants. If you pass your test AFTER submitting your application let us know in the London office and your form will be amended.
10. Some camps are very strictly NO SMOKING (this can even extend to counsellors in the local town during days/evenings off). Others are more lenient and do allow smoking but usually only in certain areas and not infront of the campers. Equally some families will not permit smoking in their homes. If you state that you are a non smoker you must expect NOT TO SMOKE for the entire 9 weeks of your assignment so do not answer NO to this question unless you are absolutely sure you can honour the commitment.

SECTION C

You are required to enter the EARLIEST date in JUNE that you can depart for the United States. An early day will ensure a better chance of placement.

SECTION D

The majority of American summer camps continue until approximately August 20th some until later. You **MUST** be available to stay in the U.S. at least until our first return flight on August 25. The date you enter here will in no way be taken as your return date choice — you will be asked to make that selection once your placement is arranged. The date you enter here should be the LATEST date you are available to stay in the U.S.

SECTION E

Please tick the MAIN programme to which you are applying — you should essentially apply to one programme. You are given the option of also indicating that you would accept a Family Companion placement — please think very carefully before answering YES, if you have any doubts do not answer this question until your interview. You should not answer YES in an attempt to increase your placement chances — seek your interviewer's advice. **If you wish to apply to the campower programme you must be a student.**

SECTION F

Answer yes if you have spent a summer at an American Summer Camp. Give the years you were in attendance and name the camp. Detail your position at camp ie Counsellor or Camper.

SECTION G

If you are not religiously active leave this section blank. If you are active please be as specific as possible ie orthodox Jewish, Lutheran etc.

SECTION H

You do not necessarily need to have experience of the Scouts or Guides in order to be willing to work at such camps. If you are experienced please indicate this, state the level you achieved ie Guide or Ranger or Scout etc.

SECTION I

Some camps cater for children who have special educational needs. At such camps children will be required to spend sometime in lessons (taught by qualified American staff) in addition to doing normal camp activities. These children will often require counsellors with greater patience but the satisfaction you can derive from working with such children can be great. Tick YES if you would accept placement at such a camp.

SECTION J

Don't let this daunting area put you off — you do not have to be an olympic champion in order to apply to Camp America. You are not expected to cover all these areas by any means — indeed Campower/Nursing Aide applicants for instance need not complete it at all. If you have a particular problem with this section you can initially complete it in pencil and pen over it at your interview. To complete this section enter a 1 against any activity which you can teach and organise (those in which you have teaching experience usually). Put a 2 after those activities you can assist in teaching. Please remember that the degree of competence required will vary from one camp to another! Also you will not generally teach or assist ALL the activities that you mark. This is not necessarily to be taken as an indication of your expected duties at camp rather it is a devise whereby Camp Directors/Families can see at a glance the areas in which you can be called upon to help if necessary.

SECTION K

There are many openings for counsellors in camps for the mentally and physically handicapped — you must however be aware of the extraordinary demands of such positions. Work on such camps is the most difficult area of work available through Camp America (but can also be the most rewarding). It is our opinion that ONLY applicants with EXPERIENCE of caring for the handicapped should answer YES to these questions. If you do answer YES please note that assignment to such a placement is highly likely. If you are experienced in this type of work but do not wish for placement at such a camp do NOT answer yes but DO detail your caring experience on page 3 of this form (under experience with children), include a statement in this description that you do not wish to be placed at such a camp.

N.B. CAMPERS AT HANDICAPPED CAMPS USUALLY INCLUDE A HIGH NUMBER OF ADULT CAMPERS. Many specialised camps cater for both handicapped groups (ie both mentally and physically handicapped).

SECTION L

On page 2 of this form you will be required to detail your experience, qualifications etc regarding your ability to teach or assist in your 3 best (strongest) activities (as indicated in section J). These 3 activities should be listed in this section.

SECTION M

List any practical (not academic) awards and certificates that you have — indicate levels ie **RLS Bronze Medallion Life Saving** etc. Copies of your life saving certificates etc must be included with your application. If you hold a bronze medallion it should be taken to your interview for viewing.

State any other activities in which you are experienced (that are not already listed in section J. These activities can be basically anything from tight-rope walking to paper craft, candle making to lama treking!

SECTIONS N/O

Complete these sections fully and clearly.

SECTION P

Only complete this section if you are applying to the Campower programme. Campower applicants must be students.

SECTIONS Q/T

Complete with as much detail as possible.

SECTION U

Take special note of this statement. Camp America is rigorous in its selection procedure.

SECTION V

Ensure you have read the brochure completely, and understand the programme conditions. Unsigned applications will not be accepted.

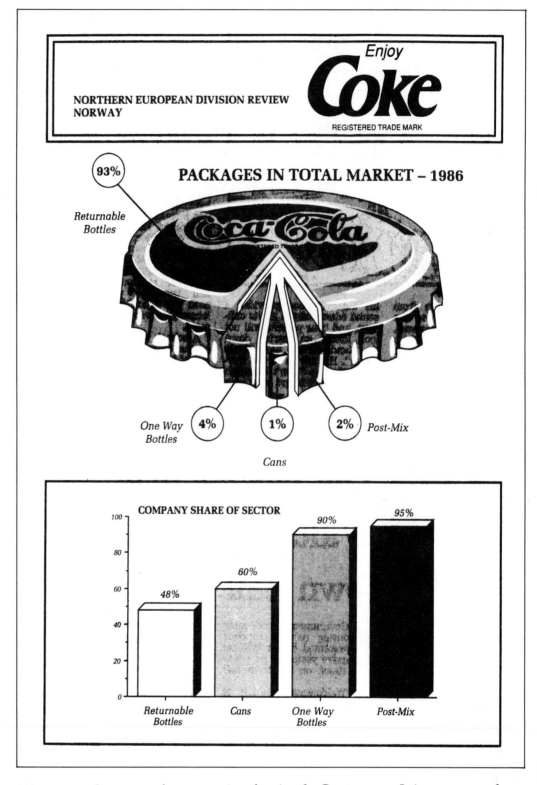

(A) appeared as part of a promotion for Apple Computers. It is meant to show how an Apple Computer can be used to design pages, not to advertise Coke. How successful do you think it is? (B) appeared in a local paper as part of an article about the dangers of excessive beer drinking. Both present information by means of graphics.

Questions

1. In 1986 what percentage of Coke was not sold in returnable bottles?
2. What percentage of cans sold in Norway in 1986 were not cans of Coke?
3. Why do they take the United States as the means of determining the wealth index?

4. From your reading of the paragraphs under the heading of Promotions, what do you understand a promotion to be?
5. How many pints of beer does the 'heavy drinker' consume per week?
6. In how many areas of Britain do people drink more than the GB average?
7. What is the figure for the area in which you live? Does it surprise you?
8. Comment on how the beer glass and the Coca Cola top are used in the diagrams, AND the two different Coca Cola logos.
9. There are ways of showing information in these two pieces of evidence. Which one presents its information most clearly? Give your reasons.

Statistics and Information Writing

The following article appeared in the *Guardian*.

Pupils take pub and homework in moderation

THE parents of Britain's preteens and early adolescents can forget what they read in newspapers about 14-year-olds taking part in drunken orgies at unsupervised parties or watching hours of porno movies on a friend's video when they should be doing homework.

If the replies of 18,002 pupils aged between 11 and 16 in a survey published yesterday are sincere and honest, not even somebody else's children are doing it.

The times may be changing, with less homework, more paid work, more under-age drinking, less reading of books for pleasure, more "steadies" at 11 or 12, more dieting, more high-fibre meals. But significant numbers still do not smoke, drink alcohol, or go to discos. And many more take a lot of showers and baths, wash their hair at least twice a week, save money — and don't eat chips.

The survey was carried out last year in 88 schools by the Health Education Authority's schools health education unit at Exeter University, the sixth in the series.

The authors, headed by Professor John Balding, the unit's director, admit that it is not a balanced sample, since questionnaires used are supplied by schools wanting to take part. But they insist it is representative.

They believe they have taken steps to prevent children giving dishonest, provocative or expected answers, by instituting systematic checks.

The findings show that 1 per cent of 11 and 12-year-old boys had an alcoholic drink every day of the week before they were questioned while 0.4 per cent had drunk more than eight pints of beer or lager and 0.5 per cent had consumed more than 21 units of alcohol, with 2.3 per cent drinking between 11 and 20. Only just over half had no drink at all, compared with 66 per cent of girls at the same age.

But a further third of boys in this age group had had a drink on only one day. Proportionately more girls of the same age said the same.

The survey does show that very young adolescents are able to buy alcohol at supermarkets and off-licences (around 5 per cent), while many more (nearly 14 per cent of both boys and girls) have been to a pub or bar at least once a week.

While 6.9 per cent of 15 and 16-year-olds said they did not want to stop smoking, 13.5 per cent of boys and 18.6 per cent of girls had given up - and 14.6 per cent of boys and 16.8 per cent of girls would like to give up.

Just under a third of the 11 and 12-year-olds said they had been given no homework on the previous day, while this proportion had risen to almost three out of five by age 15 and 16.

On the topic of TV, 18.5 per cent of 11 and 12-year-old boys and 11.2 per cent of girls of the same age said they watched more than five hours the previous day. As they get older they watch less.

By the age of 15/16, 68 per cent of boys and 54 per cent of girls confessed to reading not a single book for pleasure at home on the previous day.

Quite a few children, even at the earliest ages surveyed, do paid work, with just under a half at 15/16 getting their own income, not just pocket money. Of the later group, a fifth work in the evenings during term-time; one in 10 do more than 10 hours a week; and 16.8 per cent of boys and 19.2 per cent of girls get more than £10 a week.

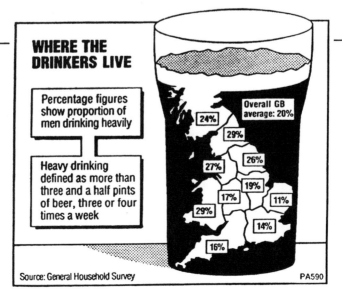

PERCENTAGE OF CHILDREN WHO CONSIDER THEMSELVES TO BE SMOKERS

Boys / Girls

Age Group	Boys	Girls
11-12	2%	1%
12-13	4%	5%
13-14	11%	14%
14-15	17%	23%
15-16	22%	24%

PERCENTAGE OF CHILDREN WHO HAD CONSUMED ANY ALCOHOLIC DRINK DURING THE PAST SEVEN DAYS

Boys / Girls

Age Group	Boys	Girls
11-12	47%	34%
12-13	58%	44%
13-14	65%	55%
14-15	69%	62%
15-16	72%	65%

WHERE THE DRINKERS LIVE

Percentage figures show proportion of men drinking heavily

Heavy drinking defined as more than three and a half pints of beer, three or four times a week

Overall GB average: 20%

24% 29% 27% 26% 19% 17% 11% 29% 14% 16%

Source: General Household Survey   PA590

Questions

1. Study the graphs. Are the results shown what you would expect?
2. Read the article. Do the findings in it match your experience or the experience of your friends?
3. Should it be made more difficult and/or more expensive to buy (a) cigarettes? (b) alcohol?

Activity

Someone has written an article in your local paper criticising young people and their lifestyles. Using the information in the *Guardian* article, write a letter to your local paper, giving what you think is an accurate picture of teenagers' lifestyles. Write about the way you live, and compare your lifestyle with the supposed lifestyle that the article in the local paper was complaining about. Call your letter 'I am not a typical teenager'.

Public Information

The Government produces many information leaflets, on topics from child nutrition to retirement pensions. Opposite is a page from a public information book on crime, which uses both words and pictures to show how you can protect your home from burglars.

Questions

1. How long does the author think it will take you to read this data? How long did it take you?
2. How many burglaries are committed by professional burglars?
3. If your home has 'louvre windows' what does the data recommend you do?
4. What should you do with ladders?
5. What is a deadlock? Where should you use it?

Activities

1. Using the information on this page, write 'An Ex-Burglar's Confession' as a speech delivered to a Neighbourhood Watch meeting.
2. Write a description of the exterior of the house, as it would appear in an Estate Agent's leaflet. To get an idea of how Estate Agents write, visit one and ask for some of their literature.
3. Imagine and describe the contents of this house.

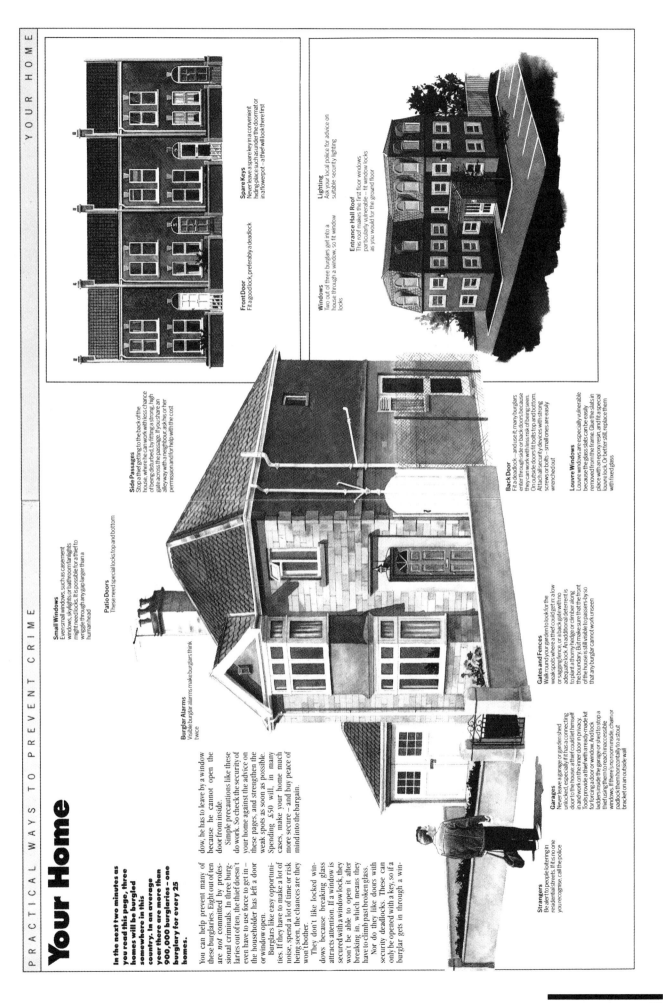

YOUR HOME

PRACTICAL WAYS TO PREVENT CRIME

Your Home

In the next two minutes as you read this page, three homes will be burgled somewhere in this country. In an average year there are more than 900,000 burglaries – one burglary for every 25 homes.

You can help prevent many of these burglaries. Eight out of ten are *not* committed by professional criminals. In three burglaries out of ten, the thief doesn't even have to use force to get in – the householder has left a door or window open.

Burglars like easy opportunities. If they have to make a lot of noise, spend a lot of time or risk being seen, the chances are they won't bother.

They don't like locked windows because breaking glass attracts attention. If a window is secured with a window lock, they won't be able to open it after breaking in, which means they have to climb past broken glass.

Nor do they like doors with security deadlocks. These can only be opened with a key, so if a burglar gets in through a win-

dow, he has to leave by a window because he cannot open the door from inside.

Simple precautions like these do work. So check the security of your home against the advice on these pages, and strengthen the weak spots as soon as possible. Spending £50 will, in many cases, make your home much more secure – and buy peace of mind into the bargain.

Strangers
Be alert to people loitering in residential streets. If it's no one you recognise, call the police

Garages
Never leave a garage or garden shed unlocked, especially if it has a connecting door to the house: a thief could let himself in and work on the inner door in privacy. Tools provide a thief with a ready-made kit for forcing a door or window. And lock ladders inside the garage or shed to stop a thief using them to reach inaccessible windows. If there's no room inside, chain or padlock them horizontally to a stout bracket on an outside wall

Burglar Alarms
Visible burglar alarms make burglars think twice

Small Windows
Even small windows, such as casement windows, skylights or bathroom fanlights might need locks. It's possible for a thief to wriggle through any gap larger than a human head

Patio Doors
These need special locks top and bottom

Side Passages
Stop a thief getting to the back of the house, where he can work with less chance of being disturbed, by fitting a strong, high gate across the passage. If you share an alleyway with a neighbour, ask his or her permission and for help with the cost

Front Door
Fit a good lock, preferably a deadlock

Spare Keys
Never leave a spare key in a convenient hiding place, such as under the doormat or in a flowerpot – a thief will look there first

Windows
Two out of three burglars get into a house through a window, so fit window locks

Lighting
Ask your local police for advice on suitable security lighting

Entrance Hall Roof
This roof makes the first floor windows particularly vulnerable – fit window locks as you would for the ground floor

Back Door
Fit a deadlock – and use it: many burglars enter through side or back doors because they can work with less risk of being seen. On outside doors fit bolts top and bottom. Attach all security devices with strong screws or bolts – small ones are easily wrenched out

Louvre Windows
Louvre windows are especially vulnerable because the glass slats can be easily removed from the frame. Glue the slats in place with an epoxy resin, and fit a special louvre lock. Or better still, replace them with fixed glass

Gates and Fences
Walk round your garden to look for the weak spots where a thief could get in: a low or sagging fence, or a back gate with no adequate lock. An additional deterrent is to plant a thorny hedge or climber along the boundary. But make sure that the front of the house is still visible to passers-by so that any burglar cannot work unseen

See units 2.1, 2.2, 2.3

Reading Different Types of Texts

Unit 2.7 First Impressions

Introduction ◆ Covers and Blurbs ◆ Titles

Introduction

This unit, and many of those that follow, focuses on books. If you are following a GCSE course you are probably aware of the importance of wider reading and the need to sample as many books as possible. This unit looks at the first impressions we get of a book.

First Impressions

Linda Gardner

I walk by you
And there is an immediate tense atmosphere
Because of the way I dress and the way I walk.
My outline is hard and cold
And maybe when I speak
It is sharp and abrupt
But why don't you stop
Talk to me
Don't judge me by my appearance
Don't talk about fighting and anger
Talk about the moon and stars
About love and friendship
The atmosphere should become relaxed and free.

Some people find it hard to show their emotional feelings
So they hide behind a suit of armour
First impressions can be deceiving!

Activities

1. Discuss your first impression of
   - your English teacher
   - a holiday town
   - your present school or college.
2. Write a story called 'First Impressions' or write about the way first impressions influence us.

Covers and Blurbs

'You can't judge a book by its cover'. You can't, but we do. In fact, we judge everything around us by its appearance. People, places, rock bands – don't we respond immediately to what they look like?

The same is true of books. The cover or jacket of a book may interest us or it may turn us off, just as film posters and television trailers sometimes make us want to see the film or programme. Here is an example.

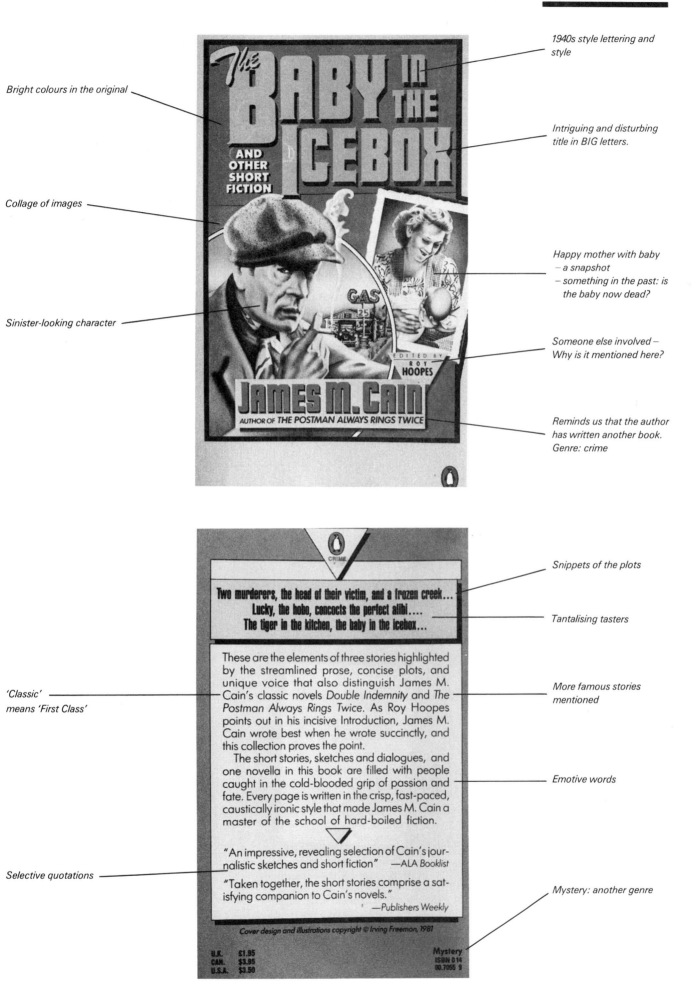

Bright colours in the original

Collage of images

Sinister-looking character

1940s style lettering and style

Intriguing and disturbing title in BIG letters.

Happy mother with baby
— a snapshot
— something in the past: is the baby now dead?

Someone else involved – Why is it mentioned here?

Reminds us that the author has written another book. Genre: crime

'Classic' means 'First Class'

Selective quotations

Snippets of the plots

Tantalising tasters

More famous stories mentioned

Emotive words

Mystery: another genre

Activity

♦ Here are six book covers and six blurbs (the enticing descriptions publishers put on the back of their books).

♦ Decide which blurb goes with which cover. Look carefully at the cover and see if you can match images to words. Does the blurb tell you anything the cover illustration does not? Does the illustration give further information?

♦ Look again at each cover and then decide which ones strike you immediately as interesting and which ones do not.
  a What is attractive about the covers you like? Is it the picture? Is it the way that the title is printed? Is it the print size?
  b What would you expect to find in the books with the covers you like best? What kind of story? Look at Catch 22, for example. Is it likely to be a Western, a horror story, a comic story, a war novel or something else?

♦ Choose a book which you have read recently and design a cover for it. If you are not very good at drawing just concentrate on the layout of the title and author's name: you do not have to include a picture. When you have done this, draw the outline of the back cover on a piece of paper, and in this write a blurb that would encourage someone to buy the book.

The verse we have chosen is meant ... to amplify notions of what poetry is. We have, for example, included a number of poems from oral cultures – hunters' prayers, charms, incantations of various kinds – which fill an emotional space that literary verse tends to leave empty. We have used much contemporary verse in translation because this often reaches its way towards awareness not commonly touched on by the vernacular literature. And we have fetched material from America fairly deliberately since this part of the English language inheritance is not as current here as it might be.

IN THE GREEDY, GRASPING MEDIA BUSINESS, MARRIED MEN DON'T STAY THAT WAY FOR LONG . . .
DAVID COOPER CHEATS . . . HIS WIFE DOESN'T . . . BUT THEN CLAUDIA COMES INTO HIS LIFE AND DAVID WANTS OUT OF HIS MARRIAGE. BUT CLAUDIA WANTS HER NAME IN LIGHTS AND DOESN'T CARE HOW SHE GETS IT THERE . . .
PHONY SHOWBIZ PROMISES . . . HUSTLERS WITH LITTLE TALENT AND NO PRINCIPLES . . . THE POWER OF THE CASTING COUCH . . . ALL PLAY THEIR PART IN THIS DEVASTATINGLY RAUNCHY EXPOSÉ OF LIFE IN THE FASTEST LANE OF ALL.

This is one of the most significant novels to have appeared this century. It was the first novel to reveal the true reality of the subjection and destitution of working class life in 'the good old days' of the Edwardian age – an age when everybody knew his place and because of it was supposed to be content. It is a masterpiece of its kind, a passionate, bitter journey through hell: 'a real hell inhabited by real people, a hell made by one's fellow men'.

RAVE REVIEWS FOR THIS TOTALLY ORIGINAL NOVEL.
"Remarkable, mind-spinning, rave of a novel. Uniquely funny." Kenneth Allsop, DAILY MAIL.
"Comic, macabre, knockabout, nightmarish, ironic, bawdy, illogical, formless, Shavian." BOOKS AND BOOKMEN.
"Blessedly, monstrously, bloatedly, cynically, funnily, and fantastically unique. No one has ever written a book like this." FINANCIAL TIMES.
"A wild moving, shocking, hilarious, raging, exhilarating, giant roller-coaster of a book." NEW YORK HERALD TRIBUNE.

This guide is not an arid list of Dos and Don'ts, though it is very practical in the advice it gives. It is a witty and engaging discussion, aims to stimulate literary and historical research on the one hand, while disciplining it on the other. Although written primarily with students of literature and history in mind, it deals with issues no less of concern to students of law, social science and the physical sciences. Any student faced with a thesis, dissertation or extended essay should find it helpful and entertaining in equal measure.

This fantasy of the future is one of the author's best-known books. Its impact on the modern world has been considerable. Abandoning his mordant criticism of modern men and morals, the author switches to the future and shows us life as he conceives it may be some thousands of years hence. Written in the thirties when – whatever the immediate outlook may have been – people believed that ultimately all would be for the best in the best of all possible worlds, this novel is a warning against such optimism. With irrepressible wit and raillery, the author satirizes the idea of progress put forward by the scientists and philosophers; and his world of test-tube babies and 'feelies' is uncomfortably closer now than it was when the book was first published.

THE RATTLE BAG

edited by
Seamus Heaney
and
Ted Hughes

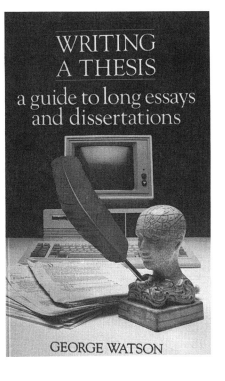

WRITING A THESIS

a guide to long essays and dissertations

GEORGE WATSON

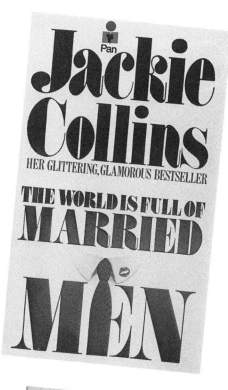

Pan

Jackie Collins

HER GLITTERING, GLAMOROUS BESTSELLER

THE WORLD IS FULL OF MARRIED MEN

THE RAGGED TROUSERED PHILANTHROPISTS

Robert Tressell
With an introduction by
ALAN SILLITOE

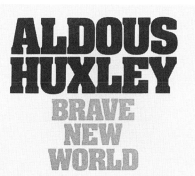

ALDOUS HUXLEY

BRAVE NEW WORLD

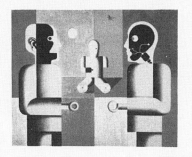

JOSEPH HELLER

THE POLYMESMERIC NOVEL THAT NO ONE WILL FORGET

CATCH 22

With a new introduction by
ANTHONY BURGESS

Titles

The title of a book is very important. *Jaws* is a title which suggests very snappily what a book is about. A successful title will:

a reflect the book's content
b be memorable.

What makes a title attractive? Is the *Field of Blood* more likely to appeal than *Rambling down the Manchester Ship Canal*? Is it more eyecatching than *The Naked Nun and the Axe Man*? It obviously depends on the reader.

Activities

Here are 50 book titles – the 50 most popular books in Britain in 1987. Choose 20 that immediately create a picture in your mind. Write the titles down and compare your selections and descriptions with those chosen by the rest of the class.

1. Write a blurb for five of these books.
2. Choose one of these titles and draft or write a story using the title you have chosen.
3. Get the current 100 best sellers list (it appears in the *Bookseller* magazine in January of each year) and compare it with this list.
4. What title would you give to:

> YOUR AUTOBIOGRAPHY

> A HISTORY OF YOUR COMMUNITY/TOWN

> THE HISTORY OF THE SCHOOL/COLLEGE

> A CLASS OR COLLEGE MAGAZINE

> A COMPILATION OF YOUR FAVOURITE MUSIC

> BIOGRAPHY OF A PERSON YOU ADMIRE

> A REFERENCE BOOK OF COURSES AND TRAINING AVAILABLE IN YOUR COMMUNITY

Which type of book is most popular?	No.	TITLE	GENRE	AUTHOR
	1	Hold the Dream	Saga	B. Taylor Bradford (Br)
	2	The Burning Shore	Yarn	Wilbur Smith (Br)
	3	Lucky	Novel	Jackie Collins (Br)
	4	If Tomorrow Comes	Novel	Sidney Sheldon (US)
Which one word title do	5	Dinner of Herbs	Saga	Catherine Cookson (Br)
you like best?	6	London Match	Thriller	Len Deighton (Br)
Why?	7	Echoes	Novel	Maeve Binchy (Irish)
	8	Moon	Horror	James Herbert (Br)
	9	Proof	Thriller	Dick Francis (Br)
	10	Riders	Novel	Jilly Cooper (Br)
	11	Confessional	Thriller	Jack Higgins (Br)
Which authors appear	12	The Lonely Sea	Thriller	Alistair MacLean (Br)
most often?	13	Is That It?	Autobiog	Bob Geldof (Irish)
	14	How To Be A Complete Bastard	Humour	Ade Edmondson (Br)
	15	Harold	Saga	Catherine Cookson (Br)
	16	Family Album	Romance	Danielle Steele (US)
	17	Secrets	Romance	Danielle Steele (US)
Which is the longest title?	18	The Mammoth Hunters	Saga	Jean Auel (US)
How many words does it	19	Skeleton Crew	Horror	Stephen King (US)
have?	20	Wicked Willie's Guide	Humour	Jolliffe & Mayle (Br)
	21	Juggernaut	Thriller	Desmond Bagley (Br)
	22	The Sicilian	Novel	Mario Puzo (US)
	23	Paradise Postponed	Saga	John Mortimer (Br)
	24	Thinner	Horror	Richard Bachman (US)
From which country do	25	Jian	Thriller	Eric van Lustbader (US)
most of the novelists	26	Hunt for Red October	Thriller	Tom Clancy (US)
seem to come?	27	Queenie	Novel	Michael Korda (US)
	28	Creed for 3rd Millennium	Fantasy	Colleen McCullough (Aust)
	29	The Red Fox	Thriller	Anthony Hyde (US)
	30	Lily My Lovely	Saga	Lena Kennedy (Br)
	31	Lime Street At Two	Autobiog	Helen Forrester (Br)
Write down the names of	32	Goddess	Biog	Anthony Summers (Bri)
the authors you	33	Horoscopes 1987	Fantasy	Patric Walker
recognise, along with	34	Field of Blood	Thriller	Gerald Seymour (Bri)
other books they have	35	Cover Story	Thriller	Colin Forbes (Bri)
written	36	Ambassador's Women	Hist Rom	Catherine Gaskin (Bri)
	37	Red Crystal	Thriller	Clare Francis (Bri)
	38	Boy	Autobiog	Roald Dahl (Bri)
	39	Falling Towards England	Autobiog	Clive James (Aust)
	40	Dirty Beasts		Roald Dahl (Bri)
	41	Voice of Love	Ragbag	Doris Stokes (Bri)
	42	Chapter House Dune	Sf	Frank Herbert (US)
	43	Blessing In Disguise	Autobiog	Alec Guinness (Bri)
	44	A Man Cannot Cry	Saga	Gloria Keverne (S Afr)
	45	Lacocca	Biog	William Novak (US)
	46	The World, the Flesh	Novel	Reay Tannahill (Bri)
	47	Where Have All The Bullets	Autobiog	Spike Milligan (Bri)
	48	The Class	Novel	Erich Segal (US)
	49	Too Much Too Soon	Novel	Jacqueline Briskin (US)
	50	Making Rubik's Magic	Gamebook	Albie Fiore (Bri)

Reading Different Types of Texts

Unit 2.8 Openings: Mainly about Novels

Television and Film ◆ Books ◆ Openings: How they
Work ◆ Openings ◆ More Openings

◗ *See units 4.1–4.4, 4.7*

Television and Film

Raiders of the Lost Ark begins with Indiana Jones defying death to retrieve a stone idol from a cave. The film *Jaws* begins with a girl going for a midnight swim, and being attacked by a shark which we do not see. *Star Wars* begins with a rebel spaceship being overpowered by overwhelmingly superior forces. Television and radio serials often begin with a dramatic event – the continuation of the cliffhanger with which the last episode ended.

Books

Once the cover, the blurb or someone's recommendation has encouraged us to pick up a book, we then usually leaf through it, noticing the length, the contents list, the presence or absence of illustrations, and perhaps the size of the type. We may then go on to sample the opening paragraph and this will influence our first impression of the book.

Not all novels begin with action. They often open quietly, setting the scene. Good openings work on lots of levels. They set both the general period and the specific time, give some basic information about what is going to happen and who is in the book.

Here is the opening of *Wuthering Heights*, which does all of these things.

Wuthering Heights

Emily Brontë

Precise date: 1801
Setting: remote country area of England
Plot interest: why is Heathcliff suspicious and why has the narrator withdrawn from society? A character—Heathcliff—is introduced.

1801 – I have just returned from a visit to my landlord – the solitary neighbour that I shall be troubled with. This is certainly a beautiful country! In all England, I do not believe that I could have fixed on a situation so completely removed from the stir of society. A perfect misanthropist's Heaven: and Mr. Heathcliff and I are such a suitable pair to divide the desolation between us. A capital fellow! He little imagined how my heart warmed towards him when I beheld his black eyes withdraw so suspiciously under their brows, as I rode up, and when his fingers sheltered themselves, with a jealous resolution, still further in his waistcoat, as I announced my name.

Here is an opening that concentrates on setting the scene, but also suggests a future time.

Brave New World Aldous Huxley	A squat grey building of only thirty-four storeys. Over the main entrance the words CENTRAL LONDON HATCHERY AND CONDITIONING CENTRE and in a shield, the World State's motto COMMUNITY, IDENTITY, STABILITY.

Here is an opening that provides the first step in the plot.

I'm the King of the Castle Susan Hill	Three months ago, his grandmother died, and then they moved to this house.

Here is an opening that sets the tone.

Catch 22 Joseph Heller	It was love at first sight. The first time Yossarian saw the chaplain he fell madly in love with him.

Which words would you use to describe the tone here:

ROMANTIC?	SERIOUS?	HUMOROUS?	ANGRY?	SUSPICIOUS?

Openings: How they Work

The opening page of a novel does not always make clear where we are supposed to be – future, past or present – but it is worth looking for clues just the same. The author may send us an early signal, telling us the kind of world we are in. Several writers have set their stories in a world after a nuclear war. How soon can we recognise this?

Openings

Here is an early signal, on the first page of a novel called *Z for Zachariah* by Robert C. O'Brien. The book opens with a description of smoke rising from a camp fire on Claypole Ridge; ordinary enough. But then there is this:

> Beyond Claypole Ridge there is Ogden town, about ten miles further. But there is no-one left alive in Ogden town.

This sentence signals to us that the events in the novel take place in a particular world – a world in which there has been some kind of terrible disaster.

The next sentence reinforces this:

I know because after the war ended and all the telephones went dead . . .

On the second page there is another disturbing signal:

There were dead birds all over the streets.

All of these clues or signals prepare us for the awful truth: there has been an atomic war.

More Openings

Here are four more openings of novels.

1984
George Orwell

1. 'It was a bright cold day in April, and the clocks were striking thirteen. Winston Smith, his chin nuzzled into his breast in an effort to escape the vile wind, slipped quickly through the glass doors of Victory Mansion, though not quickly enough to prevent a swirl of gritty dust from entering along with him.'

The Day of the Triffids
John Wyndham

2. 'When I was quite small I would sometimes dream of a city . . . the traffic in the streets was strange, carts with no horses to pull them, and sometimes there were things in the sky, shiny fish-shaped things that were certainly not birds . . . Dreams were funny things . . . so it might be that what I was seeing was a bit of the world as it had been once upon a time – the wonderful world that the old people had lived in, as it had been before God sent tribulation.'

Sometimes authors plunge straight into a story. Here is the beginning of Robert Leeson's *It's My Life*:

It's my Life
Robert Leeson

3. Peter Carey cut across the scrum by the gate as the school yard emptied and stopped in front of Jan.
   "Doing anything on Friday night?"
   For a second she was stuck for words, embarrassed. She made a face and shrugged. He went on, "There's a disco at the college . . ."
   Their eyes crossed. The wind whipped the scarf across his face and Jan thought of Dick Turpin. He wasn't asking her. He was telling her.
   "I'll let you know."

Instead of waking up with a toothache, or a temperature, Gregor Samsa wakes up with an unusual problem:

Metamorphosis
Franz Kafka

4. As Gregor Samsa awoke one morning from uneasy dreams he found himself transformed in his bed into a giant insect. He was lying on his hard, as it were, armour-plated back and when he lifted his head a little he could see his dome-like brown belly divided into stiff arched segments, on top of which the bed quilt could hardly keep in position and was about to slide off completely. His numerous legs, which were pitifully thin compared to the rest of his bulk, waved helplessly before his eyes.

Questions

1. What information are we given in these openings about:
   a the specific time?
   b the period – past, present or future?
   c the setting?
   d the characters in the book?
2. What would you expect to happen next after each of the openings 2, 3, and 4.
3. In pairs, discuss and compare openings 3 and 4. Which would you find easier to continue if you were asked to do so in an examination? Why?

Reading Different Types of Texts

Unit 2.9 Plot and Narrative

Plot ◆ Plots in Novels ◆ Gulliver's Travels ◆ Example of Narrative

◗ *See units 3.12, 4.7*

Plot

For many readers the greatest pleasure to be had from a book is in wondering how a story is going to end. People like to read stories with a distinct plot. A plot is a series of events, one of which leads to another.

Activity

Borrow a copy of Grimms' Fairy Tales from the junior section of your local library. Read two or three of the stories. Then write your own story in the same style.

Plots in Novels

We will now look at some novels and see how the plots build up, and how each important incident is built into another. You probably know *Lord of the Flies*, by William Golding. Here is the plot, presented as a graph. As well as showing the *events* of the novel, it also shows how the plot moves from 'civilisation' to 'evil' through the novel.

Activities

1. Produce a similar graph to show the plot movement in terms either of action (peaks for action-packed chapters, troughs for quiet, reflective or descriptive ones) or emotion (peaks for strong or violent emotions, troughs for lighter, gentler ones) from a book of your choice.
2. Write about what your graph reveals about the plot.

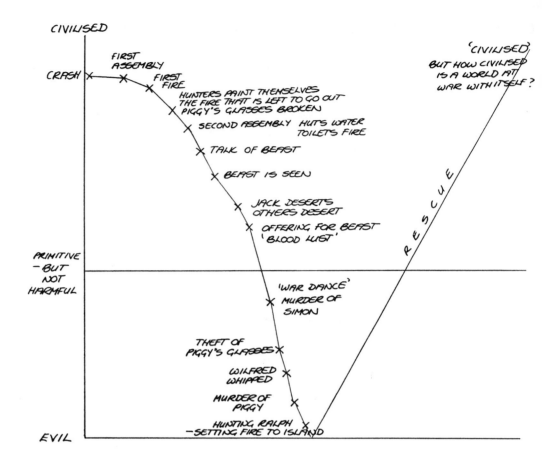

Gulliver's Travels

Here is another way of seeing how a plot develops. This is the contents page of *Gulliver's Voyage to Lilliput* from *Gulliver's Travels* by Jonathan Swift.

PART ONE – A VOYAGE TO LILLIPUT

Chapter I

Chapter II

Chapter III

Chapter IV

Chapter V

The author by an extraordinary stratagem prevents an invasion. A high title of honour is conferred upon him. Ambassadors arrive from the Emperor of Blefuscu, and sue for peace. The empress's apartment on fire by an accident; the author instrumental in saving the rest of the palace   48

Chapter VI

Of the inhabitants of Lilliput; their learning, laws, and customs. The manner of educating their children. The author's way of living in that country. His vindication of a great lady   55

Chapter VII

The author being informed of a design to accuse him of high treason, maketh his escape to Blefuscu. His reception there   65

Chapter VIII

The author, by a lucky accident, finds means to leave Blefuscu; and, after some difficulties, returns safe to his native country   74

1. How much of the Contents is plot? How much is description? Take a sheet of paper and write numbers one to eight in a narrow column down the left hand side. Divide the rest of the sheet into two columns, with the headings PLOT and DESCRIPTION. For each of the eight chapters of the contents, list the events of Gulliver's voyage under PLOT, and descriptive elements under DESCRIPTION.
2. Try to tell the story of *Gulliver's Voyage to Lilliput* in 1,000 words from the information in the contents list.
3. Make up a chapter title for each of the eight chapters.
4. Choose a novel you have read, and write out a contents list in the same way as *Gulliver's Voyage to Lilliput*. Try to keep the contents list to the same style as the novel you have chosen.

Plot as Episodes

Here is how a plot unfolds, episode by episode. The novel *Hard Times*, by Charles Dickens, was originally published in 20 parts in a magazine *Household Words*. Here are the parts:

Plot Questions	Episodes	Significant Plot Development
Early episodes establish a number of separate plots	Part 1	Circus girl Cecilia (Sissy) starts at Mr Gradgrind's strict school in Coketown. Other pupils include Mr Gradgrind's children, Tom and Louisa. Later, Tom and Louisa are discovered at the circus.
	Part 2	Factory and bank owner Mr Bounderby is introduced. He is an arrogant, self-made man and a great friend of Gradgrind's.
	Part 3	Bounderby and Gradgrind visit the circus people and tell them to take Sissy away,

Plot Questions	Episodes	Significant Plot Development
		because she is making Gradgrind's children interested in the circus.
What will Tom do?	Part 4	Tom plans to get revenge for his strict schooling.
What will Stephen do?	Part 5	One of Bounderby's poor factory workers, Stephen Blackpool – an alcoholic – is introduced. He wants to be divorced but Bounderby says he must accept his lot.
Who is this woman? (Answer – Part 17)	Part 6	A mysterious woman appears and asks questions about Bounderby.
Will they marry? (Answer – next Part)	Part 7	The awful Bounderby wants to marry Louisa. She loathes his kisses but has no fight in her.
Will they stay together (Answer – Part 11)	Part 8	Louisa marries Bounderby to help her brother, who wants to work in Bounderby's bank.
Will Louisa be tempted by him?	Part 9	A handsome man appears, and takes an interest in Louisa.
Will they run away together?	Part 10	He flirts with Louisa and she begins to respond.
What will Stephen do?	Part 11	Stephen Blackpool is sacked for defending the men in the trade union.
Where has Stephen gone?	Part 12	Tom tells him there might be a job at the bank for him. But Stephen then disappears.
	Part 13	The handsome man continues to worm his way into Louisa's affections, playing on her worries about her brother.
Who robbed the bank?	Part 14	Bounderby's bank is robbed.
PLOT QUESTIONS ARE ANSWERED IN THE LAST SIX EPISODES.		
	Part 15	Mrs Gradgrind dies.
	Part 16	Louisa has arranged to run away with the man. She leaves Bounderby, but goes instead to her father, and collapses at his feet.
	Part 17	The woman who was watching Bounderby is found and brought face to face with him.
Where is Stephen?	Part 18	Stephen fails to reappear, although he promised he would clear his name.
	Part 19	Stephen Blackpool is found. We learn exactly who robbed the bank.
	Part 20	Loose ends are tied up. Stephen dies.

Group-Created Plot

- Divide into six groups.
- Each group chooses a different plot opening from the list below:

  a A girl decides to run away from home and stow away on a plane.
  b A boy discovers he has X-ray vision.
  c A woman invents a time-travelling machine.
  d The world starts to enter a new ice age.
  e A child is born and begins to grow at five times the normal rate.
  g A new dinosaur is discovered and brought to England.
  h A girl finds an invitation to a party at Buckingham Palace.

- As a group, decide what is going to happen next in the plot you have chosen; write your idea on a piece of paper and pass it on to the next group.
- As a group, read the new story you have been given; write down your idea for the next episode and pass it on.
- This process continues until each group gets back the plot it started off with, and you write an ending for that story.

Each group now has the complete plot of a story in seven episodes. The task of writing up episodes into chapters is divided up between the members of the group. (There are probably fewer people in your group than there are episodes, so you will have to work out carefully who is going to write what.) When all the episodes have been written up into chapters, the whole group edits and finalises the story.

Example of Narrative

Here is a complete short story with a clear and simple plot. The story has been annotated to show the first three important plot items.

Neighbour in Distress

D. Ann Graham

A ringing phone sets the plot in motion

Nikki's visit to Marsha's house

An ordinary morning. The eggs had gone hard and I'd burned the toast. Jimmy forgot his lunch and missed the bus. But schedules being what they are, the hustle ended at 8.15 when the door slammed for the last time.

Now I could enjoy a long, luxurious half-hour before the baby woke up. Suddenly, though, the phone rang, and I scrambled to catch it before the second ring so that it wouldn't wake Peter.

"Hello, Nikki?" It was Marsha, next-door. "You've got to come over right away. I . . . I think I've just killed Harry."

"Marsha!" I couldn't believe it. "Marsha, what did you say?"

"Please, please just hurry!" Click.

Peter was not asleep. Somehow, he'd managed to reach up to the box of tissues on his dresser and obviously had been occupying himself for quite some time, pulling them out one by one. The inside of his crib looked like a paper cloud. He delivered a sheepish grin and said, "No, no!"

Normally, I would have been irritated. Instead, I scooped him up and grabbed a banana for his breakfast before dashing out the door. Marsha's house was hardly 15 feet away, yet in that short distance, my mind was crowded with a hundred troubled thoughts.

There must have been an accident. Marsha had always been overemotional and, as always, had probably just exaggerated the situation. Harry was a 6'2" bricklayer. Frail Marsha couldn't have killed him if she tried.

The door wasn't locked. "Marsha?" I didn't wait for an asnwer but settled Peter in a chair and peeled his banana. "Marsha?" I called again.

"In the kitchen," came the reply.

Marsha was standing at the counter in her housecoat, face flushed, eyes so bright that they seemed almost glazed, and her luxuriant hair, which was usually pinned up, falling loosely down to her shoulders.

"What happened?" I asked. "Where is he?"

She discovers that Harry is dead

"Over here, by the stove," she replied. "But wait, let me explain -"

"Explain." I walked over to the counter anyway. "Did you call the ambulance? Oh, Marsha -"

Harry was dead. I don't know how I knew, but I knew. He looked like any number of victims I'd seen on TV, stretched out full length on the linoleum. He might've been sleeping had it not been for the little tell-tale pool of blood gathering around his head.

He was dressed in a blue bathrobe and had a spatula in his hand. My mind absurdly flashed back to last Saturday when I'd seen him barbecuing on the patio. One of the burgers caught fire, and he had doused the orange flames with the beer he'd been drinking.

"Nikki, you're not even listening!" The rising panic in Marsha's voice brought me back. "I said they'll put me in jail! My kids'll be sent to foster homes – "

"Not jail," I protested, "just because of an accident."

"Everybody knows the trouble we were having!" She began to pace the floor, gesturing with her hands as she went on. "The fights! The separation! Now this! Who's going to believe what really happened?"

"What did happen?"

"You see?" she wailed. "Even you don't believe me! My own neighbour!"

"Oh, Marsha, you didn't tell me anything yet. I'm sure it's all ... logical. Things got out of hand, there was an accident ... It was an accident, wasn't it?"

"Of course it was an accident!" she cried. "Am I the type of person who could kill my own husband on purpose? I have wanted to kill Harry a hundred times, but I couldn't really kill him."

"Did you call the police?"

"What should I say? I want to report a murder?"

"You've got to call the police."

"No! I mean, of course I'll call. But first, I need to work some things out ... And I need your help."

"What kind of help?"

"Just to make sure they don't arrest me. You said if I ever needed anything

"But, Marsha, this is -"

"Let me tell you what I had in mind," she interrupted. "You know how we fight." She paused long enough to light a cigarette with the steady ease of habit. "I mean, I'm always clouting him with something."

"But, look, you know Harry." She waved the cigarette emphatically. "Strong as an ox! Only, I caught him off guard, and, well, Harry slipped."

"So what do you want me to do?" I asked.

"I want you to help me get him into the bathroom – so it looks like he just slipped in the shower."

"Marsha!"

"It's not lying, really. He slipped, after all. It's just that it would look better if I hadn't been so – helpful."

"But it's wrong."

"It'd be wrong if I had to spend the rest of my life in jail, for something I didn't do! Nikki, I'd go crazy in jail! I'd rather kill myself!"

She was hysterical again. "He probably planned it this way, the -"

"Oh, all right. But you've got to promise to call the police right afterward, do you hear?"

"I will, I promise."

"Goes against my better judgment. I mean, it's downright illegal. You know that don't you?"

"So, what's legal? There's no justice anymore. It's the system that runs the country these days, Nikki, and I could get trapped in it and never get out ... My kids would end up in foster homes!"

"Don't talk about foster homes."

"I can't help it." She looked over at Harry for the first time since I'd been there. "Come on, we'd better hurry."

I don't know why I did what I did in those next few moments. I was a little surprised at my own coolness, but everything seemed so unreal.

At first, Marsha was going to take his head, but when it came right down to trying to move him, she began to fall apart. "Oh, Nikki, I just can't – I can't bear to look at him."

"We better just forget this and call the police." I was having second thoughts.

"No!" She pulled herself together. "Maybe if I close my eyes -"

"Oh, here. You take his feet, and I'll take his head."

It was a struggle. He was so heavy, and the hall actually seemed to get longer and longer. Marsha didn't say anything, and I was so busy trying to keep up my end of Harry and keep moving, I didn't look at her. We made it to the bedroom and finally, to the bathroom. By then, we were both panting and breathless.

"Okay. Help me get his bathrobe off."

"Marsha, I couldn't."

"People don't take showers with their clothes on, Nikki. We have to."

The doorbell rang.

"See who it is!" Marsha whispered frantically.

I turned to the window and carefully lifted an edge of the curtain. There were two policemen on the porch. "Marsha -" My voice came out as a whisper. I was scared stiff, but I couldn't take my eyes off them.

Then, I watched the unbelievable happen. The door swung open slowly, and there stood Peter in his nappy. He looked up at the visitors with a smile and said, "Bye-bye."

"Marsha . . . Peter just -"

There was no answer. I turned to her. She had taken off her housecoat and was standing in front of the mirror, stuffing her disheveled hair into a chic-looking black hat with a net veil. Under her housecoat she'd been wearing a sleek black dress, a string of pearls ...

"Marsha, what do you think you're -"

She turned, looked at me and – to my horror – began to scream, loud, long, hysterical shrieks that shocked and unnerved me. A policeman came running up the hallway behind her, and she staggered back and fell against him, crying, "That woman! In my house – Harry! Harry! Oh, the blood, the blood!" I looked down at myself and gasped at the bright red stains on my yellow bathrobe.

The officer backed carefully away and led her crying and moaning down the hall. In a moment, the other policeman appeared at the doorway. All I could do was stare at him in disbelief. I was in Marsha's bedroom – wearing a bloodstained bathrobe – with Harry lying naked a few feet away ...

"Could you tell me your name, please?" the policeman asked. He had a very gentle voice.

"Nikki Stevens," I managed. "But there's been a mistake, a terrible mistake." I was trying to stay calm and logical ... Don't cry, don't ...

"We'll straighten things out," he assured me. "Would you mind coming with me, Mrs. Stevens?" He seemed so kind and so levelheaded. I was sure that he'd understand. I moved toward him, and he continued, "First of all, I want you to know that you have the right to remain silent ..."

Activities

1. Complete the list of plot items that apear in the margin.
2. Imagine you are the detective giving evidence at the murder trial. You have interviewed the two suspects, Marsha and Nikki. Write out in note form the evidence you would present, including the versions of events the two suspects gave you.
3. Write out the versions of events that Marsha and Nikki might present as evidence at the ensuing murder trial.
4. Write a newspaper report of the case.

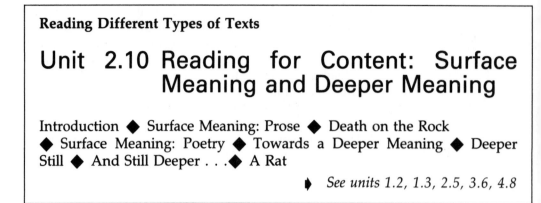

Introduction

As you try to respond to and understand a piece of writing, it is important to ask yourself if the writing has different layers of meaning. Let us look more closely at this.

Surface Meaning: Prose

In much writing the surface meaning is the important meaning.

| **Delia Smith's Complete Cookery Course** | *Frying Eggs*
 A very personal thing, how you like your egg fried but for absolute beginners here is my method, which might prove helpful. For me frying requires a bit more heat than other methods, because I like a faint touch of crispness around the edge of the egg: so – a medium heat, a fresh egg and | some hot but not smoking bacon fat or pure lard (butter goes too brown for frying, I think). Let the egg settle in the pan and start to set; then, using a tablespoon, tip the pan and baste the top of the egg with the fat until it's done to your liking. Lift it out carefully with a fish slice. |

This is about frying eggs – how the writer likes to fry them, and how to fry them. It has no deeper meaning.

Deeper Meaning: Prose

In literature the surface meaning may be coupled with a deeper meaning. When you are presented with a literary text, read for the deeper meaning as well as for the surface meaning.

Here is a passage from *The Chocolate War* by Robert Cormier. On the left-hand side are notes on the surface meaning, on the right-hand notes on the deeper meaning.

The Chocolate War

Robert Cormier

SURFACE MEANING		DEEPER MEANING

SURFACE MEANING

it's about a man who gets hit by three people

he's wearing a helmet

they're playing a game

on a big field – 50 yards

it's a team game

On the third play, he was hit simultaneously by three of them: one, his knees; another, his stomach; a third, his head – the helmet no protection at all. His body seemed to telescope into itself but all the parts didn't fit, and he was stunned by the knowledge that pain isn't just one thing – it is cunning and various, sharp here and sickening there, burning here and clawing there. He clutched himself as he hit the ground. The ball squirted away. His breath went away, like the ball – a terrible stillness pervaded him – and then, at the onset of panic, his breath came back again. His lips sprayed wetness and he was grateful for the sweet cool air that filled his lungs. But when he tried to get up, his body mutinied against movement. He decided the hell with it. He'd go to sleep right here, right out on the fifty yard line, the hell with trying out for the team. Screw everything, he was going to sleep, he didn't care anymore . . .

DEEPER MEANING

it's about pain that takes you over

almost like death

the pain is so bad that you just want to lie still

it makes you forget everything else

Responses

A written response concentrating on content might look like this:

> In this passage a boy or man is knocked down in some kind of ball game. It could be rugby or football, except the character is wearing a helmet and so perhaps it is American football.

A written response concentrating on the deeper meaning might look like this:

> The passage is about playing a team game, but this is just a vehicle for the writer to talk about the experience of pain. It is also about how pain is very solitary. There is a comparison between the team and the main character's solitary pain.

Activity

Talk or write about a time or times when you were in great pain. You could write about a fight, an illness or a sports accident, for instance.

Death on the Rock?

This is the opening paragraph of a novel. The surface meaning of the passage is simply that a man is going to be murdered in a seaside resort.

Brighton Rock

Graham Greene

Hale knew, before he had been in Brighton three hours, that they meant to murder him. With his inky fingers and his bitten nails, his manner cynical and nervous, anybody could tell he didn't belong – belong to the early summer sun, the cool Whitsun wind off the sea, the holiday crowd. They came in by train from Victoria every five minutes, rocked down Queen's Road standing on the tops of the little local trams, stepped off in bewildered multitudes into fresh and glittering air, the new silver paint sparkled on the piers, the cream houses ran away into the west like a pale Victorian water-colour; a race in miniature motors, a band playing, flower gardens in bloom below the front, an aeroplane advertising something for the health in pale vanishing clouds across the sky.

Response

Nothing really 'happens' in this passage but there are still things to say about it. The first thing that is striking about this is the opening sentence. A man, Hale, is going to be murdered! But the passage is not just about this: it is about Brighton, a seaside resort. We know the town is on the sea because it mentions the piers. The passage as a whole is more concerned with the town – the band, the trams, the flower gardens, than the man. Yet the opening sentence is unforgettable: it overshadows everything else. The two contrasting pieces of information – about the bright seaside town and the murder threat – work on our feelings in a way the Delia Smith extract does not. There is a deeper meaning.

Activity

Continue the story suggesting why they want to murder Hale, and who 'they' are. Write the next two or three paragraphs (limit yourself to 200 words), keeping to the style of the original.

Surface Meaning or Deeper Meaning?

But not all fiction works on deeper levels. Bear this in mind as you read the following passage:

Dancing in the Dark Carolyn Ross	I was the first one out of the door when the bell finally rang. I raced down the hall, dumped my books in my locker, and stopped in the girls' room to brush my hair and put on some blusher and lip gloss. My hair was newly trimmed so it would look nice for the contest. I was trying the positive approach. Eric just had to be allowed to enter with me. That was all there was to it. I was wearing a cotton sweater in our school colors, blue and white. I also figured a little luck wouldn't hurt, so the night before, I'd put the rose Eric had given me in an envelope in my purse. I wasn't really superstitious, but everything had gone right when I carried it before. I was willing to try anything to make sure Eric won the match.

Activities

1. In groups, talk about the extract. What event are the girl and Eric going to? What clues are there that this story is not set in England? And what is the surface meaning? Is there a deeper meaning? What type of person is the narrator – the person telling the story?
2. How do you think the story would continue? Write the next three paragraphs, keeping to the style of the original, then compare your ideas with others in the same group.
3. Rewrite the passage changing the girl into a boy. How many changes do you have to make?
4. Write a chapter of a teenage novel set in a school. You should write in the first person, but if you are a boy you must write as if you are a girl, and vice versa. Read your chapter out to somebody else in your class. How authentic does it sound? Have you managed to make your chapter sound like it was really written by someone of the opposite sex?

Surface meaning: Poetry

It is perhaps more difficult to write about a poem than about a piece of prose, but the approach is basically the same. (Refer back to 'How to Read a Poem' in Unit 2.5 to refresh your memory). Read the poem at least twice and ask yourself what is happening in the poem. Is the surface meaning the whole meaning? It probably is not; most poems do have deeper meaning. Even an apparently straightforward poem describing an autumn day may – through its mood or use of symbols – be hinting at deeper themes such as old age or the passing of time.

There are poems – particularly narrative poems or nonsense rhymes – whose meaning is only surface meaning. But poetry as a genre is not really used for putting across surface meaning only. See if you can find a poem that has no deeper meaning – you may spend a long time looking! Poetry is a genre in which writers use striking images, symbols and METAPHORS (See Language Reference Section, p.233) to put across a point or to invite the reader to reflect upon a theme.

Towards a Deeper Meaning

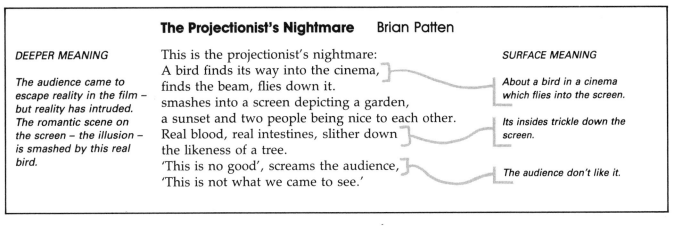

The Projectionist's Nightmare   Brian Patten

DEEPER MEANING

The audience came to escape reality in the film – but reality has intruded. The romantic scene on the screen – the illusion – is smashed by this real bird.

This is the projectionist's nightmare:
A bird finds its way into the cinema,
finds the beam, flies down it.
smashes into a screen depicting a garden,
a sunset and two people being nice to each other.
Real blood, real intestines, slither down
the likeness of a tree.
'This is no good', screams the audience,
'This is not what we came to see.'

SURFACE MEANING

About a bird in a cinema which flies into the screen.

Its insides trickle down the screen.

The audience don't like it.

A response

This is a poem about a bird, flying into a cinema screen and killing itself, and the horrified reaction of the audience. But it is more than that – because it is also about the difference between what people were watching on the screen – a pleasant romantic scene depicting a garden and a sunset – and the bloody, broken body of a real bird that replaces it. It is a poem about the way reality destroys illusion – and the title tells us that the projectionist dreads this: the moment when the film breaks down, and the outside world intrudes.

Deeper Still

Here is another poem in which birds play a part.

Love without Hope

Robert Graves

Love without hope, as when the young bird-catcher
Swept off his tall hat to the Squire's own daughter,
To let the imprisoned larks escape and fly
Singing about her head as she rode by.

A response (Limited to surface content)

Here the bird catcher takes off his hat when he sees the Squire's daughter. The birds – larks, which presumably he keeps under his hat, escape and fly about the woman's head.

Questions on Deeper Meaning

The poem clearly describes an episode – but what does it all really mean? Looking for answers to the following questions may help you get closer to the 'deeper meaning' of the poem.

1. What does the title mean?
2. Why has the poet chosen the two characters?
3. Would the bird-catcher really keep larks under his hat? Do the larks perhaps have a 'deeper meaning'? If so, what?

And Still Deeper . . .

Sometimes there may be little surface meaning, or the surface meaning may in fact mislead us:

Not Waving But Drowning

Stevie Smith

SURFACE MEANING

A man has nearly drowned. Is this a 'dead' man speaking?

Onlookers see him and comment.

Nobody heard him, the dead man.
But still he lay moaning:
I was much further out than you thought
And not waving but drowning.

Poor chap, he always loved larking
And now he's dead
It must have been too cold for him his heart gave way
They said

Oh, no no no no, it was too cold always
Still the dead only lay moaning
I was much too far out all my life
And not waving but drowning.

DEEPER MEANING

How can you hear a dead man?
Does it mean dead, not literally, but about to die?

Waving – cheerful, happy, friendly.
Drowning – desperate, waving for help, dying.

Simple explanation. He died of shock from the cold water.

Cold here means something like 'difficult'.
He couldn't cope.
It's always been this way.

A response

This is more difficult. It seems to be about a man who has drowned. He is introduced (line 1) as a 'dead man', yet he is still moaning, and the poem goes on to quote the actual words of the 'dead man', 'I . . . was not waving but drowning'. This is all very confusing, but perhaps provides us with clues as to the poem's deeper meaning. The comment 'I . . . was not waving but drowning' suggests the poem is about being misunderstood. People who appear to be cheerful and sociable may in fact be desperately lonely or depressed.

A Rat

This poem is about a rat, but there may be more to it than this. When you have read the poem once, answer the questions which follow it; then read it again, and write your response to it.

**An
Advancement
of Learning**

Seamus Heaney

I took the embankment path
(As always, deferring
The bridge). The river nosed past,
Pliable, oil-skinned, wearing

A transfer of gables and sky.
Hunched over the railing,
Well away from the road now, I
Considered the dirty-keeled swans.

Something slobbered curtly, close,
Smudging the silence: a rat
Slimed out of the water and
My throat sickened so quickly that

I turned down the path in cold sweat
But god, another was nimbling
Up the far bank, tracing its wet
Arcs on the stones. Incredibly then

I established a dreaded
Bridgehead. I turned to stare
With deliberate, thrilled-care
At my hitherto snubbed rodent.

He clockworked aimlessly

The tapered tail that followed him,
The raindrop eye, the old snout,
One by one I took all in,
He trained on me. I stared him out.

Forgetting how I used to panic
When his grey brothers scraped and fed
Behind the hen-coop in our yard,
On ceiling boards above my bed.

This terror, cold, wet-furred,
  small-clawed
Retreated up a pipe for sewage.
I stared a minute after him,
Then I walked on and crossed the bridge.

Questions

1. In your own words describe the writer's surroundings at the beginning of the poem (lines 1–12).
2. Write down three words or short phrases that suggest the unpleasantness of the rats.
3. What are the various feelings shown by the poet towards the rats he meets?
4. The poet uses several words to suggest movement. What is suggested by each of the words in italics below:
   - The river *nosed* past (line 3);
   - Another was *nimbling* past (lines 14–15):
   - He *clockworked* aimlessly (line 21).
5. What do you think the poet is suggesting by the title of the poem?
6. Suggest two reasons why the last line is a good ending to the poem.

Activity

Write your own response to the poem, trying to look both for surface meaning and and deeper meaning.

Reading Different Types of Texts

Unit 2.11 Noticing the Words

Introduction ◆ The Meaning of Words ◆ Made-up Words ◆ What Words Suggest to us: Connotations ◆ Words in Advertising ◆ Words in Poetry ◆ Colloquial Words and Language ◆ Drafting ◆ Selecting the Right Word ◆ Finding Words: Using a Dictionary

◗ *See units 1.2–1.4, 2.1, 2.2, 2.4–2.6, 2.8, 2.9, 3.1–3.11*

Introduction

Words can do interesting things to us, if we let them. If a book captures our interest it can take us into another world, and we forget about the world we are in. Poems, too, can take us out of ourselves. If we read attentively, and pay close attention to the words that the author has chosen to use we may notice interesting patterns. Most important of all our own writing may improve, as we write more ambitiously and with greater awareness.

The Meaning of Words

'When I use a word . . . it means just what I choose it to mean – neither more nor less.'

So says Humpty Dumpty in Lewis Carroll's *Alice Through the Looking Glass*. Let us see whether we all mean the same thing when we use a word. Here are five simple sentences:

1. A *boat* appeared on the horizon.
2. There was a *hat* on the chair.
3. A *tree* had been drawn in the sand.
4. He opened the *window*.
5. There was a *shoe* in the road.

Activities

1. Discuss what pictures formed in your minds when you read the underlined words.
2. Draw a simple picture to show what the following words stand for:

| BOAT | HAT | TREE | WINDOW | SHOE |

3. Divide into pairs and compare your pictures to see if you have visualised the words in the same way. Have you drawn the same kind of boat, hat or tree?

Made-up Words

Several prose writers have enjoyed making up words. You may like to do a library search and look at the first page of each of the following:

| DYLAN THOMAS : UNDER MILK WOOD | JOHN LENNON : IN HIS OWN WRITE |
| RUSSELL HOBAN : RIDDLEY WALKER | JAMES JOYCE : ULYSSES |

Poets, too, have invented – or 'coined' – words. Here is part of a very long poem by the author of *Alice Through the Looking Glass*.

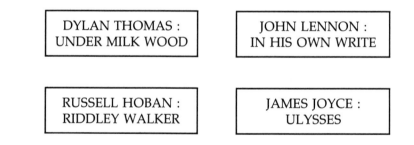

| **Jabberwocky**

Lewis Carroll | Twas brillig, and the slithy toves
did gyre and gimble in the wabe
all mimsy were the borogroves
and the mome raths outgrabe |

Activities

1. The whole of this poem is 'translated' in Chapter Six of Lewis Carroll's *Alice Through the Looking Glass*. Find a copy of this book in your local library and write out the translation.
2. Make up your own word for an everyday object and then write a paragraph using this word. Read your paragraph to someone else and see if he/she can work out what your word means.

What Words Suggest To Us: Connotations

Some words – such as 'shoe' – have a definite meaning but they do not produce such a strong reaction in us as words like 'cancer' or 'diamond'. As well as meaning (or denoting) dangerous disease and precious stone respectively, cancer and diamond have associations in our minds of fear and death, and of wealth and luxury. We call this sort of extended meaning 'connotation', to distinguish it from basic meaning, or 'denotation'. These terms are useful ones to know since they enable you to talk about types of language.

Read the following passage about the connotations of car names and then answer the questions that follow it.

Car Names

It is easy to think that car names tell us something about cars, but a moment's reflection will show that in most cases this is not so (exceptions include, Mini, Reliant, Maxi and Space Wagon). The names that are chosen tell us something about the driver or owner as an individual, and the whole range of names may say something about our overall attitude to cars and driving. What we are dealing with here is a prime example of the power of connotation – the associations, vague or definite – that a word has. Many people are ignorant of the denotations (actual meanings) of car names, but the connotations are still powerful enough to affect their choice.

First, let us look at manufacturer's own names. These fall mainly into three groups. Most are named after the original owner of the company, eg Ford, Peugeot, Renault, Rolls-Royce (two separate people), Ferrari, Porsche, to name but a few. Some are named after places, often the site of the factory, such as Vauxhall, Humber or Moskvich. The glamour of Rolls-Royce or Porsche is therefore nothing to do with the actual denotation of the words, but is something they have acquired over the years. The same is true of the third group of car names – initials. BMW, for example, stands for Bavarian Motor Works, and FIAT for Fabbrica Italiana Automobili Torino (The Italian Auto factory of Turin) – both rather mundane! MG stands for Morris Garages, and VW for Volkswagen, which means 'people's car' in German.

There are several types of names given to the cars themselves. The first type I want to consider is those that relate to aggression, competition and speed. Here is a selection of fast or aggressive animals:

Stag, Jaguar, Manta, Panther, Tercel, Mustang, Pinto, Cobra, Cougar, Barracuda, Mako, and Stingray. (Many of these are American, but much of our car culture emanates from across the Atlantic.)

Here are some weapons:

Scimitar, Stiletto, Magnum, Interceptor, Spitfire, Colt.

Here are some names of aggressive people:

Hunter, Cavalier, Corsair, Lancer.

Here are some names relating to winning:

Triumph and Victor.

And, finally, two names suggesting speed:

Vitesse, Allegro.

I would suggest that these names are aimed much more at men than at women, for whom these characteristics are frequently less important. The use of these names perhaps encourages drivers to see the road as a place of competition, where winning is significant, being able to drive fast is valued, and success is equated with, if not arriving first, then at least not being overtaken on the way.

Another popular group of names is places. These tend to be holiday locations, often from abroad: Granada, Cortina, Capri, Montego, Alpine, Marina, Dolomite, Mulsanne, Mexico (in fact named after the World Cup). Other names with these cheerful holiday associations are Sunny, Horizon and Sunbeam. Perhaps there is some element of escape inherent in these names: step into your car and it takes you out of the drudge of your normal environment. To take you further out of this world we have Zodiac, Orion and Astra. British places have also been used in the past – Oxford, Devon, Somerset, Cambridge, Anglia – perhaps to encourage or exploit nationalism on the part of the owner/ driver. As with cigarettes there is a long list of names with glamorous or sophisticated associations: Consul, Ambassador, Princess, Senator, Sovereign, Mayfair, Prestige, Commodore, Sceptre, Corona, Viceroy, Royal. We hope that some of the glamour and sophistication will rub off on us.

In recent years car names have undergone a number of changes. A significant one is that the number of aggressive names has decreased. There are several reasons for this. One is the enormous increase in petrol prices in the 1970's. Motoring was perceived less as the carefree luxury it had been. We also became more safety conscious, thus names that encourage dangerous attitudes also became less desirable; wielding a scimitar is seen as anti-social, so the name becomes attractive to a smaller proportion of the target population. A third reason for the reduction in aggressive names is that women have become more significant as purchasers of cars, so names have been used to attract women as well as to pander to men's pseudo-combative fantasies. As a result we have an increase in the number of 'soft' names: Panda, Kitten, Rabbit (the American Golf) and Pony. These perhaps portray the car as a pet. There are women's names – Cressida, Violet and Estelle, and musical terms: Quintet, Celeste, Galant, Prelude, Stanza, Caprice, Samba, and Maestro. Other 'soft' names include Charade, Laurel, Domino, Civic, Escort, Bluebird and Acclaim. Notice how names like Accord (= agreement) and Charmant (= charming) emphasise co-operation rather than competition.

A fourth factor is the increase in the use of foreign words as names for cars; British cars as well as foreign ones. While these have always been popular they have increased considerably in recent years: Maestro, Strada, Uno, Viva, Nova, Astra, Sierra, Fiesta, Metro, Esprit, Elan, Eclat, Elite, Quattro, Fuego, Micra,

Avant, Argenta, Beta, Delta, Gamma. One advantage of these is that they are easily exported, doing away with the need to have a different name for each country you sell in. Notice, however, that names are still adapted to the perceptions of the buyers. The FIAT Ritmo (Italian for rhythm), a name that does not roll easily off the English speaker's tongue, is called the Strada (Italian for street) in Britain.

A trend in names that avoids unfortunate connotations is to use invented names: Starion, Tredia, Solara, Camry, Tagora, Celica. These have only vague connotations, and would appear to have been chosen for the right sort of sound. Other names, such as Carina (a keel-like ridge) and Corolla (the inner whorl of floral envelopes), are presumably chosen primarily for their sound rather than their denotations.

All cars perform essentially the same function of transporting people from A to B. The names serve to create differences in the minds of the consumers. People are affected, in a small but significant way, by the names cars have, so car manufacturers spend a lot of time and money (£50,000 in the case of Ford and the Ford Granada) in selecting the best names. When we buy the car we buy the name with it, and in a way we are also buying a part of ourselves. The type of car one drives is often taken as an indicator of the type of person one is. One way of emphasising the significance of names is to ask yourself if you would be happy driving, or being a passenger in, a car called Grapefruit, Granite, Cudgel, Birmingham, Duchess of York or Lettuce. The connotations of these names are all wrong, and this seems naturally so, but remember that the values associated with cars reflect our culture, and to that extent are artificial. After all, the car has only been around for 100 years, and attitudes towards it would have developed quite differently in that time. They may well do so in the years to come.

Questions

1. What do the names Mini, Reliant and Maxi tell us about the cars?
2. Why does the writer think that aggressive names are aimed at men rather than women?
3. Why are some cars named after places?
4. In your own words, give three reasons why aggressive names for cars are less frequently used now.
5. How does the writer explain the frequent use of foreign words for car names?
6. How does the writer introduce humour into the last paragraph?

Activities

1. Under the appropriate headings – manufacturers' own names, musical terms, animals, etc. – list as many examples of different types of car names as you can think of. Then write a more up-to-date account of car names and their connotations.
2. Do you think the name of a car matters or not?
3. Think up an appropriate name for a: **a** new sports car; **b** new van; **c** new small town car.
4. Using the passage on car names as an example, write your own article, aimed at the readers of a consumer magazine, on one of the following topics: **a** names of sweets; **b** magazine titles; **c** names of cosmetics.
5. Explain the difference between denotation and connotation.

Words in Advertising

We all know how frequently advertisers use enticing words like 'new', 'free', and 'improved'. These words are sometimes described as 'advertiser's hype'. On the next page is an advertisement with many such words. Those in the top half of the advertisement have been underlined.

Activities

1. Take each of the underlined words, write it down and explain why you think it was chosen. Describe the visual images. Do they add much to the advertisement?
2. Pick out similar enticing words from the second half of the advertisement.
3. Does the advertisement try to use any technical language to sell the radio? What is the effect of this technical information? Do you notice anything about the picture of the Soviet Union presented in the advertisement?
4. Write a letter to a friend describing the radio you have bought from this advertisement. Make sure you avoid advertiser's hype!
5. Your new radio goes wrong only a week after you bought it. Write a letter of complaint to the manufacturer.

BEST

JUST

SPECIAL

STYLISH

EXCLUSIVE

SUPER

BEST

BRILLIANT

Words in Poetry

Let us look at the role and effect of words in poems and literary prose.

In the following poem Wendy Cope has chosen to write in the style of an Infant Reading Scheme book, which uses simple words to teach young children to read. Some Reading Schemes have been criticised for offering a very narrow vocabulary, and for using sexist and stereotypical images of boys and girls and mothers and fathers. This poem is not, however, aimed at children who are learning to read. The author is poking fun at Reading Schemes by using the style of writing in them to describe an event which certainly would not occur in an Infant Reader . . .

Reading Scheme

Wendy Cope

Here is Peter. Here is Jane. They like fun.
Jane has a big doll. Peter has a ball.
Look, Jane, look! Look at the dog! See him run!

Here is Mummy. She has baked a bun.
Here is the milkman. He has come to call.
Here is Peter. Here is Jane. They like fun.

Go Peter! Go Jane! Come, milkman, come!
The milkman likes Mummy. She likes them all.
Look, Jane, look! Look at the dog! See him run!

Here are the curtains. They shut out the sun.
Let us peep! On tiptoe Jane! You are small!
Here is Peter. Here is Jane. They like fun.

I hear a car, Jane. The milkman looks glum.
Here is Daddy in his car. Daddy is tall.
Look, Jane, look! Look at the dog! See him run!

Daddy looks very cross. Has he a gun?
Up milkman! Up milkman! Over the wall!
Here is Peter. Here is Jane. They like fun.
Look, Jane, look! Look at the dog! See him run!

Activities

1. Describe in your own words what is happening in the poem.
2. Show what it is in the poem that reminds us of a book for young children.
3. Write your own 'Reading Scheme' in verse or prose.
4. Simple words are often short words. All of the words in the Wendy Cope poem have either one or two syllables. Write a sentence using only one-syllable words, and then a sentence using only two-syllable words. Try sentence 'sandwiches'. Write a sentence made up of words of one syllable, then a word of two syllables, then another one of one syllable, and so on.

Colloquial Words and Language

Here is a poem written in the style of speech, with many words and spellings you would not find in standard English.

Rythm

Ian Crichton
Smith

They dunno how it is. I smack a ball
right through the goals. But they dunno how the words
get muddled in my head, get tired somehow.
I look through the window, see. And there's a wall
I'd kick the ball against, just smack and smack.
Old Jerry, he can't play, he don't know how,
not now at any rate. He's too flicking small.
See him in shorts, out in the crazy black.
Rythm, he says and ryme. See him at back.
He don't know nothing about Law. He'd fall
flat on his face, just like a big sack,
when you're going down the wing, the wind behind you
And crossing into the goalmouth and they're roaring
the whole great crowd. They're on their feet cheering.
The ball's at your feet and there it goes, just crack.
Old Jerry dives – the wrong way. And they're jeering
and I run to the centre and old Bash
Jumps up and down, and I feel great, and wearing
my gold and purple strip, fresh from the wash.

Activities

1. Like *Reading Scheme*, this poem has short words. But is it as easy to understand? Give your reasons for your answer.
2. Write your response to this poem, focusing in particular on the following:
   ◆ What is the surface meaning and what is the deeper meaning?
   ◆ Who seems to be speaking?
   ◆ Why has the poet mis-spelt a number of words?
3. Discuss the importance of spelling. Can you think of any situations where it is essential to spell correctly? Does it matter if you cannot spell? Is there anything you can do about it?

Drafting

All published writers choose their words carefully, and rewrite things a number of times before they are satisfied. When you are writing, always ask yourself whether the words you have chosen are the best – or most appropriate ones for what you want to say. Write at least two versions – a 'draft' version, and a final version of your piece of writing, aiming to make your second version more polished than the first. Here are examples of two versions of a piece of writing. Read them both, noticing the differences between them. Are the changes made in the second version an improvement? If so, why?

**London –
First Attempt**

There is rubbish on the streets, and the paving slabs don't fit. The shops overflow, and in side streets abandoned cars rust. In every corner there are polystyrene take away food containers, and the grey people move through the drizzle without comment or expression.

**London –
Second
Attempt**

Rubbish gathers like dirty snow in the corners of the streets and the paving stones erupt like gravestones on the Last Judgement. All the skips are full, and in the suburban side streets abandoned cars rust. In every high street you find the soiled and crushed Big Mac containers, ignored by the people who move through the drizzle without comment or expression.

Activity

Imagine wandering through your own home town or neighbourhood. Jot down half a dozen or so sights or sounds you might encounter as you wander through the streets. Then shape these images into a poem or a description, first in a draft version and then in a finished version.

Selecting the Right Word

Here is an extract from *The Lost World*, a novel by Sir Arthur Conan Doyle, in which a group of explorers find a remote plateau where dinosaurs are still living. One of the explorers' first encounters with a dinosaur is described below. Some of the words which the author chose to make the animal more frightening have been removed. Choose the word that you would insert, to create the most frightening impact.

The Lost World

A. Conan Doyle

strong/long/powerful

safe/gentle/harmless

frightening/loud/ferocious

animal/brute

I stood like a man paralysed, still _____ at the ground which I had traversed. Then suddenly I saw it. There was movement among the bushes at the far end of the clearing which I had just traversed. A great _____ shadow disengaged itself and hopped out into the clear moonlight. I say 'hopped' advisedly, for the _____ moved like a kangaroo, springing along in an erect position upon its _____ hind legs, while its front ones were held bent in front of it. It was of _____ size and power, like an erect elephant, but its movements, in spite of its bulk, were exceedingly alert. For a moment, as I saw its shape, I hoped that it was an iguanodon, which I knew to be _____ but, ignorant as I was, I soon saw that this was a very different creature. Instead of the gentle, deer-shaped head of the great three-toed leaf-eater, this beast had a broad, squat, _____ face like that which had alarmed us in our camp. His _____ cry and the horrible energy of his pursuit both assured me that this was surely one of the great flesh-eating dinosaurs, the most _____ beasts which have ever walked this earth. As the huge _____ loped along it dropped forward upon its forepaws and brought its nose to the ground every twenty yards or so. It was smelling out my trail. Sometimes, for an instant, it was at fault. Then it would catch it up again and come bounding swiftly along the path I had taken.

Even now when I think of that _____ the sweat breaks out upon my brow. What could I do?

staring/gazing

big/black/dark

animal/creature/beast

incredible/gigantic/enormous

unpleasant/toad-like/ugly

terrible/enormous/unusual

situation/nightmare/experience

Finding Words: Using a Dictionary

Dictionaries list words in alphabetical order, and can be used to check or find out
  a Spelling ('tabioca' or 'tapioca'?)
  b Meaning ('tantalise' – to tease or torment)

and sometimes to check and find out
  c Part of speech ('tall' is an adjective)
  d Pronunciation
  e Origin

Some basic dictionaries do not bother with **d** and **e**.

Questions

Using this page from a dictionary, answer the following questions.

1. Check the correct spelling of the fruit:

   tangarine or tangerine?

2. What is a military tattoo?
3. What would 'TARE 3 TONS' mean on the side of a lorry?
4. A noun is an object or an idea; a verb expresses action. Find three words which can be both nouns and verbs (e.g. tailor). Then use them in sentences to show that you understand the difference.
5. Find a word which has two completely different meanings.

Activities

1. Create your own dictionary. Use a different page of a notebook for each letter of the alphabet and write in it new words that you discover, together with their meanings.
2. A thesaurus is a collection of words grouped under headings. All the words under a particular heading have a similar or related meaning. For example:

TALK: speak, utter, say, reply, retort, suggest, respond, enquire

---

See if you can add more words to this list.

---

tailor *n.* a person who makes suits and other garments. fem. TAILORESS. TAILOR *v.* to make garments.

taint *v.* to infect; to corrupt.

TAINT *n.* a trace of something unpleasant or bad.

take *v.* 1 to get hold of. 2 to grasp; to seize. 3 to guide; to accompany. 4 to photograph. 5 to consider; to suppose.

takings *n.pl.* money received; the total receipts.

tale *n.* 1 a true or fictitious story. 2 a mischievous report.

talent *n.* a special skill or ability. TALENTED *adj.*

talk *v.* 1 to speak; to express in spoken words. 2 TALK OVER OR ABOUT to discuss.

TALK *n.* 1 a conversation or discussion. 2 a lecture. 3 gossip.

tall *adj.* 1 of more than average height. 2 of a particular height.

tallow *n.* animal fat melted down for use in making candles, soap, etc.

talon *n.* the claw of a bird of prey, such as an eagle or hawk.

tambourine *n.* a small, one-sided drum with bells round its side.

tame *adj.* 1 not wild; domesticated 2 gentle and obedient.

TAME *v.* to make tame; to subdue. TAMELY *adv.*

tamper (with) *v.* to meddle with; to interfere.

tan *v.* 1 to make an animal skin into leather by treating with acid. 2 to become brown by exposure to the sun.

TAN *n.* 1 oak bark used for tanning. 2 sunburn. 3 a yellowish-brown colour. TANNED *adj.* TANNING *n.*

tandem *n.* a bicycle for two riders.

tang *n.* a sharp or strong taste.

tangent *n.* a straight line which touches a curve at a point but does not cross it.

tangerine *n.* a small, sweet orange.

tangible *adj.* 1 that can be touched. 2 real; definite.

tangle *v.* 1 to become confused and muddled. 2 to twist or jumble together.

TANGLE *n.* a muddle; a mix-up.

tank *n.* 1 a container for a liquid or a gas. 2 an armoured fighting vehicle moving on caterpillar tracks.

tankard *n.* a large drinking mug.

tanker *n.* a ship or road vehicle for carrying liquids.

tantalise *v.* to tease or torment.

tantrum *n.* a fit of bad temper.

---

tap *n.* 1 a device for controlling the flow of a liquid or gas. 2 a light pat or touch.

TAP *v.* 1 to draw off liquid by means of a tap. 2 to pat or touch.

tape *n.* 1 a narrow strip of cloth. 2 a magnetic ribbon used to make sound recordings.

TAPE *v.* 1 to fasten with tape. 2 to record (sound) on tape.

taper *v.* 1 to become narrower towards one end. 2 to make thinner towards one end.

TAPER *n.* 1 a narrowing. 2 a long thin candle.

tapestry *n.* a piece of cloth with patterns or pictures woven into it.

tapioca *n.* a white, starchy food obtained from cassava root.

tar *n.* a thick, black substance obtained from coal and used for road surfacing and wood preservation.

TAR *v.* to coat with tar.

tare *n.* 1 a weed found growing among corn. 2 the weight of a container or vehicle when empty.

target *n.* 1 a mark or object for shooting at. 2 something to be aimed at.

tarmac *n.* a mixture of tar and gravel used on road surfaces, playgrounds, etc.

tarn *n.* a small, mountain lake.

tarnish *v.* to make or become dull and discoloured. TARNISHED *adj.*

tarpaulin *n.* a large, thick, canvas sheet, tarred to make it waterproof.

tart *n.* a piece of pastry containing fruit or jam, a shallow pie. TART *adj.* sharp or sour in taste.

tartan *n.* woollen cloth woven in the colours of a Scottish Highland clan.

task *n.* a piece of work set to be done.

taste *n.* 1 the ability to taste. 2 flavour. 3 a person's judgement in liking things. 4 a small quantity.

TASTE *v.* 1 to distinguish a taste or flavour. 2 to test a small quantity. TASTEFUL *adj.* TASTELESS *adj.* TASTY *adj.*

tasty *adj.* of pleasant flavour; savoury.

tattoo *n.* 1 a military display at night. 2 a drumbeat calling soldiers together. 3 a design on the skin made by pricking it and applying dyes.

TATTOO *v.* to prick a design into the skin.

taunt *v.* to mock or sneer at; to ridicule. TAUNT *n.* mockery; ridicule.

taut *adj.* tightly stretched. TAUTLY *adv.*

Reading Different Types of Texts

Unit 2.12 Making Your Own Pictures

Introduction ◆ Pictures in Imaginative and Transactional Writing ◆ Pictures that Form in Our Minds ◆ More Pictures ◆ Two Tigers ◆ Towards Writing ◆ Pictures of Creation ◆ Pictures in Prose

◗ *See all units relating to poetry and prose*

Introduction

Last night I had a bad dream. What pictures form in your mind when you dream? Here are some questions to consider:

- ◆ Do dreams mean anything?
- ◆ Are they significant?
- ◆ Have you had any bad or recurrent dreams?
- ◆ Do dreams predict the future?
- ◆ Do you talk in your sleep?
- ◆ Do you sleepwalk? (How do you know?)
- ◆ Do you dream in colour?
- ◆ Can you remember pictures from your dreams?

Pictures in Imaginative and Transactional Writing

Imaginative writing is full of images or pictures. Here is a piece of imaginative prose, by Dylan Thomas, with the pictures identified.

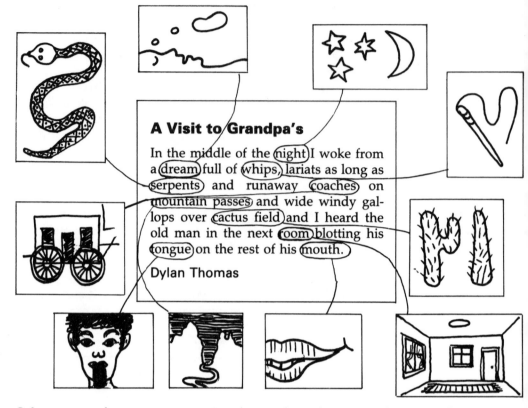

A Visit to Grandpa's

In the middle of the night I woke from a dream full of whips, lariats as long as serpents and runaway coaches on mountain passes and wide windy gallops over cactus field and I heard the old man in the next room blotting his tongue on the rest of his mouth.

Dylan Thomas

Other types of prose – transactional or technical writing, for example – contain few images.

Dream Interpretations	The attempt, mainly by dream analysis through free association to explain various features of and elements in a dream. In psychoanalytical theory the dream form and the dream material or content are first of all distinguished, and the interpretation consists mainly in explaining the form which the content has been given.
Penguin Dictionary of Psychology	

Pictures that Form in Our Minds

As we read words our minds provide us with pictures: we do the imagining because there are no pictures on the page. Some people say they prefer television programmes, films and comic books because they give us these pictures ready made. But beware! Somebody invented the costumes and sets which appear in the pictures that make up any film or TV programme you choose to mention; somebody imagined Asterix and Mickey Mouse. If we just become consumers, then we are at the mercy of the producers; we let other people do our thinking for us. So the argument for using our own imagination – making our own pictures in our minds – is that it makes us more independent. When we read poems and stories, making use of our imaginations is exactly what we have to do. To demonstrate this process, here are the pictures that form in my mind when I read *Chips* by Stanley Cook:

CHIPS

Is this a metaphor?

Out of the paper bag
Comes the hot breath of chips
And I shall blow on them
To stop them burning my lips

The 'hot breath' of the chips is good. I came back to this when I read the last verse. I knew it would be winter.

Before I leave the counter
The woman shakes
Raindrops of vinegar on them
And salty snowflakes

Here's a word picture that's two pictures in one. The crystals of salt are also 'snowflakes'. We know they're not real snowflakes, but this helps us to picture the shape of the big salt grains. Look out for more examples of metaphors in other poems and literary extracts in Do You Read Me?

Is 'frosty pavements' a metaphor?

Outside the frosty pavements
Are slippery as a slide
But the chips and I
Are warm inside.

'Frosty pavements' reminds me of cold winter nights when I have eaten delicious hot chips. I'm inside and warm and the chips are inside me!

Stanley Cook

Activity

Think about the simple things in life that have brought you pleasure, like eating a bag of chips on a cold night, going fishing on a wet summer's day, wearing something new you have just bought or getting ready to go out. Write about the things, either in verse or prose. Make a list first, then picture those happy moments.

More Pictures

Here is Alan Ross's poem about a wartime night patrol. Opposite I have written the pictures that form in my mind. Here is the first half of the poem.

Night Patrol

Alan Ross

We sail at dusk. The red moon
rising in a paper lantern, sets fire
To the water; the black headland disappears,
Sullen, in shadow, clenched like a paw.

'At dusk' – no clear, precise picture. 'Red Moon' – I can picture this. Paper lantern – very helpful – I know what paper lanterns look like but this doesn't help me to picture this moon . . . can guess – paper clouds? 'Black headland' – easy to picture. Why 'Like a paw'?

The docks grow flat, rubbered with mist
Cranes, like tall drunks hang
Over the railway. The unloading of coal
Continues under blue arc-lights

Mist acting like bits of an eraser left on a surface? 'Like tall drunks' – at odd angles, lurching – I can imagine this.

Turning south, the moon like a rouged face
Between masts, the knotted aerials swing
Taut against the horizon, the bag
Of sea crumpled in the spray-flecked blackness

Like a red face – masked, like a prostitute's? 'The bag of sea' – I like this line – perhaps it's a crumpled bag. I can picture this quite easily.

Towards midnight the cold stars, high
Over Europe, freeze on the sky
Stigmata above the flickering lights
Of Holland. Flashes of gunfire

Why stigmata? Look up the word in a dictionary.

Activity   Copy out verses 5–8 and write or draw next to them the pictures that form in your mind as you read. You may wish to draw (and label) the pictures that form in your mind or you could write comments as I have.

Lick out over meditative coastlines, betraying
The stillness. Taking up position, night falls
Exhausted about us. The wakes
Of gunboats sew the green dark with speed.

From Dunkirk red flames open fanwise
In spokes of light; like the rising moon
Setting fire to the sky, the remote
Image of death burns on the water.

The slow muffle of hours. Clouds grow visible
Altering course the moon congeals on a new
Bearing. Northwards again and Europe recedes
With the first sharp splinters of dawn.

The orange sky lies over the harbour.
Derricks and pylons like scarecrows.
Back in the early light and minesweepers
Pass us, moving out slowly to the North Sea.

Two Tigers

Below are two poems about tigers. Each represents a personal, individual picture of the tiger. The picture that emerges from each is like a collage – that is, a picture that has been assembled from a lot of little pictures.

Tiger

He stalks in his vivid stripes
The few steps of his cage
On pads of velvet quiet
In his quiet rage.

He should be lurking in shadow
Sliding through long grass
Near the water hole
Where the plump deer pass

He should be snarling around houses
At the jungle's edge.
Baring his white fangs, his claws.
Terrorising the village!

But he's locked in a concrete cell
His strength behind bars
Stalking the length of his cage
Ignoring visitors.

He hears the last voice at night
The patrolling cars
And stares with his brilliant eyes
At the brilliant stars.

Leslie Norris

The Tiger

Tiger! Tiger! burning bright
In the forest of the night
What immortal hand or eye
Could frame thy fearful symmetry.

In what distant deep or skies
Burnt the fire of thine eyes
On what wings dare he aspire?
What the hand dare seize the fire?

And when thy heart began to beat,
Could twist the sinews of thy heart?
And why the heart began to beat,
What dread hand? And what dread feet!

What the hammer? What the chain?
In what furnace was thy brain?
What the anvil? What dread clasp?
Dare its deadly terrors clasp?

When the stars threw down their spears
And water'd heaven with their tears
Did he smile his work to see?
Did he who made the Lamb make thee?

Tiger! Tiger! burning bright
In the forests of the night
What immortal hand or eye
Dare frame thy fearful symmetry.

William Blake

Activities

1. In which of the two poems do you feel more strongly the presence of an actual tiger, a big cat – a real animal? Explain your choice.
2. Pick out the word pictures and metaphors from these poems. Isolate them and then – in note form – explain how the image works on you. For example:

   . . . *burning bright*: a tiger does not really burn, but 'burning bright' gives a sense of clarity and power – a clearly burning flame.
   . . . *forests of the night*: does this mean "dark forests" – night – dark, or does it mean that night is like a forest, a tangled web of vegetation where you can get lost. In either case, the tiger is shown as a bright light in a dark place.

3. Write your response to both poems, considering surface meaning and deeper meaning (see Unit 2.10).

Towards Writing

Here are two more poems about weather and the sea, and the feelings that they arouse in people.

Abersoch

There was that headland, asleep on the
  sea,
The air full of thunder and the far air
Brittle with lightning; there was that girl
Riding her cycle, hair at half-mast,
And the men smoking, the dinghies at
  rest
On the calm tide. There were people
  going
About their business, while the storm
  grew
Louder and nearer and did not break.

Why do I remember these few things,
That were rumours of life, not life itself
That was being lived fiercely, where the
  storm raged?
Was it just that the girl smiled,
Though not at me, and the men smoking
And the look of those who have come
  safely home?

R. S. Thomas

Sea Fever

I must down to the seas again, to the
  lonely sea and the sky,
And all I ask is a tall ship and a star to
  steer by,
And the wheel's kick and the wind's
  song and the white sail's shaking,
And a grey mist on the sea's face and a
  grey dawn breaking.

I must down to the seas again, for the call
  of the running tide
Is a wild call and a clear call that may not
  be denied:
And all I ask is a windy day with the
  white clouds flying,
And the flung spray and the blown
  spume, and the seagulls crying.

I must down to the seas again, to the
  vagrant gypsy life,
To the gull's way and the whale's way
  where the wind's like a whetted knife;
And all I ask is a merry yarn from a
  laughing fellow-rover,
And a quiet sleep and a sweet dream
  when the long trick's over.

John Masefield

Activities

1. Read the poems carefully and make a list of all the pictures that make up the scene.
2. There are some images in the poems which a photograph could not show, such as the metaphor 'the wind's song'. List other metaphorical images in the poems which a photograph could not show.

3. Compare these two poems, using the skills you developed in Units 2.10 and 11. Look at the meanings (both surface and deeper) and content (what is the poem about?). Look at the words the poets use, and at the images (or pictures) that the poets create through language. You must also be able to respond to the poems yourself. Which one do you like better? Which one speaks more clearly to you?

4. If you have visited the sea think about the experience and write an account of it. If you prefer, make up a story which is set either on or by the sea. If you have not been to the sea you will still have an idea of what the sea is like from books, television programmes and films. In a piece of writing describe what you associate the sea with.

Pictures of Creation

If we think about the immensity of the sea, the sky and the stars we may wonder where it all came from. Here are two explanations: the first is a creation story from the Bible; the second is a creation story from China.

This extract from the book of Genesis is full of 'pictures'. It could be presented dramatically or as a group reading exercise, reading in the round.

The Creation

from
The Book of Genesis

In the beginning God created the heaven and the earth.

And the earth was without form, and void; and darkness was upon the face of the deep. And the Spirit of God moved upon the face of the waters.

And God said, Let there be light: and there was light.

And God saw the light, that it was good: and God divided the light from the darkness.

And God called the light Day, and the darkness he called Night. And the evening and the morning were the first day.

And God said, Let there be a firmament in the midst of the waters, and let it divide the waters from the waters.

And God made the firmament, and divided the waters which were under the firmament from the waters which were above the firmament: and it was so.

And God called the firmament Heaven. And the evening and the morning were the second day.

And God said, Let the waters under the heaven be gathered together into one place, and let the dry land appear: and it was so.

And God called the dry land Earth: and the gathering together of the waters called he Seas: and God saw that it was good.

And God said, Let the earth bring forth grass, the herb yielding seed, and the fruit tree yielding fruit after his kind whose seed is in itself, upon the earth: and it was so.

And the earth brought forth grass, and her yielding seed after his kind, and the tree yielding fruit, whose seed was in itself, after his kind: and God saw that it was good. And the evening and the morning were the third day.

And God said, Let there be lights in the firmament of the heaven to divide the day from the night; and let them be for signs, and for seasons, and for days, and years. And let them be for lights in the firmament of the heaven to give light upon the earth: and it was so. And God made two lights; the greater light to rule the day, and the lesser light to rule the night; he made the stars also.

And God set them in the firmament of the heaven to give light upon the earth.

And to rule over the day and over the night, and to divide the light from the darkness: and God saw that it was good. And the evening and the morning were the fourth day.

And God said, Let the waters bring forth abundantly the moving creature that hath life, and fowl that may fly above the earth in the open firmament of heaven.

And God created great whales, and every living creature that moveth, which the waters brought forth abundantly, after their kind, and every winged fowl after his kind: and God saw that it was good.

And God blessed them, saying, Be fruitful, and multiply, and fill the waters in the seas, and let fowl multiply in the earth. And the evening and the morning were the fifth day.

And God said, Let the earth bring forth the living creature after his kind, cattle, and creeping thing, and beast of the earth after his kind: and it was so.

And God made the beast of the earth after his kind, and cattle after their kind, and everything that creepeth upon the earth after his kind: and God saw that it was good.

Activities

1. Read this passage aloud. Notice the rhythm created by repetition. Note the repeated words and phrases.

2. Write down two words that you find difficult to understand. Look them up in a dictionary and see if you can replace them with easier words with the same meaning. Now find five old fashioned words or phrases in the extract and give the modern equivalents.

3. What pictures form in your mind as you hear this read aloud? Write down the words or draw the pictures.

4. In a film called *The Bible*, an attempt was made to film the Creation! Imagining that the words are the soundtrack of the film, what images would you show on the screen? You could present your ideas for images in the following way:

SOUND	PICTURE
"And God said, 'Let there be light' and there was light."	Shot of big sun rising behind a mountain

Here is a creation story from China. Read it and make a list of the most vivid pictures in your mind. Compare the images with those from the Christian creation story. Every culture has its own creation story.

Creation Story

O listener, let it be told of a time when there was nothing but chaos, and that chaos was like a mist and full of emptiness. Suddenly into the midst of this mist, into this chaos of emptiness, came a great, colourful light. From this light all things that exist came to be. The mist shook and separated. That which was light rose up to form heaven, and that which was heavy sank, and formed the earth.

Now from heaven and earth came forth strong forces. These two forces combined to produce yin and yang. Picture, O listener, this yang like a dragon – hot, fiery male, full of energy. Imagine, O listener, this yin as a cloud – moist, cool, female, drifting slowly. Each of these forces is full of great power. Left alone, they would destroy the world with their might, and chaos would return. Together they balance each other, and keep the world in harmony.

This then is yin and yang, and from them came forth everything. The sun is of yang, and the moon, yin. The four seasons and the five elements – water, earth, metal, fire and wood – sprang from them. So did all kinds of living creatures.

So now there was the earth, floating like a jellyfish on water. But the earth was just a ball, without features. Then the forces of yin and yang created the giant figure P'an Ku, the Ancient One. P'an Ku, who never stopped growing every year of his great, long life, set to work to put the earth in order. He dug the river valleys and piled up the mountains. Over many thousands of years he shaped and created the flow and folds of our earth.

But such work took its toll. Even mighty P'an Ku could not escape death, and worn out by his struggle he collapsed and died. His body was now so vast that when he fell to the ground, dead, his body became the five sacred mountains. His flesh became the soil, his bones the rocks, his hair the plants and his blood the rivers. From his sweat came the rain, and from the parasite – the tiny creatures living on his body – came forth human beings.

The people at first lived in caves, but soon Heavenly Emperors came to teach them how to make tools and houses. The people also learned how to build boats, to fish, to plough and plant, and to prepare food. O listener, this is how it all began.

Activities

1. Write your own creation story in the style of one of these.
2. Write a humorous account of Creation, as if you were the Creator of the world.
3. Write a scientific explanation of the beginning of the world.

Pictures in Prose

The language of the Bible – that is, the translation of the Bible made in 1611 – with its rhythms, its pictures, and its short verse form, has influenced many English writers. In this extract from *Sons and Lovers* by D. H. Lawrence, a drunken miner pushes his pregnant wife out into the garden:

Sons and Lovers

D. H. Lawrence

He came up to her, his red face, with its bloodshot eyes, thrust forward and gripped her arms. She cried in fear of him, struggled to be free. Coming slightly to himself, panting, he pushed her roughly to the outer door, and thrust her forth, slotting the bolt behind her with a bang. Then he went back into the kitchen, dropped into his arm-chair, his head, bursting full of blood, sinking between his knees. Thus he dipped gradually into a stupor, from exhaustion and intoxication.

She hurried out of the side garden to the front, where she could stand as if in an immense gulf of white light, the moon streaming high in face of her, the moonlight standing up from the hills in front, and filling the valley where the Bottoms crouched, almost blindingly. There, panting and half weeping in reaction from the stress, she murmured to herself over and over again: "The nuisance! the nuisance!"

She became aware of something about her. With an effort she roused herself to see what it was that penetrated her consciousness. The tall white lilies were reeling in the moonlight, and the air was charged with their perfume, as with a presence. Mrs. Morel gasped slightly in fear. She touched the big, pallid flowers on their petals, then shivered. They seemed to be stretching in the moonlight. She put her hand into one white bin: the gold scarcely showed on her fingers by moonlight. She bent down to look at the binful of yellow pollen; but it only appeared dusky. Then she drank a deep draught of the scent. It almost made her dizzy.

Activities

1. Is the passage about the same thing throughout or does it move from one thing to another? Look at the first part of the passage (the first two paragraphs) and the second part (the last paragraph). Say what the writer is doing in each part.
2. Which words help build up an unpleasant picture of the miner? You could write your anwer down like this (the inverted commas show that you are taking the words from the passage):

The miner has a "red" face. He has "bloodshot" eyes . . . and so on.

3. Which paragraph or paragraphs contain most vigorous action? Pick out the words which tell us about these actions and write them down, as you did for Question 2.
4. Look at the last two paragraphs. An effect is created here by introducing lots of words relating to light. Find as many words as you can associated with light.
5. There is evidence of repetition in the final two paragraphs, too. Write down the four sentences that begin with 'she'. New rewrite these sentences so that they contain the same information but do not begin with 'she'. Read the original version, and then your 'new' version with the changed sentences to someone else. Ask this person to comment on the differences between the two versions and write down their comments.
6. Continue the story by writing two paragraphs following on from the extract above. The woman is locked out. The husband has fallen asleep. What happens next? You could write as if you are the woman, telling a neighbour what happened, or the miner telling a friend in the pub.
7. Write a paragraph showing how Lawrence uses words in this extract. Say what pictures form in your mind as you read this passage.

Reading Different Types of Texts

Unit 2.13 Reading and Listening

Reading and Listening: The Receptive Side of Language ◆ From Reception to Production ◆ There's more to Talk than Talking ◆ Role Play ◆ Talking Points: From Reading to Writing

◗ *See units 1.5, 3.8*

Reading and Listening: The Receptive Side of Language

So far most of this book has been about the reception of written language. But the reception of spoken language – listening – is also important both in everyday life and in first English examinations. In an oral assessment, you will be rewarded, not just for your ability to talk, but for your ability to listen to other people.

How do we receive language? How do we listen? How do we read? The answer is complex, but it is partly physical: we need ears and eyes, as these two pieces of writing show:

How We See

Our eyes tell us more about our surroundings than any other organ. Through them we become aware of the objects around us, and learn their size, shape, and colour. But our eyes tell us not only about objects near to us, but also about those that are a long distance away – far beyond the range of our hearing, taste or smell. Though our eyes are the organs that collect all this information, 'seeing' takes place in our brains.

from *The Doom Machine* Sackett and Marshall

How Do We Hear?

Sound vibrations from the *eardrum* are picked up by the *hammer*, the *anvil*, the *stirrup* – the body's three smallest bones. The stirrup vibrates strongly against a smaller 'eardrum' – the *ear window*. These stronger vibrations cause pressure waves in the *perilymph* fluid in the *cochlea*. In turn, the pressure waves activate special sense cells, called ham cells, in the basilar membrane. These cells transmit impulses along the auditory nerve to the brain – and we hear sound.

Questions

1. Which one of these is an example of technical writing (writing which uses specialist terms)? Give some examples of technical language from the passage.
2. Read 'How we see' and then, without looking at it, jot down the main points of the passage. At the end of the lesson ask someone to read it to you, and then jot down the main points you can remember after hearing it. Did you jot down more points after reading the passage, or after hearing it?

Activities

1. Look at different sorts of print and handwriting in any books, papers, or folders that are ready to hand. Take six examples. Comment on how easy or difficult they are to read.
2. Listen to a ten minute news broadcast on the radio and then write down as much of it as you can remember. Comment on the newsreader's voice.
3. Ask four different people to read the same news item. Then discuss which reading was the clearest and easiest to listen to and why.
4. Listen to three different kinds of talk programme on TV (these include chat shows, political debates, news broadcasts and sports commentaries). Listen carefully to the programmes and then compare the way the people are talking on each of them. You may wish to consider the following points in particular:

   ◆ Are the people on the programme talking to each other or to the viewers at home?
   ◆ Are they talking in a formal or an informal way?
   ◆ Are they using technical language?

From Reception to Production

To understand what someone is saying, we need to understand two things:

◆ The meaning of the words which the person is using
◆ The way in which these words are put together.

In the English language, words tend to be used in a certain order, and we expect that order of words to be used when people speak to us, so that we can make sense of what they are saying. For example:

"The bulls chased us across the field"

is more readily understood than

"Across the fields, us, the bulls chased".

This is because the word order in the first example is more familiar to us. We could use the second order – but it takes time to 'tune in' to that pattern. It is unconventional. (The words we use are technically called LEXIS. The order in which we put them is SYNTAX.)

There's More to Talk Than Talking

As well as being aware of the need to use words that are appropriate for the audience to whom you are speaking, you must also be aware of the way in which your audience responds to you. If you speak too slowly your audience will become bored. If you speak too quickly you may create anxiety and confusion in your audience as they try to keep up with what you are saying. Speak in a monotone and your audience will probably drop off to sleep as you 'drone on'!

When you are talking you are doing other things as well – often without being aware of them. You may be moving your hands. You will certainly be moving your eyes – fixing them on one listener, flickering between members of your audience or averting your eyes from them. Your eyes and hands can have the effect of either holding the attention of your audience or acting as a distraction.

Role Play

Preparing a talk is only one part of the oral course work you will be required to do for your English examination. Other components of the examination include discussion, reading, narrating an anecdote, solving a problem in a simulation, improvisation and role play.

Activity

Choose one of the situations listed below and then take a card or sheet of paper for each of the two parts involved in the role play. Write the name of one of the characters at the top of the sheet. On the first sheet write down the questions and statements to be spoken by one character, and on the second sheet the responses to be spoken by the other.

Write a card for each character, filling in details of the role.

1. A parent complains to a headteacher about his/her child being given too much homework.
2. A customer goes into a shop and asks for a refund on a damaged pair of shoes.
3. A TV chat show host interviews a celebrity.
4. An employer interviews somebody who has applied for a job.
5. An MP listens to a constituent's worries about the threatened closure of a local factory.
6. A policeman interviews a suspect in connection with an armed robbery of a bank.
7. A character from a play such as *Romeo and Juliet* is interviewed by a school student.

Talking Points: From Reading to Writing

As we move towards a section which concentrates on producing writing, it is an appropriate time to pause and decide – through discussion – what kind of guidance you want with your own writing.

Activities

1. Either in groups or as a class, discuss and agree on a marking strategy for written work:

    ♦ Do you want misspelling corrected?
    ♦ Do you want marks?
    ♦ Do you want comments?
    ♦ Do you want to hand in drafts?
    ♦ Do you want to discuss the draft with your teacher?
    ♦ Do you want to mark each other's work sometimes?

2. You have probably seen TV viewers airing their views or responding to other people's claims or criticisms in the *Video Box* on Channel 4's *Right to Reply*. Write your own two minute speech responding to the claim: 'Young people

today are entirely thoughtless, inconsiderate and selfish'. Deliver your speech to the class, or in front of a video camera!

3. In small groups, have a discussion about reading, focusing on the following questions:

- When and how often do you read?
- Why do you read?
- What type of books do you read?
- What do you think are the purposes of reading?
- What do you think you gain from reading novels?
- When you leave school, what use will you put your reading to?

After the group discussion, move on to a general class discussion, in a circle.

4. In small groups, talk about writing. Focus on the following:

a Why do people write novels or poems?
- for money?
- for fame?
- because they are lonely? (Writing is a substitute for talking.)
- because they have the urge to tell people something?
- because they enjoy writing and are good at it?

b Would you ever write (i) a novel, (ii) a poem, (iii) a short story? (Give a reason for your answer in each case.)

c When you write something, do you always hope someone is going to read it? Do you ever write anything which you do not wish anyone else to read?

d Do you write letters? Do you always have plenty to say? Is writing (i) easy? (ii) necessary?

e Can we learn anything from reading novels and poems? What can we learn?

PART 3: APPROACHES TO WRITING

Part 3 of *Do You Read Me?* is mainly about writing – about how communication in written form takes place. The units look at *why* we write (Unit 3.1), then at some different forms of writing – writing which:

◆ informs and persuades (Unit 3.2)
◆ describes (Unit 3.3)
◆ tells stories, makes us laugh or provides fast action (Unit 3.4)
◆ conveys strong feelings and atmosphere (Unit 3.5)

Through these units, the text looks at the purposes and the audiences of writing.

See units To the student, 1.1, 3.2

> **Approaches to Different Types of Writing**
>
> # Unit 3.1 Why Write?
>
> Introduction: Reasons for Writing ◆ Do We Need to be able to Write? ◆ Who is the Author Writing for? ◆ Language Appropriate to Audience: Register ◆ Writing to Order ◆ Writing for Young Adults ◆ Writing for Something you Want ◆ Writing for Pleasure

Introduction: Reasons for Writing

Every writer – you, me, Shakespeare – writes for some reason, with some end in view. Graffiti writers spray subways to be noticed, remembered or to make some political point:

Although we may doodle sometimes, we rarely write just for the sake of it. Here is a letter. Why might the author have written it?

Dear Uncle Bill,

Thank you for the five pound note. I am going to buy a record with it.

Pam

In writing this letter the author may have wanted to:

• show her gratitude to her uncle
• silence her nagging parents
• do what was conventional in the situation.

As a student you have to do a lot of writing and you may do this writing for any, or all of these reasons:

• for pleasure, the joy of expressing yourself on paper
• to have something to put into an examination coursework folder
• to satisfy the teacher.

The careful author always has a reason for writing – an aim and an audience in mind. As you read any piece of writing it may help to ask yourself the questions:

• WHAT IS THE AUTHOR TRYING TO DO?
• WHO IS THE AUTHOR WRITING FOR?

Do We Need to be Able to Write?

Although many of you would say yes, there may be some who need convincing, because they know successful people who cannot read or write very well. Imagine that when the world wakes up tomorrow no one is able to remember how to write. Working in groups, discuss how this would affect one or more of the following:

SCHOOLS	JOB CENTRES	THE POLICE
FACTORIES	SHOPS	OFFICES
CINEMAS	HOSPITALS	SPORT
TRANSPORT	THE ARMED FORCES	TELEVISION

Decide whether these institutions and organisations could carry on running in their usual way for very long. Would some of these be more affected than others?

Who is the Author Writing For?

When you write do you think about who will read your work? Do you actually think, 'Oh yes, my teacher will read this, probably at home with the cat next to him on the sofa, and a cup of coffee on my work'? Probably not, but should you think about the impact your work will have on the reader?

For example, do you think that Stephen considered that this piece of coursework would be read by a teacher?

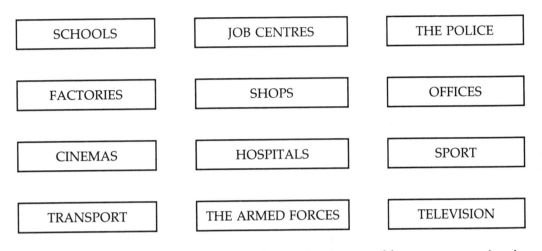

TEACHERS

Teachers have an easy life. They sit there while the children have to do all the work and they get paid as much as anyone even though they have long holidays. They finish early (at 4 o'clock). They don't have to work on Saturdays.

I wouldn't be a teacher if you paid me.

Stephen

This is clear; it expresses forcefully a point of view. But what doesn't it do?

When you are writing you may not be aware of thinking very much, if at all, about your teacher reading your work, but you might be upset if your teacher gave the piece of work to somebody else to read. Would you choose to write differently if you thought that the rest of the class was going to read your story? If you would – then it shows that you have a sense of audience. This means that you are writing with a particular person or group of people – a readership – in mind.

Language Appropriate to Audience: Register

The kind of language we use when we speak varies according to the situation we are in and according to whom we are talking to. Here are some different ways of saying goodbye:

> 'Cheers then!'
> "Bye.'
> 'Goodbye.'
> 'Goodbye Mrs. McClusky.'

You might say 'Cheers then' to friends in the street; "Bye' to your parents; 'Goodbye' to a stranger; and 'Goodbye Mrs. McClusky' to a headteacher or elderly neighbour. These are different REGISTERS of language – ranging from the informal register you would use when talking to your friends, to the more formal register you would use when addressing an older person or a person in authority. We use a particular register with a particular person because it is what they *expect*. People switch registers quickly and automatically. Teachers do not talk to each other in the way that they talk to pupils; pupils do not talk to each other in the way that they talk to their parents. Although this is common sense and automatic in speech, it is sometimes forgotten when it comes to writing.

Activities

1. Divide into groups of three and prepare the following role-play. One of you is a student who has virtually given up doing any schoolwork, one of you a concerned friend, and the other a worried parent.
   - Write role cards for:
     a a scene in which the friend talks with the student about the problem;
     b a scene in which the parent talks with the student about the problem.
   - Act out the role play.
   The person who is 'offstage' in each scene should observe and see if the appropriate language (i.e. register) is being used in each case.

2. Imagine that you have secretly made up your mind to join the army. You have been along to the army careers office, and have been accepted. This will mean leaving home, but you cannot pluck up courage to tell anyone what you intend to do. Write the note or letter you will leave for – or send to – each of the following, explaining the reasons for your decision to join the army and leave home.

| PARENTS | BOYFRIEND/GIRLFRIEND |

| THE EMPLOYER YOU WORK FOR ON SATURDAYS | THE CAPTAIN OF THE SPORTS TEAM YOU PLAY FOR ON SUNDAYS |

Writing to Order

Some people write because they are employed to do so. Newspaper journalists are usually told by their editors what to write about. They may have to describe rather ordinary things such as farming or local news, because the editor wants the story.

Okehampton's Farmers' Union decided not to change the town's market day from Saturday to Thursday, as has been requested.	Celebrating their diamond wedding anniversary are Mr. Bill Read and his wife, Edith, from Mincinglake Road, Stoke Hill.

This is called WRITING TO A BRIEF. This means writing according to a set of instructions. A journalist might be asked to write a review, a news story or a features article.

REVIEW

The tinny men

IN THE LAND OF OZ by Howard Jacobson/Hamish Hamilton, £12.95

HOWARD JACOBSON has made his name as an author with three witty, irreverent, and invective-filled novels.

He brings the same talents to this journey through Australia, the land where he worked in the '60s as a university lecturer and in the '70s as a plasterer's labourer.

Armed with a publisher's advance and accompanied by his Australian wife, Ros, Jacobson set off on a tour around Oz that provided plenty of scope for his acid pen.

NEWS

Lorry load smashes phone box

EGGESFORD's only telephone box is no more after 20 tons of steel girders smashed it to pieces.

The kiosk ended up in bits when a lorry on the A377 Exeter to Barnstaple road shed its load on a bend by Eggesford railway station.

But the telephone itself was still in working order.

FEATURES

A Star's scents of direction

NO OFFENCE to Henry but Mr. Cooper's "splash it all over" days seem well and truly numbered. However, there's no shortage of sports personalities willing to use their names to promote men's smellies.

Bjorn Borg, the Seventies tennis superstar, is about to launch his own exclusive men's fragrance in the United Kingdom – Signature and 6-0. Borg has been busy since his Wimbledon days: he is Ambassador for Tourism in Sweden, has a men's fashion line, as well as cashing in on the ever-increasing market for men's toiletries.

SPORT

ANGLING

THE WELCOME INN to Clapperbrook Bridge length of the Exeter Canal was in disappointing form for the popular Mandrake Motors sponsored event that attracted 38 seniors and 15 juniors.

For most competitors, fish were very hard to tempt and there were many dry nets.

It seemed that several nights of low temperatures had contributed to the poor result which saw anglers gaining points in the Express and Echo League with just ounces.

Activities

1. As a journalist on a local paper, you have been asked to cover a darts contest. Here are your notes. You have to write between 175 and 200 words for the sports page. You *do not* have to give a headline.

> S.W. Darts Contest at Dryons Centre
> 100 entries
> 3 categories: men, women, over 65s
> Crowd of 4-600 attended
> 1st round over 9.10; 2nd round by 11;
> semi final - midnight.
> Final finished at 12.58 a.m.
> Men's winner: Peter Heppa; runner-up - Martin Rolfe
> Women's winner: Ruth Hooper, runner-up - Eve Spencer
> Highest score: 180 - prize won by Mary Bell
> Over 65s - winner: Roy Ebb; runner-up
> Alice Cooper
>
> First prize in each category £50; second prize £30; highest single score £20.
> Youngest competitor: Tracy Butler (13½)
> knocked out in 2nd round.

Include all the names (local papers always do so). Numbers count as one word.

2. Write a review of a book, video, album, television programme or film for your local paper. You should write between 175 and 200 words.

3. Write a report of a sporting event for the sports pages of a broadsheet paper like *The Times* or the *Guardian*, and then one for a tabloid like the *Daily Mirror* or the *Sun*. Write 200 words for each.

Writing for Young Adults

Bernard Ashley is a popular writer of stories for older children. But does he aim his writing at teenagers? Does he have an audience in mind?

Kid's Stuff

Bernard Ashley

Bernard Ashley was born in Woolwich in 1935. He now lives with his wife and three sons in London and is Headmaster of a Junior school not far from the scene of his early childhood. He writes adventure stories mostly about children in difficulties and his serial RUNNING SCARED was seen on BBC Children's Television.

One of the most difficult questions an author gets asked is, 'Who do you write for?' The quick cop-out answer, always leaving an after-taste of smug in the mouth, is 'I write for me – to please myself.' It's never true, of course, not in a one-hundred-per-cent sense. Can there ever have been an author who was unaware of any sense of audience, who knew no constraints? The reality is that you write for many different people, sometimes all of them at the same time, sometimes individually; that 'significant other' varying by sentence. There's yourself, yes, or you wouldn't be sitting at a desk at all; but there's also a thick glass screen of other people between you and the book-buying public you're waving at. Now it might be your mother, who'd appreciate that old family word; now your wife, or your children, or a friend (writing about an experience you've shared with someone else can't fail to have you imagining the acclaim when they see what you made of it); and always there's your publishing editor, sitting on your shoulder like a mother bird with a meal in her beak, watching you earn it. Not forgetting the social consciences (like the anti-racist or anti-sexist campaigners) who must know what side you're on. Finally, though, there's the main audience – or the main partnership as I prefer to think of it (for every book is a sharing between writer and reader with the latter needing to bring his/her own experience to the page). Again, this imagined partnership will vary within the book; sometimes it's with a child you know, sometimes with a wider group – like Asian girls in London through parts of RUNNING SCARED. How simple it would be if, eschewing the 'writing for me' idea, you could instead adopt that single phantom personality described by some writers: because in contemplating a piece on 'Writing for Teenagers' the title already seems more than a little removed. Perhaps 'Being Marketed for Teenagers' fits the bill better.

So when I'm asked who my books are for I always answer, 'Everyone.' I'd be disappointed if an adult threw down one of my books as being only for children. I never write with one hand behind my back; poor as it might be, it's always the best I can do at the time. Sometimes the output from an evening's session is one word, and you can't be trying harder than that.' Actually, it happened just once. I was revising a section from HIGH PAVEMENT BLUES, written in the first person, and I had the central character Kevin, the son of an ex-soldier, describing the impermanence of wherever he lived. One phrase ran: 'pigsty or palace you always live a temporary sort of life when your father's a soldier.' For some reason I wasn't happy with it, and after a think and a Scotch I narrowed it down to that word temporary; it didn't ring true coming from the boy and it had a juddering effect on the sentence flow (it's that sort of word). I thought of the soldiers we see around Woolwich hurrying to the station on leave, and suddenly I had it: out went temporary and in came suitcase, giving a mental picture and alliterative flow. I went to bed happy.

Questions

1. What does Bernard Ashley do for a living apart from writing?
2. What are most of his stories about? (Use your own words.)
3. Does he write simply to please himself? (Give a reason.)

4. What picture does he intend to put in our minds by comparing this publishing editor to a mother bird?
5. Who are anti-sexist and anti-racist campaigners?
6. Does he modify the way he writes because he is writing for teenagers?
7. What information are we given about the book *High Pavement Blues*?
8. Why did he not like the word 'temporary'?
9. How did he come to think of the word 'suitcase'?
10. What does he mean by 'alliterative flow'?

Writing for Something You Want

Often we write either to request, or provide information. Here is a typical letter of the kind you might write:

> 40 Magdalen Road,
> Exeter, EX8 4BG.
> 26·3·95
>
> Channel 4,
> Charlotte Street,
> London.
>
> Dear Sir,
>
> I would be grateful if you would send me the booklet which goes with the Channel 4 programme "Eat Healthy – Stay Young". I enclose a cheque for £3.95.
>
> Yours faithfully,
>
>
> Richard Wilson

Activities

1. Write a letter
   a to Wallace Arnold coaches asking for information about the cost of hiring a coach to take 50 people on a day trip to the National Exhibition Centre in Birmingham on a week day.
   b to a local car hire firm – Kastners – asking if they have any job vacancies.
   c to an old teacher, asking if you can use his/her name as a reference in your application to a college.
2. This activity requires you to write three letters all relating to holidays. You can base the details of your letters either on a holiday you have had, or on a holiday you hope to have. Write
   a a letter inviting a friend to stay with you for two weeks. Explain in your letter what you could do during the two weeks, and where you could go.
   b a letter to a travel agent booking a holiday you saw advertised in a brochure.
   c a letter telling a friend about the holiday you are having.

Writing for Pleasure

Most of the books and poems that you will be reading during your examination course were written by people who *chose* to write! They were not forced to write – nor was there a simple, practical reason for writing. They wrote for pleasure, or for personal reasons.

Why I Write

George Orwell

From a very early age, perhaps the age of five or six, I knew that when I grew up I should be a writer. Between the ages of about seventeen and twenty-four I tried to abandon this idea, but I did so with the consciousness that I was outraging my true nature and that sooner or later I should have to settle down and write books.

I was the middle child of three, but there was a gap of five years on either side, and I barely saw my father before I was eight. For this and other reasons I was somewhat lonely, and I soon developed disagreeable mannerisms which made me unpopular throughout my schooldays. I had the lonely child's habit of making up stories and holding conversations with imaginary persons, and I think from the very start my literary ambitions were mixed up with the feeling of being isolated and under-valued. I knew that I had a facility with words and a power of facing unpleasant facts, and I felt that this created a sort of private world in which I could get my own back for my failure in everyday life. Nevertheless the volume of serious – i.e. seriously intended – writing which I produced all through my childhood and boyhood would not amount to half a dozen pages. I wrote my first poem at the age of four or five, my mother taking it down to dictation. I cannot remember anything about it except that it was about a tiger and the tiger had "chair-like teeth" – a good enough phrase, but I fancy the poem was a plagiarism of Blake's "Tiger, Tiger". At eleven, when the war of 1914-18 broke out, I wrote a patriotic poem which was printed in the local newspaper, as was another, two years later, on the death of Kitchener. From time to time, when I was a bit older, I wrote bad and usually unfinished "nature poems" in the Georgian style. I also, about twice, attempted a short story which was a ghastly failure. That was the total of the would-be serious work that I actually set down on paper during all those years.

However, throughout this time I did in a sense engage in literary activities. To begin with there was the made-to-order stuff which I produced quickly, easily and without much pleasure to myself. Apart from school work, I wrote vers d'occasion, semi-comic poems which I could turn out at what now seems to me astonishing speed – at fourteen I wrote a whole rhyming play, in imitation of Aristophanes, in about a week – and helped to edit school magazines, both printed and in manuscript. These magazines were the most pitiful burlesque stuff that you could imagine, and I took far less trouble with them than I now would with the cheapest journalism. But side by side with all this, for fifteen years or more, I was carrying out a literary exercise of a quite different kind: this was the making up of a continuous "story" about myself, a sort of diary existing only in the mind. I believe this is a common habit of children and adolescents. As a very small child I used to imagine that I was, say, Robin Hood, and picture myself as the hero of thrilling adventures, but quite soon my "story" ceased to be narcissistic in a crude way and became more and more a mere description of what I was doing and the things I saw. For minutes at a time this kind of thing would be running through my head: "He pushed the door open and entered the room. A yellow beam of sunlight, filtering through the muslin curtains, slanted on to the table, where a matchbox, half open, lay beside the inkpot. With his right hand in his pocket he moved across to the window. Down in the street a tortoisehell cat was chasing a dead leaf." etc. etc. This habit continued till I was about twenty-five, right through my non-literary years. Although I had to search, and did search, for the right words, I seemed to be making this descriptive effort almost against my will, under a kind of compulsion from outside. The "story" must, I suppose, have reflected the styles of the various writers I admired at different ages, but so far as I remember it always had the same meticulous descriptive quality.

When I was about sixteen I suddenly discovered the joy of mere words, i.e. the sounds and associations of words. The lines from Paradise Lost,

> So hee with difficulty and labour hard
> Moved on: with difficulty and labour hee,

which do not now seem to me so very wonderful, sent shivers down my backbone: and the spelling "hee" for "he" was an added pleasure. As for the need to describe things, I knew all about it already. So it is clear what kind of books I wanted to write in so far as I could be said to want to write books at that time. I wanted to write enormous naturalistic novels with unhappy endings, full of detailed descriptions and arresting similes, and also full of purple passages in which words were used partly for the sake of their sound. And in fact my first completed novel, *Burmese Days*, which I wrote when I was thirty but projected much earlier, is rather that kind of book.

I give all this background information because I do not think one can assess a writer's motives without knowing something of his early development. His subject matter will be determined by the age he lives in – at least this is true in tumultuous, revolutionary ages like our own – but before he ever begins to write he will have acquired an emotional attitude from which he will never completely escape. It is his job, no doubt, to discipline his temperament and avoid getting stuck at some immature stage, or in some perverse mood: but if he escapes from his early influences altogether, he will have killed his impulse to write. Putting aside the need to earn a living, I think there are four great motives for writing, at any rate for writing prose. They exist in different degrees in every writer, and in any one writer the proportions will vary from time to time, according to the atmosphere in which he is living. They are:

1. Sheer egoism. Desire to seem clever, to be talked about, to be remembered after death, to get your own back on grown-ups who snubbed you in childhood, etc etc. It is humbug to pretend that this is not a motive, and a strong one. Writers share this characteristic with scientists, artists, politicians, lawyers, soldiers, successful businessmen – in short, with the whole top crust of humanity. The great mass of human beings are not acutely selfish. After the age of about thirty they abandon individual ambition – in many cases, indeed, they almost abandon the sense of being individuals at all – and live chiefly for others, or are simply smothered under drudgery. But there is also the minority of gifted, wilful people who are determined to live their own lives to the end,

and writers belong in this class. Serious writers, I should say, are on the whole more vain and self-centred than journalists, though less interested in money.

2. Aesthetic enthusiasm. Perception of beauty in the external world, or, on the other hand, in words and their right arrangement. Pleasure in the impact of one sound on another, in the firmness of good prose or the rhythm of a good story. Desire to share an experience which one feels is valuable and ought not to be missed. The aesthetic motive is very feeble in a lot of writers, but even a pamphleteer or a writer of textbooks will have pet words and phrases which appeal to him for non-utilitarian reasons; or he may feel strongly about typography, width of margins, etc. Above the level of a railway guide, no book is quite free from aesthetic considerations.

3. Historical impulse. Desire to see things as they are, to find out true facts and store them up for the use of posterity.

4. Political purpose – using the word "political" in the widest possible sense. Desire to push the world in a certain direction, to alter other people's idea of the kind of society that they should strive after. Once again, no book is genuinely free from political bias. The opinion that art should have nothing to do with politics is itself a political attitude.

What I have most wanted to do throughout the past ten years is to make political writing into an art. My starting point is always a feeling of partisanship, a sense of injustice. When I sit down to write a book, I do not say to myself, "I am going to produce a work of art". I write it because there is some lie that I want to expose, some fact to which I want to draw attention, and my initial concern is to get a hearing. But I could not do the work of writing a book, or even a long magazine article, if it were not also an aesthetic experience. Anyone who cares to examine my work will see that even when it is downright propaganda it contains much that a full-time politician would consider irrelevant. I am not able, and I do not want, completely to abandon the world-view that I acquired in childhood. So long as I remain alive and well I shall continue to feel strongly about prose style, to love the surface of the earth, and to take pleasure in solid objects and scraps of useless information. It is no use trying to suppress that side of myself. The job is to reconcile my ingrained likes and dislikes with the essentially public, non-individual activities that this age forces on all of us.

It is not easy. It raises problems of construction and of language, and it raises in a new way the problem of truthfulness. Let me give just one example of the cruder kind of difficulty that arises. My book about the Spanish civil war, *Homage to Catalonia*, is, of course, a frankly political book, but in the main it is written with a certain detachment and regard for form. I did try very hard in it to tell the whole truth without violating my literary instincts. But among other things it contains a long chapter, full of newspaper quotations and the like, defending the Trotskyists who were accused of plotting with Franco. Clearly such a chapter, which after a year or two would lose its interest for any ordinary reader, must ruin the book. A critic whom I respect read me a lecture about it. "Why did you put in all that stuff?" he said. "You've turned what might have been a good book into journalism." What he said was true, but I could not have done otherwise. I happened to know, what very few people in England had been allowed to know, that innocent men were being falsely accused. If I had not been angry about that I should never have written the book.

In one form or another this problem comes up again. The problem of language is subtler and would take too long to discuss. I will only say that of late years I have tried to write less pictur-esquely and more exactly. In any case I find that by the time you have perfected any style of writing, you have always outgrown it. *Animal Farm* was the first book in which I tried, with full consciousness of what I was doing, to fuse political purpose and artistic purpose into one whole. I have not written a novel for seven years, but I hope to write another fairly soon. It is bound to be a failure, every book is a failure, but I know with some clarity what kind of book I want to write.

Looking back through the last page or two, I see that I have made it appear as though my motives in writing were wholly public-spirited. I don't want to leave that as the final impression. All writers are vain, selfish and lazy, and at the very bottom of their motives there lies a mystery. Writing a book is a horrible, exhausting struggle, like a long bout of some painful illness. One would never undertake such a thing if one were not driven on by some demon whom one can neither resist nor understand. For all one knows that demon is simply the same instinct that makes a baby squall for attention. And yet it is also true that one can write nothing readable unless one constantly struggles to efface one's own personality. Good prose is like a window pane. I cannot say with certainty which of my motives are the strongest, but I know which of them deserve to be followed. And looking back through my work, I see that it is invariably where I lacked a political purpose that I wrote lifeless books and was betrayed into purple passages, sentences without meaning, decorative adjectives and humbug generally.

Questions

1. Why was George Orwell a lonely child?
2. Using your own words, describe the kind of poems he wrote as a boy.
3. Apart from poems, what else did he write as a boy?
4. Using your own words, summarise the four reasons for writing given by Orwell.
5. What seems to be Orwell's main motive as a writer?

Activities

1. Imagine that you are either Orwell's mother or father and you are being interviewed on the radio about your son's childhood. Using the information in the first half of the passage, devise the questions they would be asked and the answers that they would give. Then write out a transcript of the interview. (The interview should last between five and eight minutes.)

2. Using the information contained in the second half of the passage (from 'I give all this background information'), write a description of Orwell's books and the way he writes.

Approaches to Different Types of Writing

Unit 3.2 What is the Writing Doing?

Writing that Informs ◆ Writing that Persuades

▶ *See units 3.1, 3.4–3.12, 4.1–4.3*

Writing That Informs

Before the age of books, if you wanted information you had to get it from another person – a fact which made 'teachers' very powerful people! Although television and radio provide us with a great deal of information, it is in the form of writing that most information is stored in libraries. Here is an example of writing that informs:

TEA

History – Facts — Tea was first sold publicly in England in 1657, when it was a great luxury, costing between £6 and £10 a pound. According to legend the plant took root from the severed eyelids of a Buddhist saint, which he had cut off to prevent himself from falling asleep whilst meditating. It is an Asian plant, native to India, China and Sri Lanka (Ceylon). Until the middle of the nineteenth century the bulk of tea came from China, but now the majority comes from India and Sri Lanka. The United Kingdom is the destination of about half the world's tea exports, and the Cutty Sark at Greenwich stands as a reminder of the great clippers which once brought tea to England.

Cost

Legend

Where it comes from

Indicates scale of tea drinking in UK

Romantic period of maritime history

Here the author simply gives us information in a clear, plain manner.

Activity

Do some research into a popular food or drink product, such as Coca Cola or potato crisps and, using the passage on tea as a model, write an informative piece about it. You should concentrate on the following areas in your account:
- ◆ The product's history
- ◆ the product's ingredients
- ◆ how it is advertised
- ◆ who drinks or eats it.

Writing That Persuades

Early morning comes to life with the golden flavour of Ceylon tea

Why link these two words together?

Sounds good — a golden taste? But think carefully about this!

It's not, you're told it — so it's no longer a secret!

Is it?

Value words

Don't make the mistake of keeping your lovely Ceylon tea for afternoon and company only. In fact the half-awake, oh-goodness-does-it-have-to-be-morning time is just when the rich golden taste of Ceylon tea is a necessity.

The secret of the extra flavour of Ceylon teas is the cool mountain air in which they are grown. The tea-bush grows slowly there and has time to concentrate all the true taste in its tender leaves and buds.

Obviously, the more Ceylon teas there are in any blend, the better the tea; and only blends that are more than half Ceylon have the Lion of Ceylon on the packet. So when you see the Lion, you are sure of getting the golden flavour you expect from good tea, *Join the tea set.*

Value word

Is it?

'Extra' — sounds good

What if you don't like 'golden' tea?

Invitation to the 'in crowd'

Activities

1. Compare the two passages about tea. Draw two columns, one marked 'facts' and one 'opinions'. Then fill in the two columns.
   a Which passage contains more facts?
   b Which passage contains more opinions?
   c What conclusions can you draw from these findings?

   Ceylon is now called Sri Lanka. Ceylon is the old name it had when it was a British colony. Why do you think we still talk about Ceylon tea?

2. Write a short persuasive paragraph that might appear in an advertisement for Coca Cola, milk, coffee or any other drink that you like. Before you begin, jot down as many pleasant-sounding words as you can think of that would be appropriate to use in the advertisement, such as rich, satisfying or relaxing.

Approaches to Different Types of Writing

Unit 3.3 Describing Places and People

Introduction ◆ A Landscape ◆ People

◆ *See units 4.1–4.4*

Introduction

Descriptive writing forms an important part of English course work. In descriptive writing, the focus tends to be on the scene and the people and objects on it, rather than on the story.

A Landscape

Read the following passage carefully, then answer the questions on it.

The Clark's Fork Valley, Wyoming

Ernest Hemingway

At the end of the summer, the big trout would be out in the centre of the stream: they were leaving the pools along the upper part of the river and dropping down to spend the winter in the deep water of the canyon. It was wonderful fly-fishing then in the first weeks of September. The native trout were sleek, shining, and heavy, and nearly all of them leaped when they took the fly. If you fished two flies, you would often have two big trout on and the need to handle them very delicately in that heavy current.

The nights were cold, and, if you woke in the night, you would hear the coyotes. But you did not want to get out on the stream too early in the day because the nights were so cold they chilled the water, and the sun had to be on the river until almost noon before the trout would start to feed.

You could ride in the morning, or sit in front of the cabin, lazy in the sun, and look across the valley where the hay was cut so the meadows were cropped brown and smooth to the line of quaking aspens along the river, now turning yellow in the fall. And on the hills rising beyond, the sage was silvery grey.

Up the river were the two peaks of Pilot and Index, where we would hunt mountain-sheep later in the month, and you sat in the sun and marvelled at the formal, clean-lined shape mountains can have at a distance, so that you remember them in the shapes they show from far away, and not as the broken rock slides you crossed, the jagged edges you pulled up by, and the narrow shelves you sweated along, afraid to look down, to round the peak that looked so smooth and geometrical. You climbed around it to come out on a clear space to look down to where an old ram and three young rams were feeding in the juniper bushes in a high, grassy pocket cupped against the broken rock of the peak.

The old ram was purple-grey, his rump was white, and when he raised his head you saw the great heavy curl of his horns. It was the white of his rump that had betrayed him to you in the green junipers when you had lain in the lee of a rock, out of the wind, three miles away, looking carefully at every yard of the high country through a pair of good Zeiss glasses.

Now as you sat in front of the cabin, you remembered that down-hill shot and the young rams standing, their heads turned, staring at him, waiting for him to get up. They could not see you on that high ledge, nor wind you, and the shot made no more impression on them than a boulder falling.

You remembered the year we had built a cabin at the head of Timber Creek, and the big grizzly that tore it open every time we were away. The snow came later that year, and this bear would not hibernate, but spent his autumn tearing open cabins and ruining a trap-line. But he was so smart you never saw him in the day. Then you remembered coming on the three grizzlies in the high country at the head of Crandall Creek. You heard a crash of timber and thought it was a cow elk bolting, and then there they were, in the broken shadow, running with an easy, lurching smoothness, the afternoon sun making their coats a soft, bristling silver.

You remembered elk bugling in the fall, the bull so close you could see his chest muscles swell as he lifted his head, and still could not see his head in the thick timber; but hear that deep, high mounting whistle and the answer from across another valley. You thought of all the heads you had turned down and refused to shoot, and you were pleased.

You remembered how this country had looked when you first came into it. You could remember all the hunting and all the fishing and the riding in the summer sun and the dust of the pack-train, the silent riding in the hills in the sharp cold of fall going up after the cattle on the high range, finding them wild as deer and as quiet, only bawling noisily when they were all herded together being forced along down into the lower country.

Then there was the winter; the trees bare now, the snow blowing so you could not see, the saddle wet, then frozen as you came downhill, breaking a trail through the snow, trying to keep your legs moving, and the sharp, warming taste of whiskey when you hit the ranch and changed your clothes in front of the big open fireplace. It's a good country.

Questions

1. What does this passage show about Hemingway's attitude to hunting?
2. Pick out three sentences which make the valley sound attractive or unattractive to you.
3. What kind of person would you have to be to enjoy staying in this valley?
4. Several animals are mentioned in this passage. What do you think was the author's intention in mentioning them? Say what the animals are and whether the author seems to admire them or not. Start with the grizzly bear.
5. In what ways does the valley show a different face according to the time of day or the season?
6. What do you think the author's intention was when he wrote this passage? Does he make the valley sound attractive or unattractive?

Response

In this passage, a celebration of the wilderness, Hemingway is clearly keen to communicate his enthusiasm as a hunter for Fork Valley – an unspoilt patch in the United States.

He begins by exciting us with the thought of fishing for the 'big' trout, 'sleek, shining and heavy'. 'It was wonderful, fly-fishing in September' he says. His pleasure is clear.

The whole valley is teeming with life. He describes the old ram and 'the great heavy curl of his horns'. If you woke in the night you could hear the coyotes. In the high country you could come upon grizzlies, 'sun making their coats a soft smoking silver'. Then there are the elk, 'bugling' to one another, a sound so thrilling that it makes Hemingway glad that there are some he spared. Clearly the writer wishes us to share his enthusiasm for wildlife.

The scenery too, is lovingly described.

Activities

1. Write your own response to the question, but concentrate on the scenery and the way that the landscape changes according to the seasons.
2. Think about and plan a piece of imaginative writing called 'My Dream House'. Start off by listing some of the things that would go to make up your dream house. These might include:

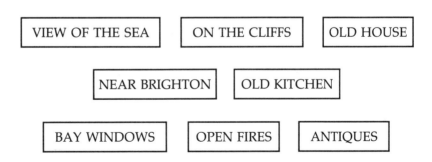

VIEW OF THE SEA   ON THE CLIFFS   OLD HOUSE

NEAR BRIGHTON   OLD KITCHEN

BAY WINDOWS   OPEN FIRES   ANTIQUES

- Decide how many paragraphs you are going to write, and what will go in them. If you decide on five paragraphs your plan might look like this:
  1 What my own house is like
  2 What my dream house would be like
  3 What its gardens would be like
  4 The landscape around it
  5 How I would acquire my dream house.
- Write your piece. (You may need to write a first draft and a final version.) Aim to write between 400 and 600 words.

3. Plan and draft a piece of descriptive writing on one of the following subjects: Imagine you are describing the scene for a radio audience.

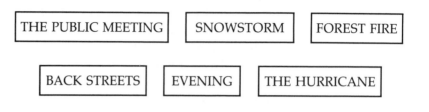

| THE PUBLIC MEETING | SNOWSTORM | FOREST FIRE |

| BACK STREETS | EVENING | THE HURRICANE |

You might find it helpful to imagine you are describing the scene for a radio audience.

People

Here are two pieces of writing that introduce memorable characters:

Cider with Rosie

Laurie Lee

Cabbage-Stump Charlie was our local bruiser – a violent, gaitered, gaunt-faced pigman, who lived only for his sows and for fighting. He was a nourisher of quarrels, as some men are of plants, growing them from nothing but the heat of belligerence and watering them daily with blood. He would set out each evening, armed with his cabbage-stalk, ready to strike down the first man he saw. "What's up then Charlie? Got no quarrel with thee." "Wham!" said Charlie, and hit him. Men fell from their bicycles or back-pedalled violently when they saw old Charlie coming. With his hawk-brown nose and whiskered arms he looked like a land-locked Viking; and he would take up his stand outside the pub, swing his great stump round his head, and say "Wham! Bash" like a boy in a comic, and challenge all comers to battle. Often bloodied himself, he left many a man bleeding before crawling back home to his pigs. Cabbage-Stump Charlie, like Jones's Goat, set the village to bolting its doors.

Ruby

Rosa Guy

Daphne, Daphne, Daphne of the smooth, tan skin. Daphne of the heavy, angry black eyebrows that were so fantastically right in combination with her gray eyes. Daphne of the thick, well-formed lips, the large white teeth. Feminine Daphne with her thick, crisply curly, black shoulder-length hair. Boyish Daphne with her thick neck, her colorful silk shirts, her tweeds. Now she will settle her six-foot frame into her seat . . . push her bookbag carelessly to the back of her desk, cross her legs . . . pat her moccasin-shod feet in time with music . . . her inner music . . . now searching her bag, she will find her file, look at her nails . . . the long nails of the tapered fingers . . . Daphne, Daphne, Daphne.

Question

Read these two passages and then compare the way in which the two characters are described. Which character do you find easier to visualise?

Activities

1. Choose somebody that you know quite well, a teacher, a brother, a sister, a neighbour, a friend. Invent an interesting name for them and then describe them as if you are starting to write a long story about them. Remember to include details about their dress, speech, mannerisms and behaviour as well as their physical appearance. Present them in some precise setting such as in a café, in a park, in a classroom or anywhere else that you think is appropriate.

2. Describe one of your teachers to a friend (without naming him/her). See how long it is before he/she is recognised.

3. Imagine that you are a missing person and write the description of yourself that might be read out in an appeal for information, broadcast by a local radio station. Start off by noting down your personal details. Then build this information up into a written description to be read out on the radio.

Approaches to Different Types of Writing

Unit 3.4 Humour and Adventure

Humour ◆ Unreliable Memoirs ◆ Adventure

◗ *See units 4.1–4.5*

Humour

Some authors produce work which is intended to amuse us. Here is an example:

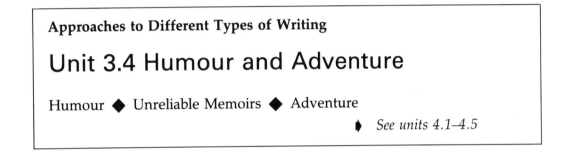

| **Distracted the mother said to her boy**

Gregory Harrison | Distracted the mother said to her boy
"Do you try to upset and perplex and annoy?
Now, give me four reasons and don't play the fool
Why you shouldn't get up and get ready for school."

Her son replied slowly, "Well mother you see
I can't stand the teachers and they detest me;
And there isn't a boy or a girl in the place
That I like, or, in turn, that delights my face."

"And I'll give you two reasons," she said, "Why you ought
Get yourself off to school before you get caught;
Because, first you are forty and next, you young fool,
You're the head of the school." |

Questions

1. How does the poet lead us to believe that he is writing about a mother and young child?
2. Did you find the poem amusing? If so, can you say why?
3. Do you think the author is doing anything else in the poem apart from amusing us? If so, what is it?

Activity

◆ Individually jot down the names of some comedians and comedy shows that make you laugh.
◆ In groups of three or four, swap ideas and see if you can decide *why* these people and programmes make you laugh.

◆ Keeping in mind your findings, write an amusing description of the funniest or most ridiculous thing that has happened to you or that you have seen. Read it to the group to see if it amuses them. Ask the group to make suggestions for improvements and then rewrite your description if necessary.

◆ Hand in both your draft and final versions, and your comments on the changes that were suggested.

Unreliable Memoirs

Here is another example. Clive James is describing how, as a boy, in Australia, he built a slow but particularly successful cart for riding down a local street, at the corner of which is formidable Mrs. Branthwaite's much cherished flower bed.

Unreliable Memoirs

Clive James

That afternoon when there was a particularly large turnout, I got sick of watching the ball-race carts howling to glory down the far side. I organised the slower carts like my own into a train. Every cart except mine was deprived of its front axle and loosely bolted to the cart in front. The whole assembly was about a dozen carts long, with a big box cart at the back. This back cart I dubbed the chuck-wagon, using terminology I had picked up from the Hopalong Cassidy serial at the pictures. I was the only one alone in his cart. Behind me there were two or even three to every cart until you got to the chuck-wagon, which was crammed full of little kids, some of them so small that they were holding toy koalas and sucking dummies.

From its very first run down the far side, my super-cart was a triumph. Even the adults who had been hosing us called their families out to marvel as we went steaming by. On the super-cart's next run there was still more to admire, since even the top flight ball-race riders had demanded to have their vehicles built into it, thereby heightening its tone, swelling its passenger list, and multiplying its already impressive output of decibels. Once again I should have left well alone. The thing was already famous. It had everything but a dining car. Why did I ever suggest that we should transfer to the near side and try the Irene Street turn?

With so much inertia the super-cart started slowly, but it accelerated like a piano falling out of a window. Long before we reached the turn I realised that there had been a serious miscalculation. The miscalculation was all mine, of course. Sir Isaac Newton would have got it right. It was too late to do anything except pray. Leaning into the turn, I skidded my own cart safely around in the usual way. The new few segments followed me, but with each segment describing an arc of slightly larger radius than the one in front. First gradually, then with stunning finality, the monster lashed its enormous tail.

The air was full of flying ball-bearings, bits of wood, big kids, little kids, koalas and dummies. Most disastrously of all, it was also full of poppy petals. Not a bloom escaped the scythe. Those of us who could still run scattered to the winds, dragging our wounded with us. The police spent hours visiting all the parents in the district, warning them that the billycart era was definitely over.

It was a police car that took Mrs. Branthwaite away. There was no point waiting for the ambulance. She could walk all right. It was just that she couldn't talk. She stared straight ahead, her mouth slightly open.

Questions

1. The first paragraph could be taken from a serious book, but there are one or two phrases that tempt us to smile. Pick out a sentence, or part of a sentence from the first paragraph that suggests that this is not going to be a serious piece.
2. Pick out the words in the second paragraph that help to create the impression that something important and splendid is happening.
3. Why does the question at the end of the second paragraph make us want to read on?
4. Can you work out why Mrs. Branthwaite is in such a shocked state at the end?
5. Clive James calls his wonderful creation a super-cart. He also calls it a monster and a scythe in the last two paragraphs. Explain why he gives it these last two names.

Activities

1. When road accidents occur and drivers want to claim on their insurance, they have to draw a diagram showing how the accident occurred. Draw a simple diagram to show how the accident in the extract occurred, showing the position of the carts before and after the accident.
2. Jokes are little comic stories which, like the poem on the previous page, or the Clive James extract, have a twist at the end. Write down a joke that you could tell **a** your grandmother, **b** your best friend, **c** a six year old child.

   How does the audience influence the kind of joke you tell?

Adventure

Here are two extracts from popular adventure stories.

| Thunderball | The little plane made a tight turn. Felix cut down the revs and just kept flying speed about fifty feet above the surface. Bond opened the door and craned out, his glasses at short focus. Yes, there were the sharks, two on the surface with their dorsals out, and one deep down. It was nosing at something. It had its teeth into something and was pulling at it. Among the dark and pale patches, a thin straight line showed on the bottom. Bond shouted, 'Get back over again!' The plane zoomed round and back. Christ! Why did they have to go so fast? But now Bond had seen another straight line on the bottom, leading off at 90 degrees from the first. He flopped back into his seat and banged the door shut. He said quietly, 'Put her down over those sharks, Felix'. Leiter took a quick glance at Bond's face. He said 'Christ!' Then, 'Well, I hope I can make it. Damned difficult to get a true horizon. This water's like glass'. He pulled away, curved | back and slowly put the nose down. There was a slight jerk and then the hiss of the water under the skids. Leiter cut his engines and the plane came to a quick stop, rocking in the water about ten yards from where Bond wanted. The two sharks on the surface paid no attention. They completed their circle and came slowly back. They passed so close to the plane that Bond could see the incurious pink button eyes. He peered down through the small ripples cast by the two dorsal fins. Yes! Those 'rocks' on the bottom were bogus. They were painted patches. So were the areas of sand. Now bond could clearly see the straight edges of the giant tarpaulin. The third shark had nosed back a big section. Now it was shovelling with its flat head trying to get underneath.

Bond sat back. He turned to Leiter. He nodded. 'That's it, all right. Big camouflaged tarpaulin over her. Take a look.' |

The Thirty Nine Steps

John Buchan

I blew my whistle.

In an instant the lights were out. A pair of strong arms gripped me round the waist, covering the pockets in which a man might be expected to carry a pistol.

'Schnell, Franz,' cried a voice, 'der Boot, der Boot!' As it spoke I saw two of my fellows emerge on the moonlit lawn.

The young dark man leapt for the window, was through it, and over the low fence before a hand could touch him. I grappled the old chap, and the room seemed to fill with figures. I saw the plump one collared, but my eyes were all for the out-of-doors, where Franz sped on over the road towards the railed entrance to the beach stairs. One man followed him, but he had no chance. The gate of the stairs locked behind the fugitive, and I stood staring, with my hands on the old boy's throat, for such a time as a man might take to descend those steps to the sea.

Suddenly my prisoner broke from me and flung himself on the wall. There was a click as if a lever had been pulled. Then came a low rumbling far, far below the ground, and through the window I saw a cloud of chalky dust pouring out of the shaft of the stairway.

Someone switched on the light.

The old man was looking at me with blazing eyes.

Questions

1. One of these passages is about a search, and the second is about a struggle and this may account for the differences in language. Describe the situation in each – compare what is happening in the *Thunderball* passage with what is happening in *The 39 Steps*.

2. Count the total number of sentences in each passage, then count how many of the sentences in each passage have fewer than ten words. Which passage has more short sentences? What is the effect of this for the reader?

3. In which passage is there more action than the other? List what happens in each. Explain why you think that more happens in one than in the other.

4. Apart from the German in the John Buchan passage (which means 'Quick, Franz, the boat!'), are there any difficult words in either passage? If so, write them down.

Activity

Choose one of the passages and then decide what might have led up to the events described in the extract, or what could have happened afterwards. Then write either the prelude (what came before), or sequel (what happened afterwards).

Approaches to Different Types of Writing

Unit 3.5 Feelings and Atmosphere

Writing that conveys strong feelings ◆ Two Cats: Creating an Atmosphere ◆ Changing the Atmosphere

◗ *See units 4.1–4.5*

Writing That Conveys Strong Feelings

Writers sometimes describe events and situations in a way that arouses feelings of anger or pity in the reader. In the last century, as today, there was a demand for the sort of writing that is so emotional – so sentimental – that it can have the effect of making the reader cry. The popular name for stories (in writing and film) that do this is 'tearjerkers'.

Here is an example of a scene in which a little girl is dying.

Uncle Tom's Cabin

Harriet Beecher Stowe

'Never mind', she said, raising her face and smiling brightly through her tears, 'I have prayed for you; and I know Jesus will help you, even if you can't read. Try all to do the best you can; pray everyday; ask Him to help you, and get the Bible read to you whenever you can; and I think I shall see you all in heaven.'

'Amen,' was the murmured response from the lips of Tom and Mammy, and some of the elder ones, who belonged to the Methodist church. The younger and more thoughtless ones, for the time completely overcome, were sobbing, with their heads bowed upon their knees.

'I know,' said Eva, 'you all love me.'

'Yes; oh, yes! indeed we do! Lord bless her!' was the involuntary answer of all.

'Yes, I know you do! There isn't one of you that hasn't always been very kind to me; and I want to give you something that, when you look at it, you shall always remember me. I'm going to give all of you a curl of my hair; and when you look at it, think that I loved you and am gone to heaven, and that I want to see

you all there.'

It is impossible to describe the scene, as, with tears and sobs, they gathered around the little creature, and took from her hands what seemed to them a last mark of her love. They fell on their knees; they sobbed, and prayed, and kissed the hem of her garment; and the older ones poured forth words of endearment, mingled in prayers and blessings, after the manner of their susceptible race.

As each one took their gift, Miss Ophelia, who was apprehensive for the effect of all this excitement on her little patient, signed to each one to pass out of the apartment.

At last, all were gone but Tom and Mammy.

'Here, Uncle Tom,' said Eva, 'is a beautiful one for you. O, I am so happy, Uncle Tom, to think I shall see you in heaven, – for I'm sure I shall; and Mammy, – dear, good kind Mammy!' she said, fondly throwing her arms round her old nurse – 'I know you'll be there, too.'

Activities

1. Pick out sentences or parts of sentences which show that the writing is intended to arouse our pity. For example, even though she is dying, the little girl says 'I have prayed for you'. This makes us feel she is so good that she should not die.

2. Write an emotional piece like this, describing one of the following events or situations:

   a the relegation of your favourite football team;

   b the bullying or persecution of someone at school;

   c the scene in the defeated cup-finalists' dressing room;

   d being ill and unable to attend an event you have been looking forward to for a long time;

   e the death of an old and much-loved pet;

   f a woman waits for the bombers to return. Her husband is an RAF pilot, and his plane is missing.

   Start off by setting the scene. Then describe the characters, and establish the situation. Do not pull your punches – the reader should be sobbing uncontrollably!

3. Try writing an emotional piece that describes a more cheerful situation or event such as:

   a news of another Royal baby or Royal wedding;

   b a happy Christmas morning;

   c breaking up for the school holidays;

   d discovering that you have won a 'Holiday of a Lifetime' competition.

Two Cats: Creating an Atmosphere

We will now look at the way in which authors use words to create a particular atmosphere. The atmosphere we will concentrate on is a sinister, frightening one – where the author is intent on scaring us.

In the following extracts some rather disturbing things are happening. In the first a man believes he has committed the perfect murder. He has killed his wife and bricked up her body behind a wall in the cellar. Rather oddly his cat has disappeared, but when the police call back to ask questions about his wife's disappearance, he is so confident that he cheerfully takes them on a tour of his house.

The Black Cat

Edgar Allan Poe

'Gentlemen,' I said at last, as the party ascended the steps, 'I delight to have allayed your suspicions, I wish you all health, and a little more courtesy. By-the-by gentlemen, this – this is a very well-constructed house.' (In the rabid desire to say something easily, I scarcely knew what I uttered at all.) 'I may say an excellently well-constructed house. These walls – are you going gentlemen? – these walls are solidly put together'; and here, through the mere frenzy of bravado, I rapped heavily with a cane which I held in my hand, upon that very portion of the brickwork behind which stood the corpse of the wife of my bosom.

But may God shield and deliver me from the fangs of the Arch-Fiend! No sooner had the reverberation of my blows sunk into silence, than I was answered by a voice from within the tomb! – by a cry, at first muffled and broken, like the sobbing of a child, and then quickly swelling into one long, loud, and continuous scream, utterly anomalous and inhuman – a howl – a wailing shriek, half of horror and half of triumph, such as might have arisen only out of hell, conjointly from the throats of the damned in their agony and of the demons that exult in the damnation.

Of my own thoughts it is folly to speak. Swooning, I staggered to the opposite wall. For one instant the party upon the stairs remained motionless, through extremity of terror and of awe. In the next, a dozen stout arms were toiling at the wall. It fell bodily. The corpse, already greatly decayed and clotted with gore, stood erect before the eyes of the spectators. Upon its head, with red extended mouth and solitary eye of fire, sat the hideous beast whose craft had seduced me into murder, and whose informing voice had consigned me to the hangman. I had walled the monster up within the tomb!

Things to notice

- As you read the passage, note where you first start to feel uneasy.
- Note any words which increase the feeling of unease.
- Predict what is going to happen, once you have read halfway through.

In the next extract a cat again appears. It is staring at a charred piece of ground in front of the fire where its master had been standing until he spontaneously combusted! (It was believed at the time that people could explode, leaving only a few charred remains.) In the extract, two men – Mr. Guppy and Tony – are waiting in an upstairs room until it is time to go down and meet the cat's master.

Bleak House

Charles Dickens

Mr. Guppy sitting on the window-sill, nodding his head and balancing all these possibilities in his mind, continues thoughtfully to tap it, and clasp it, and measure it with his hand, until he hastily draws his hand away.

"What, in the devil's name," he says, "is this! Look at my fingers!"

A thick, yellow liquor defiles them, which is offensive to the touch and sight and more offensive to the smell. A stagnant, sickening oil with some natural repulsion in it that makes them both shudder.

"What have you been doing here? What have you been pouring out of window?"

"I pouring out of window! Nothing. I swear! Never, since I have been here!" cries the lodger.

And yet look here – and look here! When he brings the candle here, from the corner of the window-sill it slowly drips and creeps away down the bricks, here lies in a little thick nauseous pool.

"This is a horrible house," says Mr. Guppy, shutting down the window. "Give me some water or I shall cut my hand off."

He so washes, and rubs, and scrubs, and smells, and washes, that he has not long restored himself with a glass of brandy and stood silently before the fire when Saint Paul's bell strikes twelve and all those other bells strike twelve from their towers of various heights in the dark air, and in their many tones. When all is quiet again, the lodger says, "It's the appointed time at last. Shall I go?"

Mr. Guppy nods and gives him a "lucky touch" on the back, but not with the washed hand, though it is his right hand.

He goes downstairs, and Mr. Guppy tries to compose himself before the fire for waiting a long time. But in no more than a minute or two the stairs creak and Tony comes swiftly back.

"Have you got them?"

"Got them! No. The old man's not there."

He has been so horribly frightened in the short interval that his terror seizes the other, who makes a rush at him and asks loudly, "What's the matter?"

"I couldn't make him hear, and I softly opened the door and looked in. And the burning smell is there – and the soot is there, and the oil is there – and he is not there!" Tony ends this with a groan.

Mr. Guppy takes the light. They go down, more dead than alive, and holding one another, push open the door of the back shop. The cat has retreated close to it and stands snarling, not at them, at something on the ground before the fire. There is a very little fire left in the grate, but there is a smouldering suffocating vapour in the room and a dark, greasy coating on the walls and ceiling. The chairs and table, and the bottle so rarely absent from the table, all stand as usual. On one chair-back hand the old man's hairy cap and coat. . .

"What's the matter with the cat?" says Mr. Guppy. "Look at her!"

"Mad, I think. And no wonder in this evil place."

They advance slowly, looking at all these things. The cat remains where they found her, still snarling at the something on the ground before the fire and between the two chairs. What is it? Hold up the light.

Here is a small burnt patch of flooring; here is the tinder from a little bundle of burnt paper, but not so light as usual, seeming to be steeped in something; and here is – is it the cinder of a small charred and broken log of wood sprinkled with white ashes, or is it coal? Oh, horror, he is here! And this from which we run away, striking out the light and overturning one another into the street, is all that represents him.

Questions

1. Re-read both passages – identify the words and phrases that build up the atmosphere. When do you start to feel uneasy? Which words, or sorts of words, does the author use? Compare your findings with others in your group. Did you all respond in the same way to the same parts of the passages?

2. Both these passages are written in a style that might seem old-fashioned to the twentieth century reader. Pick out a sentence that seems old-fashioned and then write it as you think it would be written today.

3. Who is telling the story in the first passage? Who is telling the story in the second?

4. Is the cat equally important in both passages? Give reasons for your answer. Why do you think the authors use cats and not another animal in these passages?

5. One of the extracts is actually the end of a story. Which one do you think it is? Give reasons for your opinion.

6. Choose the passage that you think is the most effective. Write a response to that passage, describing what you like about it, and focusing in particular on what you find frightening about it.

7. Pick out and write down the sentence from your preferred passage that you consider most chilling.

Activities

1. Writers can create a spine-chilling atmosphere through a combination of situation and a careful selection of words we associate with fear. You could demonstrate how this works in the first passage by drawing up a table like this:

SITUATION	DISTURBING WORDS
A murderer, carried away by his success, stands next to the police a few inches away from the concealed corpse of his wife!	fangs, arch-fiend, tomb, scream, . . .
The screaming and the howling of the cat.	
The cat sitting on the head of the corpse.	

Finish the table off by completing the list of words.

2. Now look at the second extract. Concentrate this time on the following: the situation, the words spoken, and the disturbing words. Draw three columns and write down your list under these headings:

SITUATION   DIALOGUE   DISTURBING WORDS

3. Now describe a terrifying situation from your own imagination ('Alone in the house', 'Lost in the city' or 'Crossing the moors at night'.) In your description you should attempt to include all the disturbing words you listed in 1 and 2, and lots more of your own!

Changing the Atmosphere

We should not always assume that only one thing is going on. In one short passage, or in one little poem, the writing may be doing several things. Here is a short poem in which the poet does two different things – one in the first verse and one in the second.

In the Bathroom Roy Fuller	What is that blood-stained thing – Hairy, as if it were frayed Stretching itself along The slippery bath's steep side: I approach it, ready to kill Or run away aghast And find I have to deal With a used elastoplast.

Response

In the first verse the author is trying to make us aware of his fear, to make us feel uneasy, disturbed and apprehensive with his use of the words 'hairy' and 'blood-stained'. Is he talking about a crushed spider? Or something even more repulsive? We have all seen massive spiders in the bath! In the second verse the author keeps us hanging on in suspense. What is it? But in the same verse he lets us know what it is – it's a dirty, but familiar enough object – a used sticking plaster. He has reassured us. So the writer has scared us and then reassured us. His aim was to show how our imagination can make ordinary objects frightening.

Activities

1. Consider the three following types of atmosphere:

A TENSE ATMOSPHERE	AN ATMOSPHERE OF GREAT EXCITEMENT	AN ATMOSPHERE OF GLOOM AND DEPRESSION

Think of, and write down, three situations in which you might encounter these atmospheres. Then list the ingredients that would make up the scene. You could arrange your thoughts as follows:

	TENSE ATMOSPHERE	**EXCITED ATMOSPHERE**	**GLOOMY ATMOSPHERE**
SITUATION	Tube train breaks down in a tunnel		
INGREDIENTS	Nervous people Screaming children Darkness		

2. Choose one of the situations you thought of in Activity 1 and write a description of it, bringing out the atmosphere through the words you use. A description of a situation with a gloomy atmosphere might start like this:

'The Jones family sat in the garden of their ruined house. They had returned from a day at the coast to discover that their home had been gutted by fire. Eric and Jean had squelched their way through the wet rooms, looking at their ruined possessions . . .'

Approaches to Different Types of Writing

Unit 3.6 Writing Stories, Poems and Plays

Introduction ◆ Writing Stories ◆ Writing Poems ◆ Word
Patterns ◆ Rhythm ◆ Group Poem ◆ Writing Plays

◗ *See units 1.1–1.4*

Introduction

In every area of our lives we encounter stories. Read what one writer has to say about stories at school:

'Listen in the staffroom. Listen in the bar. Listen to children as they meet again at school on Monday mornings. Listen to ourselves as we get home from a day at work that's been specially memorable. Listen to people meeting in the street. If you don't overhear stories on these occasions we'd be very surprised!'

There are stories all around us. We just have to keep an ear out for them – and to preserve them, we put them into writing.

Writing Stories

What follows is not intended to be a fail-safe recipe for writing stories, but it does provide some useful hints that may help you write better stories.

1. Where to start?
   First of all you need ideas for your story. Look for these ideas in your own experience or in the experiences you have heard recounted by your parents, relatives or friends, and then jot down notes. Use your imagination to add details to these ideas.

2. Drafting
   It is probably best to focus on a brief incident or on a series of events that take place over the course of a day or a week. Do not try to write a saga covering years or generations.
   Using your notes, write a first version of your story, paying particular attention to the beginning and the ending.

3. Criticising
   Read through what you have written. Does the opening grab the reader's attention? (See Unit 2.8). Are the characters interesting? (See Unit 3.3.) Look closely at the words and sentences and make improvements to them where necessary. Invite comments from another reader.

4. The final draft
   Write a final version of your story. You may wish to add further details describing the weather, the setting, the appearance and behaviour of the characters, even at this late stage.
   Make your handwriting as attractive as possible; remember the poor reader!

Activity

Using the hints given above, write a story based on one of the following:

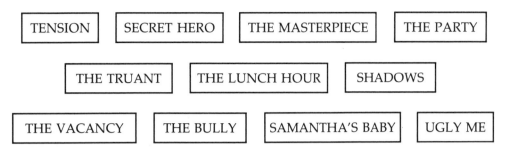

| TENSION | SECRET HERO | THE MASTERPIECE | THE PARTY |

| THE TRUANT | THE LUNCH HOUR | SHADOWS |

| THE VACANCY | THE BULLY | SAMANTHA'S BABY | UGLY ME |

Your story can, of course, come entirely from your imagination. Remember to write a first draft and to make improvements to the story before you write a final version. Aim to write between 400 and 600 words.

Writing Poems

There is no formula for writing verse but you may find the following method helps you to get started (see also Unit 2.5). Choose a subject – perhaps something inspired by a newspaper story like the one that follows.

> **CHILDREN DIE IN BLAZE**
>
> Three children died in a house blaze in Effington yesterday. Police say the fire was started by their grandfather making toast on an upturned electric fire in the sitting room. The blaze quickly spread to the upstairs rooms, trapping the children who were asleep at the time.

Then, write a sentence or sentences describing the event in a more personal and emotional way than a newspaper journalist would report it. For example:

> The old grandfather took to toasting bread on the ancient upturned electric fire.

Then divide this into lines, to make a stanza. Count the syllables in each line. Try to balance the number of syllables in each line as in the following:

> 6 The óld grándfáthér tóok   4 Ón thé áncient
> 4 Tó toástińg bréad   6 Úptuŕned éléctrić fiŕe

This stanza has a regular syllabic pattern. Try to repeat this pattern in your second stanza (and in any further stanzas).

> 6 Eýelíds clósed únáwaŕe   4 Nów bláck nów blúe
> 4 Óf smókińg bréad   6 Nów góld wíth gréedý flaŕnes

And continue.

Word Patterns

You will have noticed that so far we have not paid much attention to rhyme. This is because a lot of otherwise good poetry written by students is spoilt because the rhyme is forced. Instead, you should try to notice things about poetry other than rhyme – the use of repetition and word patterns, for example:

Witch

Jean Tepperman

They told me
I smile prettier with my mouth closed.
They said —
better cut your hair —
long, it's all frizzy,
looks Jewish.
They hushed me in restaurants
looking around them
while the mirrors above the table
jeered infinite reflections
of a raw, square face.
They questioned me
when I sang in the street.
They stood taller at tea
smoothly explaining
my eyes on the saucers,
trying to hide the hand grenade
in my pants pocket,
or crouched behind the piano.
They mocked me with magazines
full of breasts and lace,
published their triumph
when the doctor's oldest son
married a nice sweet girl.
They told me tweed-suit stories
of various careers of ladies.
I woke up at night
afraid of dying.
They built screens and room dividers
to hide unsightly desire
sixteen years old
raw and hopeless
they buttoned me into dresses
covered with pink flowers.

They waited for me to finish
then continued the conversation.
I have been invisible,
weird and supernatural.
I want my black dress.
I want my hair
curling wild around me.
I want my broomstick
from the closet where I hid it.
Tonight I meet my sisters
in the graveyard.
Around midnight
if you stop at a red light
in the wet city traffic,
watch for us against the moon.
We are screaming
we are flying,
laughing, and won't stop.

In the following poem the poet has chosen to use rhyme to create a serious, almost heroic effect, which gives the poem great power:

Still I Rise

Maya Angelou

You may write me down in history
with your bitter, twisted lies
You may trod me in the very dirt
but still like dust, I'll rise.

Does my sassiness upset you?
why are you beset with gloom?
'cause I walk like I've got oil wells
Pumping in my living room.

Just like moons and like suns,
with the certainty of tides,
Just like hopes springing high,
Still I'll rise.

Did you want to see me broken?
Bowed head and lowered eyes?
Shoulders falling down like teardrops,
Weakened by my soulful cries.

Does my haughtiness offend you?
Don't you take it awful hard
'Cause I laugh like I've got gold mines
Diggin' in my own back yard.

You may shoot me with your words.
You may cut me with your eyes,
You may kill me with your hatefulness,
But still, like air I'll rise.

Does my sexiness upset you?
Does it come as a surprise
That I dance like I've got diamonds
At the meeting of my thighs?

Out of the huts of history's shame
I rise
Up from a past that rooted in pain
I rise
I'm a black ocean, leaping and wide,
Welling and swelling I bear in the tide.

Leaving behind nights of terror and fear
I rise
Into a daybreak that's wondrously clear
I rise
Bringing the gifts that my ancestors gave,
I am the dream and the hopes of the slaves.
I rise
I rise
I rise.

Rhythm

Another important area to consider when writing poems is rhythm. Look at the following poem and try to identify the ways in which Thomas Hardy captures the movement and slowing down of the train. Look at and listen to the word 'she' at the end of the first stanza. What is happening here? (It may help you to think of the kind of engine there would have been between fifty and a hundred years ago when Hardy was writing.)

Faintheart in a Railway Train

Thomas Hardy

At nine in the morning there passed a church,
At ten there passed me by the sea,
At twelve a town of smoke and smirch,
At two a forest of oak and birch,
    And then, on a platform, she:

A radiant stranger, who saw not me.
I said 'Get out to her do I dare?'
But I kept my seat in a search for a plea,
And the wheels moved on. O could it but be
    That I had alighted there!

Group Poem

It is possible for a poem to be the product of several people's efforts. Try writing a poem using the method described here by Elizabeth Jennings.

New Poem Simply

Elizabeth Jennings

Orwell invented the idea of a machine which makes novels
ten years ago my friend and I met
for group writing
it was a bit like Consequences
we took a subject
wrote a line
turned down the paper
passed it on
sometimes we got a real poem
but it was a hazard
(who said the so-called conventional poem isn't a hazard
anyway? and what is "inspiration"?)
Our group worked better though at prose
it must be admitted
and when we had a certain amount of red wine.

Activity

Divide into groups of at least five, choose a subject and sit in a circle. Each person takes a piece of paper, writes a line of a poem, folds down the paper to hide what they have written, and then passes it on to the next person, who writes another line and then passes it on. This process continues until each member of the group has the piece of paper they started off with. The papers are then unfolded and the poems read out. (You could, if you want longer poems, pass the papers round a second or even a third time.)

Writing Plays

Plays consist of characters, dialogue and action. They require a setting and are generally made up of scenes. Perhaps the most important thing you need to remember when writing a play is that a play does not have passages of description like a story; in a play description has to be put in the mouths of the characters – it comes across through *speech*. You must ensure, too, that you choose a situation which can be portrayed through speech. Some situations – a wrestling match, for instance – are highly dramatic but would make bad material for a play because the conflict and tension cannot be expressed in words.

Here are some subjects which can be revealed mainly through speech:

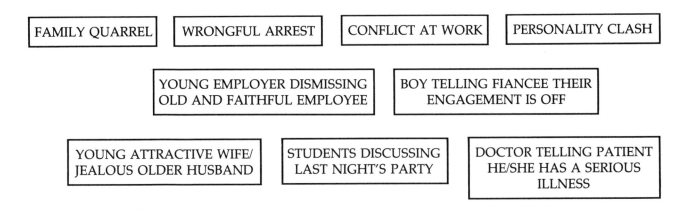

| FAMILY QUARREL | WRONGFUL ARREST | CONFLICT AT WORK | PERSONALITY CLASH |

YOUNG EMPLOYER DISMISSING OLD AND FAITHFUL EMPLOYEE

BOY TELLING FIANCEE THEIR ENGAGEMENT IS OFF

YOUNG ATTRACTIVE WIFE/ JEALOUS OLDER HUSBAND

STUDENTS DISCUSSING LAST NIGHT'S PARTY

DOCTOR TELLING PATIENT HE/SHE HAS A SERIOUS ILLNESS

There are conventions for setting out plays. The extract from Gregory's Girl on p 31 shows how plays are set out when printed. When you are laying out a play in handwriting, it is best to use the following conventions:

LINCOLN: I was shot at, gassed, reviled.
(PAUSE: LINCOLN LOOKS OUT THE WINDOW)

MICHAEL: Why did you go back?

LINCOLN: Apartheid. Soweto, Alexandra. The Third World down the road. (INCREASINGLY ANGRY) I saw my brothers and sisters on the censored news. They were still there. I wasn't.

Remember that in a play the speech should not only put across what is happening, it should also help to build up a picture of ('characterise') the speakers themselves. The extract on pxxx shows how character can be revealed through speech.

Activity

Using three or more of the following characters, write a short scene. You could involve them in one of the above situations if you wish:

MR. BAYHAM BADGER: A London Doctor.
LAWRENCE BOYTHORN: A hearty man with a pet canary.
WILLIAM GUPPY: An ambitious, 'yuppie' type, eager to make money and get on.
INSPECTOR BUCKET: A shrewd, hard working detective.
GEORGE ROUNCEWELL: An ex-soldier, young, and manager of a gymnasium.

GRANDFATHER:	A ridiculous, bad-tempered old man.
'PRINCE' TURVEYDROP:	A student.
JUDY SMALLWEED:	A student.
MRS. BAYHAM BADGER:	A middle-aged woman who dresses youthfully.
ESTHER SUMMERSON:	A level-headed young woman.
GUSTER:	A young female shop assistant.
MATTHEW BAGNET:	Another ex-soldier and trumpet player.
SIR LEICESTER DEDLOCK:	A rich man with a large country house.
JOE:	A poor, unemployed teenager without any family.
MR. KROOK:	A strange, secretive man, owner of a junk shop.
HAROLD SKIMPOLE:	A thoroughly selfish man, a sponger who neglects his family.
PHIL SQUOD:	Employed by George, and immensely strong.
LITTLE SWILLS:	A club entertainer, singer and comic.
LADY DEDLOCK:	Sir Leicester's young and attractive wife.
CAROLINE JELLYBY:	A secretary.

♦ Choose your characters and the situation in which they are going to be involved. Make sure that the situation is one that can be effectively presented through dialogue.
♦ Write a first draft of your scene, ensuring that
   a The setting and situation are quickly established
   b The characters are well-defined and contrasted and present their points of view clearly
   c The play is properly laid out with clear stage directions where appropriate.
♦ Write a final version, checking that the dialogue is as natural as possible and the scene lively and convincing.

Approaches to Different Types of Writing

Unit 3.7 Transactional Writing

Introduction ◆ Informal Letters ◆ Formal Letters: Applications and CVs ◆ Filling in Forms ◆ Writing Reports ◆ Official Reports

♦ *See units 2.6, 2.11*

Introduction

Even though we use the telephone for most of our 'instant' communication, there are still many occasions when we need to write or type (or word process!) a letter.

Informal Letters

Here is an informal letter. The annotations in type draw your attention to the usual way such letters are set out.

37 Blackwell Drive
Totnes
Devon TX3 4OL

Your address (They may have lost it or forgotten it). Reminds them when they receive it.

26th Sept.

Dear Robin,

Friendly introduction —— Just a note to let you know the latest news, which doesn't need a reply if you don't wish to start up correspondance again.

I've just had fifteen weeks of summer holiday which I've spent as a nanny for a nine-year-old boy, whilst his parents ran the new 'skippers' restaurant at Torquay's pavillion - this meant all our meals were eaten in the restaurant and days spent on the beach, playing tennis, at the zoo, circus, etc.

Paragraphs: just as important in letters as in any other prose.

Writing can help you to come to terms with unpleasant experience —— The job ended rather abruptly when I was involved in a car accident whilst driving home from work. Another girl drove into the back of my car at 60 mph when she sneezed, and my car left the ground and flew into the car in front, causing me to smash into the windscreen. Both me and my seat ended up in the back of the mini, which was totally written off. This happened three weeks ago, but I still have difficulty walking and doubt I'll ever drive again.

This evening my parents are taking me to see 'Widows' weeds' at Plymouth Theatre Royal and tomorrow we're going to north Devon for the day.

How easy is the handwriting to read?

Friendly conclusion —— I hope everything is going well for you and your family.

Best wishes,
Debbie Tapp.

Activity

Write an informal letter performing one of the following functions:

| TELLING A FRIEND ABOUT AN ACCIDENT YOU HAVE HAD | THANKING A RELATIVE FOR THE EXPENSIVE GIFT YOU HAVE ALWAYS WANTED | REPLYING TO A FRIEND'S WEDDING INVITATION (EXPRESS SURPRISE) | INTRODUCING YOURSELF TO A FAMILY YOU ARE GOING TO STAY WITH ON A FOREIGN EXCHANGE |

Your letter should be between 150 and 200 words in length.

Formal Letters: Applications and CVs

Some of the most important formal letters you will write will almost certainly be to do with applying for a course of further education, or for a job.

Imagine you are applying for a job which requires a letter of application. This may be accompanied by a Curriculum Vitae (an information sheet listing your personal details and achievements) or you may wish to include this information in the main body of the letter. The advantage of a CV is that it can be photocopied and sent with every letter of application, which can be kept short. The advantage of the individual letter is that it looks more personal. (Some employers do not require you to send a CV.) Here are examples of both kinds of letter.

Without CV

18 Mayola Road
Suntown, MZ2 3KJ
26 March 1993

The Personnel Officer
IBM Ltd
Printout Lane
Futuretown.

Ref: 5SM/ST

Dear Sir,

I would like to apply for the post of ...... advertised in 'The Western Morning News' of 25.3.93. I am presently following a full-time ..... course at South Lancashire College of Arts and Technology, and will be available for work in July. I enclose a full curriculum vitae.

I would welcome the opportunity to work for IBM and I sincerely hope that you will give my application serious consideration.

I look forward to hearing from you.
Yours faithfully,

Robert Smith

With CV

Their address

The Personnel Officer
IBM Ltd
Printout Lane
Futuretown

18 Mayola Road
Suntown, MZ2 3KJ
26 March, 1993

Your address

Date

Reference

Ref: 5SM/ST

Dear Sir

I would like to apply for the post of ..... which was advertised in 'The Western Morning News', 25.3.93.

Position applied for

I am seventeen and am at present following a..... course at South Lancashire College of Arts and Technology. At the end of the course I hope to have qualifications in the following subjects:

Present course and qualifications

From 19.. to 19.. I attended Suntown Upper School, where I obtained passes in the following subjects:

School experience and qualifications

I enjoyed my school life very much and in the fifth year was made a school prefect. I helped run the school library, was a member of the school athletics team, and helped with several drama productions.

In my spare time I like to read, listen to music and go swimming. I am a member of the Swimming Club and regularly take part in local competitions.

Hobbies, outside interests

I have had some experience of part time or temporary work. During the summer of 1992 I was employed by 'The Grand Hotel' as a waiter and for the past two years I have been employed by Tesco Stores Ltd as a checkout operator. This job was very useful because it gave me good experience of working with figures and the opportunity to use computerised machines. In both cases I formed good relationships with my employers and colleagues.

Work experience — show relevance

I would very much like to take up this post, and I feel that I have the necessary qualifications to do so. My present course finishes in June, and I will be available for work from July 1st. I look forward to hearing from you.

Polite conclusion

Yours faithfully,

Robert Smith

CURRICULUM VITAE

Personal Details

Name:	SMITH, Robert	Nationality:	British
Address:	18 Mayola Road,	Marital Status:	Single
	Suntown, MZ2 3KJ.	Date of Birth:	31.6.76.
Telephone:	(0903) 275476.		

Education

(a) Schools attended: Suntown Upper School 1986–92

(b) Examinations passed:

GCSE: SUBJECT	GRADE
English	D
Mathematics	C
CDT	B
Geography	D
Science	C

(c) Present course: Full time GCSE course, Suntown College of Arts and Technology, leading to GCSE examinations in: English Literature, History, Psychology 1993.

Work Experience

During the summer of 1992 I was employed by The Grand Hotel, Suntown, as a waiter.

For the past two years I have been employed by Tesco Stores Ltd. as a checkout operator. This job has given me experience of working with figures and with computerised machines.

Positions of Responsibility

In charge of lighting, school play 1992.
School prefect 1992.

Skills

First Aid Certificate
Swimming Certificate

Interests

Swimming, Tennis, Dancing.

Referees: Miss. R. Sullivan,
Headmistress,
Suntown Upper School,
Suntown
Tel: (0943) 793748.

Mr. G. Jones,
Store Manager,
Tesco,
138 Nelson Road,
Suntown, M43 4RF.
Tel: (0944) 223481.

Leave out any section which does not apply in your case. PRINT OR TYPE your CV and then make several photocopies. Make sure you retain your original 'master' copy.

Activity

You have seen this advertisement in your local newspaper. Apply for a job:
a with a CV,
b without a CV.

FUTUREWORLD EUROPARK

We require responsible young people (must be over 17 years old) to fill the following jobs this summer:

* Tour guides   * Lifeguards
* Information staff   * Restaurant staff
* Cleaners   * First Aid assistants

We expect to welcome many European visitors, so if you have knowledge of a foreign language (preferably French, German or Spanish), you will be in a better position to do some of the jobs. We need people who can work for at least six weeks between 15th June and 5th September. Training will be given.

Apply to: Personnel Officer (Europark),
Futureworld House,
Appian Way,
MILTON KEYNES,
MK4 4TZ.
quoting reference no: TVT 006/A.

Do not forget to include the following information in your letter:
a where you saw the advertisement,
b what kind of job you are interested in (tour guide, cleaner, lifeguard, etc.),
c when you can work.

Filling In Forms

Always observe the following procedure when filling in a form:

Read the form through first
↓
Read the notes accompanying the form carefully
↓
Fill in the form, using a ball point pen, and
writing in block letters throughout
(except, of course, for your signature!)
↓
Read through the form to check you have
completed all the appropriate parts
↓
Make a photocopy of the form and keep it for your reference
(Most Post Offices have photocopiers)

Here is a form that has to be filled in if you want to vote in a general election. If you have a copy of the form, fill that it. If not, make a copy of the main headings, boxes and columns, and fill them in.

REGISTER OF ELECTORS 1988

How to return this form

First, please check that you have read and completed 1 to 6 of the form. Then, if an extra or re-usable envelope was provided, please return the form in that — no stamp is necessary. If no envelope was supplied the form will be collected.

You are required by law to complete this form.

Please read these notes
then fill in 1 to 3, 5 and 6 (or 1, 4, 5 and 6) below.

Write in Box **1** your full address in BLOCK LETTERS.

Write in Box **2** the names of all those living in your household on 10 October 1987 **who are British, other Commonwealth or Irish Citizens** and are **aged 16 or over** on that date.
Please remember to include the following:
(a) **16 and 17 years olds** — they can vote as soon as they are 18. Please give their dates of birth in the special box. The electoral registration officer will ensure that only those who reach 18 during the life of the register will be included in it.

(b) **Those who normally live in your household but are temporarily away** — for example, on holiday, as students, in hospital (including voluntary patients in psychiatric hospitals).
(c) **Anyone who is away working,** unless his or her absence will total more than six months.
(d) **Any other residents, lodgers or guests** (but not short stay visitors) in your household, whether this is a private address, or hostel or a club, including merchant seamen who live there when not at sea.
Please do not include:
● **Foreign nationals.**
Citizens of other European Community member states are foreign nationals and (except for citizens of the Republic of Ireland) are not eligible to vote.
● **People under 16.**

● **Members of HM Forces, Crown servants and British Council staff serving abroad.***
● **Wives or husbands of members of HM Forces*** who have made a service declaration which they have not cancelled.
● **Wives or husbands of Crown servants and British Council staff serving abroad*** if living abroad to be with their husbands or wives.
*Special voting arrangements are made for these people.

3 Jury Service (People 65 and over)
Please put a tick in the 'People 65 and over' box for anyone who is eligible to vote and who will be 65 and over by 16 February 1988.
People 65 and over are not eligible for jury service. Those who are not eligible for other reasons will be able to say so if they receive a jury summons.

Don't lose your right to vote ✗

1 | Address

No. of **flat** bedsit or floor (where applicable)	No. of **house** (or name if not numbered) *followed by* name of street, road, etc. *followed by* remainder of address	If the address is preprinted and is wrong, please amend.	Postcode

2 | Names

3

Please read the Notes above before filling in.
If names are preprinted and are wrong, cross them out and fill in the correct information.

Title Mr, Mrs, Miss, etc.	Surname (BLOCK LETTERS)	Full Christian names or forenames	16/17 year olds (see note 2a) Please give dates of birth of 16/17 year olds	People 65 and over (see note 3) if 65 or over by 16 February 1988 enter a ✓

4 | No one eligible

If **no one** (including yourself) in your household is eligible to vote, please write 'NO ONE' here ►
You should not write anything in box 4 if you have written in box 2

6 | Declaration

It is an offence to give false information in completing this form. I declare that to the best of my knowledge and belief the particulars given are true and accurate and that all whose names are entered are British citizens, other Commonwealth citizens, or citizens of the Irish Republic.

Signature

5 | Other households

Is where you live part of a house or other property that has been converted into flats or bedsits? Please tick here ►   Yes   No
The electoral registration officer would like to make sure that other people living there are given a form so that they are not missed off the register.

Writing Reports

There are many different sorts of report, and 'report writing' is a skill that is needed for examinations as well as in work. A written report can be presented in many ways. It can be continuous – in the form that we see in newspapers – or broken up into sections, as official reports are.

Official Reports

Official (usually Government) reports are nearly always made up of the following parts:

◆ Terms of Reference (what the report is about);
◆ The body of the report (usually divided into sections, each section referring to a separate part of the terms of reference);
◆ Summary of the report's findings.

There is an example opposite.

Activity

Write one of the reports whose terms of reference are given below. Suggested headings are provided in each case to help you structure your report.

REPORT A

Terms of Reference: To write a report on a television programme whose running time is not less than 30 minutes.

*Name of programme	*Summary of programme
*Date/Time of broadcast	*Comments on production,
*Channel	photography, editing, acting,
*Colour or black and white	script, etc.
*Purpose of programme	*Conclusion – did the programme
*Audience aimed at	fulfil its aim?

REPORT B

Terms of Reference: To examine, analyse and report on a national newspaper.

*Name of newspaper	*Politics of newspaper
*Publisher of newspaper	*Topics that get banner headlines
*Format (tabloid or broadsheet)	*Type of goods advertised
*Price	*Readership of the newspaper
*Aim of newspaper	*Summary of editorial
*Proportion of newspaper devoted to serious news, trivia, photographs and advertisements	*Conclusion

REPORT C

Terms of Reference: To examine and report on the contents of a magazine.

*Name of magazine	*Summary of contents
*Publisher	*Amount of advertising
*Frequency of publication	*Type of goods advertised
*Price	*Conclusion
*Number of pages	

WOMEN INTO INFORMATION TECHNOLOGY
A Study of the Information Technology Industry within Torbay

CONTENTS

Approaches to Different Types of Writing

Unit 3.8 Discussion and Discursive Writing

Developing an Argument ◆ Listening ◆ Observing ◆ Responding
◆ Discursive Writing

◗ *See units 2.10, 2.11*

Developing an Argument

You are probably used to discussing issues in groups or as a class. If people are reasonably well-informed about the subject in question, have the confidence to express their views and are free from crude prejudice, such discussions can be rewarding and fruitful. The key factors that make for good debate are LISTENING, OBSERVING and RESPONDING.

Listening

To prepare for the discussion, which may become heated, you could try this exercise which focuses on the ability to listen, rather than speak. Each person in the class should spend five minutes writing down three things under the heading: 'This really annoys me'.

- The first should be something that is very personal, such as people who chew their nails, or the screech of chalk on a blackboard.
- The second should be something to do with school, college or your neighbourhood, such as overcrowded buses.
- The third should be an issue of global importance, such as the killing of whales.

Then, either in groups of five or six, in front of the whole class, people should talk for three or four minutes – without interruption or comment – about the three things that really annoy them. This is a test of people's ability to LISTEN.

Observing

Observe how discussions work, by keeping a record of them. The diagram below represents a discussion following a talk on drugs by someone called Sheila. In the diagram, P stands for Paula, C for Claudine, L for Lynda, A for Alison and S for Sheila. An arrow represents something that was said to another person or to the group as a whole.

Look at the diagram carefully and say what was wrong with this discussion.

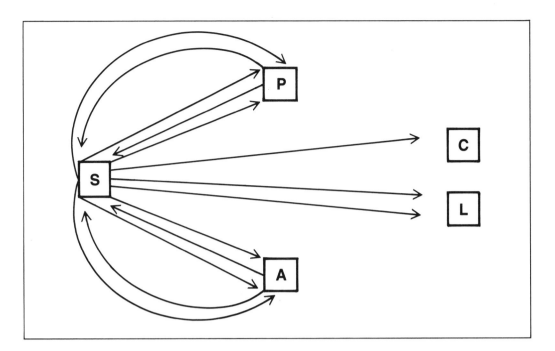

Activities

1. Here is a brief discussion of 'The Drug Problem', issued by the DHSS, and targeted at parents. You could consider the points it raises in a group discussion of your own.

THE DRUG PROBLEM.

Just because someone takes a drug it does not mean they will become addicted to it.

At times in our life, almost all of us turn to drugs of one sort or another.

Cigarettes and alcohol are, of course, the most common ones.

But many of us also turn to sleeping tablets, tranquillisers or anti-depressants to help relax and cope with the stress and tension of everyday life.

In many ways children turn to their drugs for just the same reasons.

Adolescence, as we all know, can be a difficult period.

Often it's a time when we don't get on with our parents.

There are also many pressures at school, from parents, and from friends.

It is a period of change when many choices must be made.

And at a time when work can be a major problem, there is also frustration and boredom.

All of which means that when someone, perhaps a friend, offers a child something which is supposedly 'fun' and 'everyone else' is taking it, the pressures and curiosity are so great they may try it themselves.

Fortunately, most children say 'no'.

Unfortunately, though, a disturbing number are saying 'yes'.

Most children grow out of it. Or simply decide they don't like it and then stop. But a few go on to have a serious drug problem.

That's why we all need to tread carefully when talking to a child we suspect may be taking drugs.

A wrong word at the wrong time can sometimes make a child even more rebellious.

But the right words of understanding can reinforce their decision not to take drugs.

This booklet hopes to help you find those right words, and to make you better informed.

Because the most important people when it comes to coping with the drug problem may not be the police, doctors or social workers.

They could be parents . . . like YOU.

2. Group these 20 tiny paragraphs of 'The Drug Problem' into four or five bigger ones.
3. Now write it as a discursive piece, adding your own ideas. This time imagine that your audience is teenagers, so change the language accordingly.

Responding

Remember that a discussion – even when it is about an emotive issue – should not become a row. Make your points in a reasonable way, and back them up with evidence. Listen carefully to points made by other people, judge them fairly and take them into account, and, if you wish to, counter them with arguments of your own. Try to be persuasive, rather than confrontational. Do not imitate those politicians who ridicule anyone who has the cheek to disagree with their point of view! If you do have someone in your group who tries to shout people down rather than use rational debate, you could try another listening exercise.

Activities

1. Each member of the group or class talks for two minutes – without interruption – about something he/she enjoyed doing yesterday. The focus is on the ability to listen of other members of the group.
2. Form groups of six, and divide up into four 'debaters' and two 'observers'. The four debaters discuss the merits or disadvantages of the following jobs:

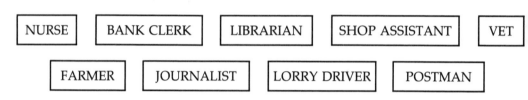

The two observers write down the names of the debaters, listen carefully to their discussion, and record the contributions made by each person with ticks and comments, e.g.:

NAME	CONTRIBUTIONS	COMMENTS
Kim Sandra Stuart Louise	√ √ √ √ √ √ √ √ √ √	Quiet – but clearly listening Fluent and convincing – not bossy Very shy – said little

3. As a class, decide on a topic for discussion. Then divide into groups of four and consider the topic chosen. Within each group, call yourselves a, b, c and d. All the as and bs from all the groups should sit in a circle; and all the cs and ds should sit in a circle outside the one formed by the as and bs.

   The inner circle now discusses the topic. Each member of the outer circle listens to and observes the contribution of the person sitting in front of him/her. After the discussion, the as and bs turn round to face their observers who tell them how well they did. The circles now change places and the whole process is repeated. Follow this up by writing a summary of the two debates.

Discursive Writing

Oral discussion tends to be random and rambling, but when you discuss something in writing it is necessary to organise your thoughts and put them in some logical order. Before we write, we carry on a debate with ourselves about our approach to a subject. It is the act of writing that helps us organise our thoughts on a subject. Here is a well argued piece of writing on a given subject. Notice how the writer gives examples to support his point of view, and presents – and answers – the opposing viewpoint.

"People who Become Heroes Have a Responsibility to set an Example to their Admirers"

20·5·86

Clear opening paragraph

I believe that people in the public eye do have this responsibility. This is because the figures will probably appeal most to teenagers, and during adolescence is the time when teenagers are most easily influenced. Most teenagers (and perhaps children in general) would probably not copy rash actions of their heroes.

Link sentence: it prepares us for new paragraph

However, there are a few rebels who will copy things like that. For instance, there is the Ian Botham case.

Ian Botham was accused by the Mail on Sunday of smoking marijuana. He categorically denied the allegations, but has now admitted that he has smoked the drug. The problem now is, that, even though he says he last smoked the drug nine years ago, because he has already lied once about it, it is all the more difficult to believe him now. So now, if his admirers copied him, Britain would have even more drug addicts on its hands, to add to the already great problem.

'Another' is a good link word which keeps flow going

Another sporting hero with a problem is George Best, one of the great players in British football. At the end of his football career Best became an alcoholic, and in fact he was recently jailed for two months or so during Christmas last year. If his admirers copied him, the "Don't Drink and Drive," campaign will have been wasted on them.

Admits opponent's case and answers it

You may say that everyone does something rash, even when they are an adult. The point is, however, that people with so much public and press attention on them ought to be more careful. This applies especially to Botham, who, as well as doing something rash, plays right into the hands of the press.

Faces another argument and deals with it

Another argument against what I am saying is that people will not copy the things that their heroes do, for they will know better because they will have seen warnings like the campaign that shows the terrors of drug addiction. The point is that, say if there is a group of people who like Ian Botham, but aren't foolish enough to copy what he does, it just takes one supporter who is in a frenzied stupor about the man, and because people are so easily influenced they will follow that person like sheep.

By dealing with each of these arguments the student is strengthening his own case

Another argument is that although people like Botham and Best do do stupid things the press hype the story up and make it seem twice as bad as it really is. However, although the press do usually hype things like that up (a) Sometimes (well occasionally actually) the press are telling the truth, and it really is as bad as they make out, and anyway, (b) the famous people should know that the press do this, so they shouldn't do anything stupid in the first place.

Conclusion that doesn't use the word 'conclusion' – good

Although there are arguments against my point of view, most of them can be rebutted. Botham committed a crime, and then he committed a moral crime, because he didn't come clean about what had happened, and lied. Just to make my point of view clear I believe that people who became heroes have a responsibility to set an example to their admirers.

When writing a discursive essay you need to decide on the line of argument you are going to follow. Take this title, for example:

'THE BEST THINGS IN LIFE ARE FREE'. Do you think this is true?

This asks you to give a 'Yes' or 'No' answer, and to support it. Personally I would argue that the best things in life – friendship, good health, the countryside – are free, though I would acknowledge that you need money for certain essential things like clothing, shelter, food and, in the twentieth century, transport. These essentials, however, are not the best things in life.

Sometimes you will need to present a more balanced view of the arguments for and against a claim or statement. Some titles invite this kind of response:

WHAT ARE THE ADVANTAGES AND DISADVANTAGES OF
VERY LARGE SCHOOLS AND COLLEGES?

You could prepare your response to this by jotting down the advantages (pros) and the disadvantages (cons):

PROS	CONS
Wide range of options	You never get to know anybody

PARAGRAPHS are really important features of discursive essays. They signal to the reader that it is time to consider another aspect of the argument. Test your own writing. Can you write in pencil in the margin what each paragraph is about? If you have to write more than one sentence, something is probably wrong! (Look at the clear paragraphs in Robert's essay.)

Activity

Produce a piece of discursive writing, using either one of the many topics above, or on one of those below:

DO YOU BELIEVE THAT WE LIVE IN A VIOLENT AGE?

ARE CARS A BLESSING OR A CURSE?

ONLY THE FOOLISH BELIEVE IN THE SUPERNATURAL

'THERE NEVER WAS A GOOD WAR OR A BAD PEACE'
SAID BENJAMIN FRANKLIN. DO YOU AGREE?

PEOPLE EXAGGERATE THE EFFECTS OF POLLUTION.
THERE IS NOTHING REALLY TO WORRY ABOUT.

♦ Put the reader in the picture in your first paragraph by indicating the points you are going to discuss in detail later on in your essay.
♦ Write a first draft, then read it through annotating the places where improvements could be made.
♦ Submit the draft to your teacher and discuss it with him/her.
♦ Write a final version and hand in both this and the draft version.

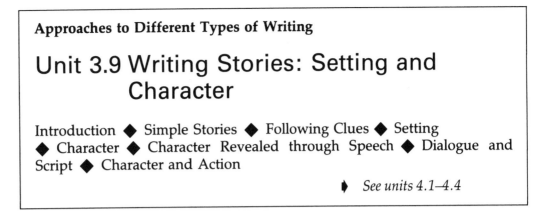

Approaches to Different Types of Writing

Unit 3.9 Writing Stories: Setting and Character

Introduction ◆ Simple Stories ◆ Following Clues ◆ Setting ◆ Character ◆ Character Revealed through Speech ◆ Dialogue and Script ◆ Character and Action

◆ *See units 4.1–4.4*

Introduction

In Units 2.7 and 2.11 we looked at some things worth noticing when we read. These included openings, plot and narrative, layers of meaning, and words and images. Here we will examine how an awareness of these and other elements of storytelling can help improve our writing.

Simple Stories

Many students like writing stories because they can be really creative and imaginative. To help the process let us look at a brief story and note the ingredients – the elements of narrative!

| SCENES (1) (2) CHARACTERS | A man called Henry was sitting at home and, as there was nothing on the television, he decided to go to the cinema. As he sat down he found himself next to a dog which seemed to be thoroughly enjoying the film, chuckling and laughing as it watched the screen. Henry turned to the dog's owner. 'I'm surprised at your dog's behaviour' Henry said. 'Yes it is surprising,' said the owner, 'he hated the book'. | PLOT SETTING ATMOSPHERE DIALOGUE |

This story contains the following narrative elements:

- A plot in which one thing leads to another.
- Three characters – two men, and a dog.
- Two scenes – one in Henry's house and the other in the cinema.
- Dialogue.
- Comic atmosphere created by the idea of a dog watching a film.

Following Clues

In the following extract P. D. James, a writer of detective stories, describes some of the elements of her stories.

P. D. James

SETTING

ATMOSPHERE

CHARACTERISATION

PLOT

CLOSED SOCIETY

SCENES

POINT OF VIEW

One of the questions a crime writer is most frequently asked is 'How do you make a beginning?' Does the book start with an idea for an original method of murder, with a character or with place? For me it is invariably the setting which sparks off my native imagination and sets in motion the complicated process which results in a novel. Setting is particularly important in a crime novel. It helps to create an atmosphere of suspense, menace and mystery, it can provide both a contrast to and a relief from horror, it influences fundamentally the details of the plot. It is also important to characterisation since people react to their own environment and are influenced by it. And like most detective writers I am fascinated by closed societies, particularly those in which human beings are flung together in involuntary and sometimes unwelcome proximity, and where the reprehensible emotions of jealousy, envy, dislike and lust can fester and erupt into the ultimate crime.

Once I have found my setting I gradually fill it with my characters and begin to devise the details of my plot. The classical English detective story must be carefully structured and meticulously plotted if one is to achieve the right balance between setting, puzzle and characterisation, and I find that I spend as much time on the planning and research as I do on the actual writing. And I never start at the beginning of the book and then work through to the end. Instead I see the novel in scenes, rather as if I am shooting a film, and I write these scenes out of order before finally putting them together to produce the finished work. One of the most difficult problems in writing a mystery is that of the writer's viewpoint in telling the story. A first person narrative can be particularly effective . . .

Activity

1. SETTINGS
    Here are six settings. Which would make the best setting for a murder mystery? Why?

    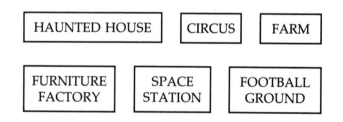

    | HAUNTED HOUSE | CIRCUS | FARM |
    | FURNITURE FACTORY | SPACE STATION | FOOTBALL GROUND |

2. ATMOSPHERE
    Which atmosphere most closely matches the feeling in (a) this lesson, (b) a maths lesson, (c) a disco, (d) a street at 3 am, (e) the local bus station:

    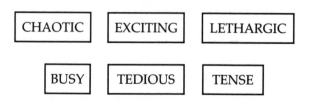

    | CHAOTIC | EXCITING | LETHARGIC |
    | BUSY | TEDIOUS | TENSE |

3. PLOT
A plot is a series of events, one leading to another. Describe one of the following:

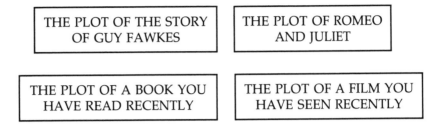

| THE PLOT OF THE STORY OF GUY FAWKES | THE PLOT OF ROMEO AND JULIET |
| THE PLOT OF A BOOK YOU HAVE READ RECENTLY | THE PLOT OF A FILM YOU HAVE SEEN RECENTLY |

Prepare by jotting down notes to show the stages so that you can describe the plot clearly.

4. CHARACTERISATION
Describe in turn:
a your mother or father
b your brother or sister
c your maths teacher
d an actor or a singer.

5. CLOSED SOCIETIES
Here are some 'Closed Societies'. What do they all have in common?

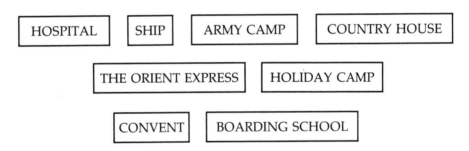

HOSPITAL	SHIP	ARMY CAMP	COUNTRY HOUSE
THE ORIENT EXPRESS	HOLIDAY CAMP
CONVENT	BOARDING SCHOOL

6. SCENES
Choose a short story or a chapter from a novel. Try to work out how many scenes there would be, if you were filming it.

7. POINT OF VIEW
What is the difference between this:

I went outside, climbed into my car and as I turned to fasten my seat belt I noticed that there was a body on the back seat.

and this?

He went outside, climbed into his car, and as he turned to fasten the seat belt noticed that there was a body on the back seat.

Setting

Many novels and short stories begin with a description of the setting – the place where the events happen.

The Trout Sean O'Faolain	One of the first places Julia always ran to when they arrived in G- was the Dark Walk. It is a laurel walk, very old; almost gone wild; a lofty midnight tunnel of	smooth, sinewy branches. Underfoot the tough brown leaves are never dry enough to crackle. There is always a suggestion of damp and cool trickle.

Feet Jan Mark	Unlike the Centre Court at Wimbledon the Centre Court at our school is the one nobody wants to play on. It is made of asphalt and has dents in it, like Ryvita. All the other courts are grass, out in the sun; Centre Court is in between the	science block and the canteen and when there is a Governors' Meeting the governors use it as a car park. The sun only shines on Centre Court at noon in June and there is green algae growing round the edges.

Commentary

Both these stories begin with detailed descriptions which fix the settings firmly in the reader's mind. The stories are set in very precise, confined places: a path shrouded by bushes, and a tennis court. The setting can create the mood for the story: the walk is dark, old and shut in – 'A lofty midnight tunnel'. If you read the rest of the story you will discover that a trout is shut in, trapped in a little well at the end of this path.

Activities

1. Write an opening paragraph of about 100 words for a horror or ghost story that is set in one of the places below:

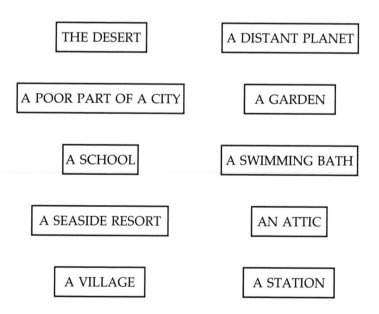

THE DESERT	A DISTANT PLANET
A POOR PART OF A CITY	A GARDEN
A SCHOOL	A SWIMMING BATH
A SEASIDE RESORT	AN ATTIC
A VILLAGE	A STATION

Read your opening paragraph to your group and ask for comments and suggestions about what could happen next.

2. Design a cover for *The Trout* or *Feet*. Draw the laurel walk or tennis court as you imagine them to be, using the details the writers supply.

Character

Here is an extract from a story about a girl who when at home has to conform with the standards of dress required by her strict Moslem family. Sumitra is a Ugandan Asian girl living in Britain. What is interesting about her character is the way that she is two people in one. As a dutiful daughter she has to behave like a traditional Moslem girl – but on Saturdays she becomes a very Western teenager. Details such as 'with a tailored jacket tossed casually over her shoulder' help to build up a picture of her and make her interesting.

Sumitra's Story

Rukshana Smith

On Saturdays, Sumitra became Sue, in swinging skirts and bright blouses, with a tailored jacket tossed casually over her shoulders. She wore her hair loose, hanging down her back. From nine to five Sue was liberated, smart and cheeky, like the other girls at work. Sue was part of the adult world, responsible for running the office while the rest of the staff served in the shop.

Explanation

Stories have characters. These characters are usually people but they do not have to be.

People can be made interesting and memorable in a number of ways, all of which involve the use of significant detail. How exactly does this work?

Novelists can make characters more interesting and easy to picture

- by describing them in detail (as we saw in *Sumitra's Story*)
- through dialogue
- by showing what they do – through their actions.

Character Revealed Through Speech

Dialogue plays a very important part in novels. We can learn a lot about people by the way they speak and what they say.

Activity

Divide into pairs or groups of three or four, and choose a passage to read aloud to the class. To prepare your reading:
- look closely at the dialogue in your chosen passage and discuss as a group what kind of person you imagine each speaker to be. How do the characters talk to each other? Are they friendly? Do they listen to one another? How do they respond?
- decide who is going to play who in your reading. (Remember that for the stories you will need a narrator – as well as characters – to speak those parts that are not dialogue.)
- write down stage directions for your reading.
  You could make a tape-recording of your reading if you wish. The passage could be one of those that follows, or one you have selected from the book box, library or the book you are currently reading.

EXAMPLE 1

This is an extract fron *Sons and Lovers* by D. H. Lawrence. In it, William, the eldest son, confronts his father, a miner who drinks and has struck William's mother, Mrs. Morel. What do we learn about these three characters from what they say?

Sons and Lovers

D. H. Lawrence

All the children, but particularly Paul, were peculiarly *against* their father, along with their mother. Morel continued to bully and to drink. He had periods, months at a time, when he made the whole life of the family a misery. Paul never forgot coming home from the Band of Hope one Monday evening and finding his mother with her eye swollen and discoloured, his father standing on the hearthrug, feet astride, his head down, and William, just home from work, glaring at his father. There was a silence as the young children entered, but none of the elders looked round.

William was white to the lips, and his fists were clenched. He waited until the children were silent, watching with children's rage and hate; then he said:

'You coward, you daren't do it when I was in.'

But Morel's blood was up. He swung round on his son. William was bigger, but Morel, was hard-muscled, and mad with fury.

'Dossn't I?' he shouted. 'Dossn't I? Ha'e much more o' thy chelp, my young jockey, an' I'll rattle my fist about thee. Ay, an' I sholl that, dost see.'

Morel crouched at the knees and showed his fist in an ugly, almost beast-like fashion. William was white with rage.

'Will yer?' he said, quiet and intense. 'It 'ud be the last time, though.'

Morel danced a little nearer, crouching, drawing back his fist to strike. William put his fists ready. A light came into his blue eyes, almost like a laugh.

He watched his father. Another word, and the men would have begun to fight. Paul hoped they would. The three children sat pale on the sofa.

'Stop it, both of you,' cried Mrs. Morel in a hard voice. 'We've had enough for one night. And you,' she said, turning on to her husband, 'look at your children!'

Morel glanced at the sofa.

'Look at the children, you nasty little bitch!' he sneered. 'Why, what have I done to the children, I should like to know? But they're like yourself; you've put 'em up to your own tricks and nasty ways – you've learned 'em in it, you 'ave.'

She refused to answer him. No one spoke. After a while he threw his boots under the table and went to bed.

'Why didn't you let me have a go at him?' said William, when his father was upstairs. 'I could easily have beaten him.'

'A nice thing – your own father,' she replied.

"'Father!'" repeated William. 'Call *him* my father!'

'Well, he is – and so –'

'But why don't you let me settle him? I could do, easily.'

'The idea!' she cried. 'It hasn't come to *that* yet.'

'No,' he said, 'it's come to worse. Look at yourself. *Why* didn't you let me give it him?'

'Because I couldn't bear it, so never think of it,' she cried quickly.

And the children went to bed, miserably.

EXAMPLE 2

This is from the opening chapter of Charles Dickens's *Great Expectations*. An orphan boy, Pip, is visiting his parents' grave in the churchyard on the marshes, when an escaped convict suddenly jumps out at him.

Great Expectations

Charles Dickens

"Hold your noise!" cried a terrible voice, as a man started up from among the graves at the side of the church porch. "Keep still, you little devil, or I'll cut your throat!"

A fearful man, all in coarse grey , with a great iron on his leg. A man with no hat, and with broken shoes, and with an old rag tied round his head. A man who had been soaked in water, and

smothered in mud, and lamed by stones, and cut by flints, and stung by nettles, and torn by briars; who limped and shivered, and glared and growled; and whose teeth chattered in his head as he seized me by the chin.

"Oh! Don't cut my throat sir," I pleaded in terror. "Pray don't do it, sir."

"Tell us your name!" said the man. "Quick!"

"Pip, sir."

"Once more," said the man, staring at me. "Give it mouth!"

"Pip. Pip, sir."

"Show us where you live," said the man. "Pint out the place!"

I pointed to where our village lay, on the flat inshore among the elder trees and pollards, a mile or more from the church.

The man, after looking at me for a moment, turned me upside down, and emptied my pockets. There was nothing in them but a piece of bread. When the church came to itself – for he was so sudden and strong that he made it go head over heels before me, and I saw the steeple under my feet – when the church came to itself, I say, I was seated on a high tombstone, trembling, while he ate the bread ravenously.

"You young dog," said the man, licking his lips, "what fat cheeks you ha' got."

I believe they were fat, though I was at that time under-sized, for my years, and not strong.

"Darn me if I couldn't eat 'em," said the man, with a threatening shake of his head, "and if I han't half a mind to't!"

I earnestly expressed my hope that he wouldn't, and held tighter to the tombstone on which he had put me; partly to keep myself upon it; partly, to keep myself from crying.

"Now lookee here!" said the man. "Where's your mother?"

"There sir!" said I.

He started, made a short run, and stopped and looked over his shoulder.

"There sir!" I timidly explained. "Also Georgians. That's my mother."

"Oh!" said he, coming back. "And is that your father alonger your mother?"

"Yes, sir," said I; "him too; late of this parish."

"Ha!" he muttered then, considering. "Who d'ye live with – supposin' you're kindly let to live, which I han't made up my mind about!"

"My sister, sir – Mrs. Joe Gargery – wife of Joe Gargery, the blacksmith, sir."

"Blacksmith, eh?" said he. And looked down at his leg.

EXAMPLE 3

Here is an extract, mainly dialogue, from *Lord of the Flies* by William Golding. You probably know the plot. Some schoolboys have crash landed on a coral island. In this scene the marooned boys decide to elect a leader.

Lord of the Flies

William Golding

"Let's have a vote."

"Yes!"

"Vote for a chief!"

"Let's vote – "

"Him with the shell."

"Ralph! Ralph!"

"Let him be chief with the trumpet thing."

Ralph raised a hand for silence.

"All right. Who wants Jack for chief?"

With dreary obedience the choir raised their hands.

"Who wants me?"

Every hand outside the choir except Piggy's was raised immediately. Then Piggy, too, raised his hand grudgingly into the air. Ralph counted.

"I'm chief then."

The circle of boys broke into applause. Even the choir applauded; and the freckles on Jack's face disappeared under a blush of mortification. He started up, then changed his mind and sat down again while the air rang. Ralph looked at him, eager to offer something.

"The choir belongs to you, of course."

"They could be the army –"

"Or hunters –"

"They could be –"

The suffusion drained away from Jack's face. Ralph waves again for silence.

"Jack's in charge of the choir. They can be – what do you want them to be?"

"Hunters."

EXAMPLE 4   In this passage two teenage girls are talking at the edge of an aerobics class. The girl called Lectric has a boyfriend who has joined the army.

Three Minute Heroes Leslie Stewart		
	RHODA:	When's he going?
	LECTRIC:	Monday, he reckons.
	RHODA:	You can become a war widow.
	LECTRIC:	Or something.
	RHODA:	You'll have to act your age and say 'ta very much' to the Queen when she gives you his medals.
	LECTRIC:	What about you, young lady? What shall we do with you?
	RHODA:	Dancer. Doctor. Prime Minister of England.
	LECTRIC:	Urban guerrilla. They're good jobs.
	RHODA:	Hooker.
	LECTRIC:	Supermum!
	RHODA:	Construction engineer.
	LECTRIC:	*(As the lights begin to fade)* Bingo winner.
	RHODA:	Something in the City.
	LECTRIC:	Tea-leaf.
	RHODA:	Pregnant.
	LECTRIC:	Prince Andrew's bit of stuff.
	RHODA:	Newspaper headline.
	LECTRIC:	War widow.
		(Blackout)

EXAMPLE 5

The Rebels of Gas Street

Jan Needle

SCENE FOUR

The Fanshawes' home. The Fanshawes have just finished tea, and **Mr. Fanshawe** *is reading a newspaper.* **Newsboy** *appears with a placard and shouts the headlines while the family remain in tableau (i.e. they freeze in position).*

NEWSBOY Chronicle, Chronicle, read all about it! Strikes in steel, cotton, coal, shipping, docks and transport. Five police horses destroyed after Liverpool riots. Troops kill two strikers in Wales. Read all about it!

MRS FANSHAWE *coming out of tableau as Newsboy leaves* Oh no! Not deaths! That is too, too terrible.

MR FANSHAWE Disgusting. Cynthia, to eat three slices of cake at one sitting is quite disgusting.

MRS FANSHAWE But can you do **nothing** about it, Charles? You are a magistrate, after all. **Deaths**!

CYNTHIA Only little bits, Daddy. I won't get fat, I promise you.

MRS FANSHAWE Charles, concentrate. Those beasts have killed five horses. Five poor, defenceless horses.

MR. FANSHAWE Terrible. Appalling. But what can one do, my dear? One cannot deport them to the Colonies any more. One does one's best, I promise you.

MRS FANSHAWE It seems to me, Charles, that the entire fabric of our dear country is being undermined. I think Mr. Churchill is quite right. They should all be shot.

CYNTHIA That's not fair, Mummy. Girls can't join the Army.

MR FANSHAWE In any case, my love, we could hardly shoot them all. At the last count there were nearly four hundred thousand men on strike. I doubt if the Army has that many bullets!

MRS FANSHAWE This is not a matter for jesting, dearest. A firm stand should be made.

CYNTHIA They could shoot just one from every factory, Daddy. Or five, perhaps.

MR FANSHAWE Darlings, we know best, I assure you. Firm action is being taken, never fear. Why, only this morning I sent one rogue to prison for three months for coming out on strike.

MRS FANSHAWE What was the charge?

MR FANSHAWE Neglecting his wife and children. Who were at the court, actually — **and one** *hundred* per cent behind him, although they are nearly starving! That will show the scum we mean business!

MRS FANSHAWE One man, for three months. It is hardly enough, Charles.

MR FANSHAWE There have been others, dear. Seventeen have been committed this week, by my hand alone. We will break their spirits, never fear.

MRS FANSHAWE And now the very schoolchildren are talking of going on strike. Those awful ragged urchins down in South Wales.

MR FANSHAWE That will not spread to this town, dear. Our authorities will treat them firmly. We will beat any such socialistic notions out of them.

CYNTHIA Anyway, Father, the boys in this place would never strike. They don't have the gumption. They are milksops, one and all.

Cyril Fanshawe rushes on, dressed in Eton-type uniform. He throws himself, crying, at his father's feet.

CYRIL Oh Father, Father, **do** something. The nasty boys have beaten me. They threw stones.

MRS FANSHAWE *comforting him* There there, Cyril, there there. Charles, this is intolerable. I insist that you take these children to a place of safety.

MR FANSHAWE A place of safety? What **can** you mean, woman?

MRS FANSHAWE *to Cyril* There there, diddums, don't you cry. Daddy will take us to the seaside for the weekend, won't you Daddy? We'll go to that nice private hotel at Blackpool.

> **CYNTHIA** Oh golly, Daddy that *would* be nice ...
>
> *They go into tableau as* **Newsboy** *returns.*
>
> **NEWSBOY** Chronicle, Chronicle – read all about it! Another school in Llanelly joins strike epidemic. Flying pickets roam the town. Mr Churchill despatches troops to deal with miners. Read all about it!

Dialogue and Script

Think about the differences between the way the dialogue is presented in the extract from novels as opposed to the play extract. In examples one and two, particularly, we are given background information and descriptions of the characters. These descriptive elements are missing from the play extract but it does have stage directions.

Activities

1. Write about the kind of people we meet in each extract. Identify the things they say that tell us things about their characters. How does the last example let us know about the kind of people the characters are?
2. Take each of the examples and imagine how the story or play would continue. Write the continuation of one of the extracts, or a story in which one of the characters appears.
3. Write the novel extracts (1–3) in the form of play scripts. You will need to think of ways of putting across the important non-spoken (descriptive) elements of the narratives.
4. Write the play extracts (4) as they would appear in a novel. You will need to think about the setting and what the characters are like.
5. For a complete unit of coursework, try adapting a whole chapter of a novel into a play, or a whole act of a play into a novel.

Character and Action

Sometimes characters reveal something significant about themselves through their actions. Here is a description of a gesture which reveals something about the character involved.

In the novel *Kidnapped* the hero David Balfour is asked by his Uncle Ebenezer, who has just poured himself a drink, if he would like one:

Kidnapped
 	
Robert Louis Stevenson
	I told him such was my habit, but not to put himself about.
	   "Na, Na," said he "I'll deny you nothing in reason!"
	   He fetched another cup from the shelf; and then, to my great surprise, instead of drawing more beer, he poured an accurate half from one cup to the other. There was a kind of nobleness in this that took my breath away. If my uncle was certainly a miser, he was one of that thorough breed that goes nearer to make the vice respectable.

Questions

1. What does this action reveal about David's uncle's character?
2. What does David think of his uncle's action?

Activities

1. The ways in which people react to situations say things about their characters. Imagine there is a fire in your classroom. How would different people react? Who would panic and who would stay cool? If you rushed to the door, knocking other people over in an attempt to get out, you would reveal a lot about your character! Divide into groups and visualise this scene. Concentrate on how individual members of the class – and the teacher – would react. Write an account of the scene that focuses on these different reactions.

2. Imagine a scene in which someone shows great heroism – by saving someone from drowning, for instance. Write two accounts of such an incident:

   a from the point of view of the hero who plays down his/her heroism
   b from the point of view of another survivor, bringing out the great courage and selflessness of the hero.

   If you wish, you could look at the next unit – 'Points of View' – before tackling this activity.

Approaches to Different Types of Writing

Unit 3.10 Who's telling the story? Point of View

Points of View ◆ First Person Narrative ◆ Third Person Narrative ◆ Not My Best Side

◗ *See units 2.1–2.3, 4.1–4.3*

Points of View

Stories can be told in different ways from a variety of viewpoints. Here P. D. James describes the problems she faces before starting to write one of her crime novels.

One of the most difficult problems in writing a mystery is that of the writer's viewpoint in telling the story. A first person narrative can be particularly effective and has the advantage that it creates immediacy, realism and credibility and encourages reader identification with the hero-narrator who is usually the detective. The disadvantage is that the reader can only experience what the hero experiences, can see only through his eyes, hear through his ears, and can learn nothing about the murder unless it is also known and experienced by the narrator. There is a similar drawback in telling the story through the hero's often less-than-brilliant partner, the Watson. The advantage of using a Watson, as Conan Doyle so brilliantly demonstrated, is that he can ask the questions the reader would like to ask and serve as a foil to the brilliant powers of the detective while representing the view of the ordinary man. But I prefer to tell my story from a number of viewpoints, moving from character to character so that the reader can sometimes experience identical events but through different eyes. It seems to me that this change of viewpoint, provided it does not take place in mid-chapter which I regard as technically maladroit, can add richness and diversity to a novel as well as an element of irony since the reader is often in possession of more information than is the detective. But the major disadvantage is that the story can never be told through the murderer's eyes since his motives and thoughts must be concealed until the last chapter if there is to be an element of surprise.

Before you start to write you should think about who is going to tell your story. There are two main modes of narrative: first person and third person.

First Person Narrative

In a first person narrative the story is told from the point of view of one of the characters in the story, as in the following examples.

| **I'm Trying to Tell You**

Bernard Ashley | Lenny Fisher is a boy in my class. But to tell the truth, he doesn't come very often. He stays away from school for a week at a time, and I'll tell you where he | is. He's at the shops, stealing things sometimes, but mainly just opening the doors for people. He does it to keep himself warm. I've seen him in our shop. |

| **Stranger with My Face**

Lois Duncan | "My name is Laurie Stratton. I am seventeen years old, and I live at the | Cliff House on the northern tip of Brighton Island." |

| **Pearls are a Nuisance**

Raymond Chandler | It is quite true that I wasn't doing anything that morning except looking at a blank sheet of paper in my typewriter and thinking about writing a letter. It is also quite true that I don't have a great | deal to do any morning, but that is no reason why I should have to go out hunting for old Mrs. Penruddock's pearl necklace. I don't happen to be a policeman. Pearls are a nuisance. |

Third Person Narrative

Many stories are told by a narrator whose identity we do not know because he/she stands outside the story. But this unknown narrator can see and describe everyone and everything – he/she knows much more about what is going on than the storyteller in a first person narrative. In a third person narrative the focus is on the story, not the storyteller.

| **Tulku**

Peter Dickinson | Theodore woke in the dark, sucked harshly out of the pit of sleep by a hand shaking his shoulder and a voice hissing in his ear. Before he could groan a question the hand covered his mouth. | He jerked himself free and sat up, making the straps of his bed creak with the strain, but by now he had recognised the voice, and guessed at the urgency. |

Commentary

We are in the room with Theodore like flies on the wall. We see him awake. We do not think about who it must be who is writing this. We do not think of the person who is telling us this.

Here is another 'third person' narrative. It is the opening of a short story. Notice how we enter into the character's thoughts this time.

A Bit of Singing and Dancing

Susan Hill

AT FIVE MINUTES to three he climbed up the ladder into the loft. He went cautiously, he was always cautious now, moving his limbs warily, and never going out in bad weather without enough warm clothes. For the truth was that he had not expected to survive this winter, he was old, he had been ill for one week, and then the fear had come over him again, that he was going to die. He did not care for his own part, but what would become of the boy? It was only the boy he worried about now, only he who mattered. Therefore, he was careful with himself for he had lived out this bad winter, it was March, he could look forward to the spring and summer, could cease to worry for a little longer. All the same he had to be careful not to have accidents, though he was steady enough on his feet. He was seventy-one. He knew how easy it would be, for example, to miss his footing on the narrow ladder, to break a limb and lie there, while all the time the child waited, panic welling up inside him, left last at the school. And when the fear of his own dying did not grip him, he was haunted by ideas of some long illness, or incapacitation, and if he had to be taken into hospital, what would happen to the child, then? *What would happen?*

Activities

1. Rewrite one of the extracts above from a different point of view. (For instance, you could rewrite the *Tulku* extract as a first person narrative.)
2. Continue one of the above extracts by writing the next paragraph from the same point of view.
3. Write a version of a story you have read recently from the point of view of one of the characters in it.
4. A boy has been accused – unjustly in his opinion – of going into another classroom at dinnertime and swearing at and bullying students from the year below. Write an account of the incident from:
   a the boy's point of view
   b the teacher's point of view
   c the point of view of a storyteller (a third-person narrator) who is able to see everything.

You should aim to write about 100 words for each. You could begin the boy's account like this:

'I do go into the first year classroom sometimes but . . .'

the teacher's account like this:

'Bernard Williams is a boy in 4S. He spends a lot of time . . .'

and the storyteller's account like this:

'It was lunchtime at Westlands School. The rain was falling and so all of the students were indoors. Bernard Williams, a tough-looking fifteen year old, was wandering down the corridor . . .'

Not my Best Side

Look at the poem by Ursula Fanthorpe (on page 156) – written from three different points of view. It is based on the painting below.

Activity

Write a response to this poem. Organise your ideas in the following way:
♦ Describe the poem
♦ Describe the person speaking in each section of the poem
♦ Describe the point of view of each person in the poem
♦ What is the point of the poem?
♦ Is it a comic poem, a serious poem, or both?
You could discuss these points in groups before making your notes. Finally, write out your response as a piece of coursework.

Not My Best Side

Ursula Fanthorpe

I

Not my best side, I'm afraid.
The artist didn't give me a chance to
Pose properly, and as you can see,
Poor chap, he had this obsession with
Triangles, so he left off two of my
Feet. I didn't comment at the time
(What, after all, are two feet
To a monster?) but afterwards
I was sorry for the bad publicity.
Why, I said to myself, should my conqueror
Be so ostentatiously beardless, and ride
A horse with a deformed neck and square hoofs?
Why should my victim be so
Unattractive as to be inedible,
And why should she have me literally
On a string? I don't mind dying
Ritually, since I always rise again,
But I should have liked a little more blood
To show they were taking me seriously.

II

It's hard for a girl to be sure if
She wants to be rescued. I mean, I quite
Took to the dragon. It's nice to be
Liked, if you know what I mean. He was
So nicely physical, with his claws
And lovely green skin, and that sexy tail,
And the way he looked at me,
He made me feel he was all ready to
Eat me. And any girl enjoys that.
So when this boy turned up, wearing machinery,
On a really dangerous horse, to be honest
I didn't much fancy him. I mean,
What was he like underneath the hardware?
He might have acne, blackheads or even
Bad breath for all I could tell, but the dragon –
Well, you could see all his equipment
At a glance. Still, what could I do?
The dragon got himself beaten by the boy,
And a girl's got to think of her future.

III

I have diplomas in Dragon
Management and Virgin Reclamation.
My horse is the latest model, with
Automatic transmission and built-in
Obsolescence. My spear is custom-built,
And my prototype armour
Still on the secret list. You can't
Do better than me at the moment.
I'm qualified and equipped to the
Eyebrow. So why be difficult?
Don't you want to carry out the roles
Sociology and myth have designed for you?
Don't you realise that, by being choosy,
You are endangering job prospects
In the spear- and horse-building industries?
What, in any case, does it matter what
You want? You're in my way.

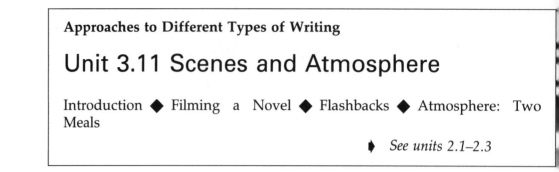

Approaches to Different Types of Writing

Unit 3.11 Scenes and Atmosphere

Introduction ◆ Filming a Novel ◆ Flashbacks ◆ Atmosphere: Two Meals

◗ *See units 2.1–2.3*

Introduction

The word 'scene' actually comes from a latin word meaning 'stage'. A scene in a play is a part of the action which occurs at one time and in one place. In novels we hardly notice the way one scene follows another. The change of scene may be marked by a gap in the text or a line of stars, or the end of a chapter. In the following extract from *Bleak House*, Dickens makes use of a bird – a crow – to take us from one scene to the next! He has been describing a scene with Mr. Snagsby in it, and he wants to move to a scene with Mr. Tulkington in it.

Bleak House **Charles Dickens**	Mr. Snagsby standing at his shop door looking up at the clouds sees a crow, who is out late, skim westward over the slice of sky belonging to Cook's Court. The crow flies straight across Chancery Lane	and Lincoln's Inn Gardens, into Lincoln's Inn Fields. Here in a large house, formerly a house of state, lives Mr. Tulkington . . .

Filming a Novel

Read the following passage from a novel by Jackie Collins. As you do so, imagine you are a film director and think about how many scenes you would need if you were going to film the passage.

The World is Full of Married Men
 	
Jackie Collins
	She vanished through the door, and David heard water running in the bathroom.
	   He thought about Claudia, and the way they had first met. Was it really only three weeks ago? He had had a particularly hard day at the office, and Linda his wife had been nagging him about all the extra work he seemed to be doing, and how she never saw him any more. It was nearly six, and he was just getting ready to leave, when Phillip Abbotson darted into his office. 'Listen, Dave.' Phillip said, 'do you have a spare moment to come down to the studio and make a decision for us? We've got two girls testing for the Beauty Maid soap product, and it's a dead heat. We just can't decide.'
	Reluctantly David went with Phillip to
		the ground floor studio in the enormous Cooper-Taylor advertising building. It was owned by his uncle, R. P. Cooper, who had two sons, and Samford Taylor, with no sons but a son-in-law. Therefore, David came sixth in the line of importance, which in a business of such a size was quite important, but not important enough as far as David was concerned. He was in charge of the TV section, and since Beauty Maid soap was to be featured quite heavily on Channel 9, it was necessary to pick the right girl.
		   They entered the studio, and David immediately spotted her. She was sprawled in a canvas chair, wearing a white terry-cloth robe. Her hair was piled high on her head, and she was eating an apple.

Activities

1. As the film director, write a report for the producer of the film version of the scene, explaining the locations and settings you will require. It might help you to start off by listing the scenes and the action they contain, as follows:

	SCENE	ACTION
1	Claudia's bedroom	Claudia goes into the bathroom David sits on the bed
2	Phillip's office . . .	

2. Choose a whole chapter from a novel, and write a similar report for a producer.

3. Read a novel of your choice. After you have read it, go back to the beginning and look carefully at the first few pages or the opening chapter, and write a scene to go before the first scene in the book: a 'prequel'.

Flashbacks

You may have noticed that the scene from the Jackie Collins novel takes us back – through the thoughts of a character – to an event that occurred earlier on. This device is known as a flashback.

In *1984* by George Orwell, Winston Smith – a man of 39 – wakes up from a dream about his mother. The story stops and we go back to an earlier scene.

1984

George Orwell

In the dream he had remembered his last glimpse of his mother, and within a few moments of waking the cluster of small events surrounding it had all come back. It was a memory that he must have deliberately pushed out of his consciousness over many years. He was not certain of the date, but he could not have been less than 10 years old.

One day a chocolate ration was issued. There had been no such issue for weeks or months past. He remembered quite clearly that precious little morsel of chocolate. It was a two ounce slab (they still talked about ounces in those days) between the three of them. It was obvious that it ought to be divided into three equal parts. Suddenly, as though he were listening to somebody else, Winston heard himself demanding in a loud booming voice that he should be given the whole piece. His mother told him not to be greedy. There was a long nagging argument that went round and round, with shouts, whines, tears, remonstrances, bargainings. His tiny sister, clinging to her mother with both hands, exactly like a baby monkey, sat looking over her shoulder at him with large mournful eyes. In the end his mother broke off three-quarters of the chocolate and gave it to Winston, giving the other quarter to his sister. The little girl took hold of it and looked at it dully, perhaps not knowing what it was. Winston stood watching her for a moment. Then with a sudden swift spring he had snatched the piece of chocolate out of his sister's hand and was fleeing for the door.

'Winston, Winston!' his mother called after him. 'Come back! Give your sister back her chocolate!'

He stopped, but he did not come back. His mother's anxious eyes were fixed on his face. Even now he was thinking about the thing, he did not know what it was that was on the point of happening. His sister, conscious of having been robbed of something, had set up a feeble wail. His mother drew her arm round the child and pressed its face against her breast.

Something in the gesture told him that his sister was dying. He turned and fled down the stairs, with the chocolate growing sticky in his hand.

He never saw his mother again. After he had devoured the chocolate he felt somewhat ashamed of himself and hung about in the streets for several hours, until hunger drove him home. When he came back his mother had disappeared.

Questions

1. How does the author let us know that this is a flashback?
2. If you were filming the scene how would you show that it involves a character remembering something from the past?

Activity

Rewrite this extract as a scene from a play. Remember that your scene will consist only of dialogue and stage directions.

Atmosphere: Two Meals

Atmosphere is hard to define. We know what it means when we say 'this house is creepy', or that a club has 'an incredible atmosphere'. Atmosphere is the feeling you pick up from the surroundings and events. If you go into a room where two people have been having a row, there is a tense atmosphere. Here is an example of a jolly atmosphere. The Cratchit family are settling down to dinner, and the mood is a happy one.

A Christmas Carol

Charles Dickens

Such a bustle ensued that you might have thought a goose the rarest of all birds; a feathered phenomenon, to which a black swan was a matter of course – and in truth it was something very like it in that house. Mr. Cratchit made the gravy (ready beforehand in a little saucepan) hissing hot; Master Peter mashed the potatoes with incredible vigour; Miss. Belinda sweetened up the apple sauce; Martha dusted the hot plates; Bob took Tiny Tim beside him in a tiny corner at the table; the two young Cratchits set chairs for everybody not forgetting themselves, and mounting guard upon their posts, crammed spoons into their mouths, lest they should shriek for goose before their turn came to be helped. At last the dishes were set on, and grace was said. It was succeeded by a breathless pause, as Mrs. Cratchit, looking slowly all along the carving knife, prepared to plunge it in the breast; but when she did, and when the long expected gush of stuffing issued forth, one murmur of delight arose all round the board, and even Tiny Tim, excited by the two young Cratchits, beat on the table with the handle of his knife, and feebly cried Hurray!

There was never such a goose, Bob said that he didn't believe that there was ever such a goose cooked. Its tenderness and flavour, size and cheapness, were the themes of universal admiration. Eked out by apple sauce and mashed potatoes, it was a sufficient dinner for the whole family; indeed, as Mrs. Cratchit said with great delight (surveying one small atom of a bone upon the dish), they hadn't ate it all at last! Yet everyone had had enough, and the youngest Cratchits in particular, were steeped in sage and onion to the eyebrows!

Activity

Although there is a happy atmosphere, there are hints that the Cratchit family are being jolly in spite of their problems. Divide a piece of paper into two columns and draw up a list of

a words and phrases that suggest pleasant activity and a happy atmosphere;

b words and phrases that suggest that all is not perfect.

The first few words and columns have been provided for you.

WORDS AND IDEAS CREATING THE IDEA OF A HAPPY ATMOSPHERE	WORDS AND IDEAS SUGGESTING THAT ALL IS NOT PERFECT
Bustle Mashed the potatoes with incredible vigour Sweetened up the apple sauce Dusted the hot plates Two young children set chairs for everybody, etc.	First sentence suggests goose is rare sight in that house. Tiny Tim cries "feebly".

Here is a contrasting description of a miserable meal eaten in a dingy canteen in George Orwell's *1984*. As you read it, look out for the details that contribute to the idea of a squalid atmosphere.

1984

George Orwell

The gin was served to them in handleless china mugs. They threaded their way across the crowded room and unpacked their trays on to the metal-topped table, on one corner of which someone had left a pool of stew, a filthy liquid mess that had the appearance of vomit. Winston took up his mug of gin, paused for an instant to collect his nerve, and gulped the oily tasting stuff down. When he had winked the tears out of his eyes he suddenly discovered he was hungry. He began swallowing spoonfuls of the stew, which in among the general sloppiness, had cubes of spongy pinkish stuff which was probably a preparation of meat. Had food always tasted like this? He looked round the canteen. A low ceilinged, crowded room, its walls grimy from the contact of innumerable bodies, battered metal tables and chairs, placed so close together that you sat with elbows touching, bent spoons, dented trays, coarse white mugs, all surfaces greasy, grime in every crack; and a sourish composite smell of bad gin and bad coffee and metallic stew and dirty clothes.

Activities

1. List the words or phrases which help create an atmosphere of squalor and misery in this piece.
2. Write up to 500 words about a miserable or happy event in your life. Look at the two examples above to see how the description of an event can be made more vivid by reflecting your feelings in the description of the place or surroundings in which the event happened.

Approaches to Different Types of Writing

Unit 3.12 Conflict, Structure and Message

Conflict: Clash of Wills ◆ Physical Conflict ◆ Structure ◆ What's the Point?

◗ *See units 4.1–4.6*

Introduction

We will briefly consider two further elements of storytelling – conflict and structure.

Conflict: Clash of Wills

In most stories there is a conflict of some sort – a physical conflict, or a clash of wills, or personalities.

Roll of Thunder Hear Me Cry, by Mildred Taylor, is a novel set in the state of Mississippi at the height of the American depression. It explores the real and persistent problem of racial prejudice. Although defeat for the South in the American Civil War had brought an end to slavery, attitudes towards black people had not changed, and an organisation called the Ku Klux Klan had been formed to terrorise and hunt down black people. Read the following poem and passage – they both come from the novel – and explain how they are linked.

Roll of Thunder Hear Me Cry

Mildred Taylor

It was then that I bumped into Lillian Jean Simms.

"Why don't you look where your're going?" she asked huffily. Jeremy and her two younger brothers were with her.

"Hey, Cassie," said Jeremy.

"Hey, Jeremy," I said solemnly, keeping my eyes on Lillian Jean.

"Well, apologize," she ordered.

"What?"

"You bumped into me. Now you apologize."

I did not feel like messing with Lillian Jean. I had other things on my mind. "Okay," I said, starting past, "I'm sorry."

Lillian Jean sidestepped in front of me. "That ain't enough. Get down in the road."

I looked up at her. "You crazy?"

"You can't watch where you going, get in the road. Maybe that way you won't be bumping into decent white folks with your little nasty self."

This second insult of the day was almost more than I could bear. Only the thought of Big Ma up in Mr. Jamison's office saved Lillian Jean's lip. "I ain't nasty," I said, properly holding my temper in check, "and if you're so afraid of getting bumped, walk down there yourself."

Roll of thunder
  hear me cry
Over the water
  bye and bye
Ole man comin
  down the line
Whip in hand
  To beat me down
But I ain't
  Gonna let him
  Turn me 'round.

Physical Conflict

This story has as its central character a boy, Bernard, who befriends a Pakistani boy called Shofiq. Before he gets to know Shofiq Bernard displays all the ignorance and prejudice that he has been taught. In this extract Bernard has not yet befriended Shofiq.

My Mate Shofiq

Jan Needle

Bernard pondered on the subject of Pakistanis for a bit, but not in a serious way. His eyes and nose were running, and he reckoned that if he was cold, in jeans, two jumpers and his anorak with the real fur-trimmed hood, that lot must be freezing brass monkeys. They ought to feel it more, by rights, being as how they came from a hot country, or their mums and dads did, but there they were, quite plain now, in some sort of silky trousers and smock-things, some of them. Nuts. Even the ones in ordinary gear didn't have anoraks on, just coats, not half so good. He wondered what the Whitehead lot would do to them.

Bobby Whitehead's gang clattered past. They took the school side of the next derelict terrace, he went behind. By the time they'd got along its length he was already hidden, waiting for them. He had a good view of the whole of that part of the croft, the part where the fight would be. Fight! He grinned again. Battering more like. Them poor little kids would get a right hammering; they didn't stand a chance.

Now he was closer, he could see them clearly. There were seven or eight of them, and they were very small, about four or six, that's all. He vaguely thought he recognised a couple of them, but then they all looked the same really, so he wasn't that sure. There were two little girls out front, holding hands, then a gap, then a knot of jabbering boys, then a couple more girls. Close to, he could make out that they had on jerseys under their pyjama-things. Not as green as they were cabbage-looking then; but they still looked ruddy cold.

The white kids who'd been near them had raced off towards the fence by now, and the rest were at the Whiteheads' mercy. For a moment Bernard switched sides in his head. He was with them, a lone waggon-train going across the Wild West prairies. He'd been out scouting for redskins, and on coming back to the main body of explorers he'd found a band about to attack. What should he do? Could he beat them single-handed, or should he gallop down to the waggons, form them in a circle, and prepare to fight off the attacking Indians? He almost laughed out loud. A band of Indians attacking that lot! They were Indians! Well it was different, at least – a waggon-train of Indians being attacked by a band of cowboys.

The Pakistani kids were just coming into good brick-bunging range, and he'd seen Whitehead's lot getting up a nice pile of good-size rocks to fling, when Bernard caught a movement out of the corner of his eye, away over to his right. He looked round, risking missing the first shot of the war, to see if he could pick it out.

Over that way it was a right jumble of old, half-down houses, the beginnings of a new estate, and the ruins of another mill, the Muscovy, that still had some bits of old wrecked weaving machines in it. Bernard stared, into the wind, with his eyes watering badly. He'd almost given up, decided he'd been mistaken, when he saw it again. There was someone, someone hiding among the remains of the third terrace along, and creeping towards him.

He flicked his eyes from the shape, to the victims, to the Whiteheads. He squeezed his frozen finger-ends into his eyes to get the tears out, to get a clearer view. One of the little kids out front began to giggle at something, high and squeaky. Pat Broome weighed up a stone in her hand; she'd soon put a stop to that!

The figure along the way moved from behind an old outside lav, full into Bernard's view. He knew him! He was in the same class! It was a bloke called Shofiq, or something. Shofiq Rahman, or something. The two little girls who'd looked familiar clicked. They were his sisters, all dressed up in silk pyjamas while Shofiq wore jeans and a jumper. Blimey – even in this weather he never had a coat on, just jeans and a jumper.

Bernard watched with extra interest, because he knew Shofiq. Not to talk to, of course, because he didn't talk much, not even in class, when Miss told him to. He was very quiet, and very dark brown, and he had a funny smell to him, like an Indian restaurant, like all the Pakis. But he'd thumped some lad once, not so long ago, and none of the kids that liked to bash up the blackies ever touched him. He couldn't take on Bobby Whitehead though, that was obvious. Bobby Whitehead was the champ, he was an ace fighter.

Bernard felt very excited, his chest got tight. This lad was coming along fast now, and he had a dirty great wallbrick in his mitt.

Suddenly there was a big row. He looked back over the wall in time to see Bobby Whitehead, and Patsy Broome, and the three little 'uns, all leap out from their hidey-hole and start bunging bricks. The air was full of them, and the little Pakistani kids just stood there for something like ages, with the rocks flying past their ears and bouncing off the soggy ground all round them. It was a miracle that none of them got hit, but they didn't seem to have the sense to do anything about it. Bernard the Black Hand almost forgot he was only there as a spy. He very nearly leapt up and yelled at them to run.

Bobby Whitehead and his lot were yelling all right, though. And they started to move slowly forward as they kept up the bombardment of stone. Some of the little kids started to dart about, as if they didn't know which way to turn. Bernard saw a rock bounce off the shoulder of a little girl of about five, and she fell into the cold mud, crying. Another little girl bent down to try and help her, with her long black pigtail hanging right down into a puddle. Two of the boys had started to pelt across towards the wire fence, and the hail of bricks followed them. It was a real rout.

Out of the corner of his eye again, Bernard saw a flashing movement at the same time as he heard a loud shout. He turned right, to see the Shofiq lad come roaring out of the garden of an old dumpy house like an express train. He'd dropped the wallbrick and picked up something that looked like a length of old rubber hose. It was about ten feet long, and grey, and an inch thick. What's more, he was swinging it round and round, faster and faster, as he ran.

Bernard was amazed. The lad was swaying with the weight of the hose whizzing round his head, sort of rocking as he ran. If it had gone much faster he would have taken off for sure, he looked so much like a helicopter. He shot towards Bobby Whitehead's lot at a terrific lick, yelling the top of his head off as he ran. The hail of rocks at the little kids stopped. They all got their wits back at once, even the girl that had been hit. They flashed across the croft bawling, a group of little frightened mice.

Bobby Whitehead shouted something, and Patsy Broome bent down to pick up a lump of iron at her feet. But it was too late, much too late, Bernard watched fascinated as the Pakistani lad got closer. The little 'uns dropped their bricks and ran. Pat looked at Bobby and she'd gone white. He just stared, shocked, as the helicopter whirled towards him. He opened his mouth. Patsy pulled back her arm as if she was going to bung the lump of iron, then she dropped it. She started to back away. She looked terrified. The whooshing noise of the whirling hosepipe came clearly to Bernard's ears. The Pakistani lad's mouth was open, his face all twisted up. Bit Patsy turned on her heels and ran.

It was obvious to Bernard that Bobby Whitehead was going to scarper too, it just had to happen. But he didn't get the chance. His gob was still wide open and he looked as if he'd wet himself. As he half turned, looking to where Pat was whistling over the croft towards the school, the helicopter arrived. As Bobby got his legs into action the hosepipe-end came whirling round, whooshing as it came. The tail-end of it caught him right across the side of the head, and he went down into a puddle with an icy splash.

Bernard, his own mouth wide open in admiration and horror, looked at the still form of the terrible Bobby Whitehead. His face was like a sheet and he wasn't moving. From under the hair above his ear a long curtain of blood started to flow.

The Pakistani lad had let go of the hosepipe and rubbed his hands on his jeans. He walked over to Bobby White-head's body and looked down at it. Then he looked towards the school and started to walk towards it. He was still panting, but that was all. Bernard skirted the fallen giant and scuttled in by a different gate. He felt quite peculiar; not at all like a secret agent.

Activity

Choose one of the examples of conflict given below and write
a a story which illustrates this conflict,
b an article in which you discuss the problems raised by the conflict.
Write between 400 and 600 words for each. (You could prepare for the story by writing notes on setting, plot, characters and atmosphere.)

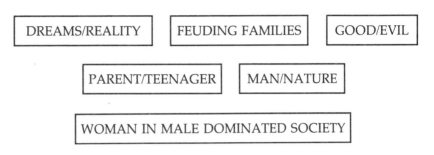

| DREAMS/REALITY | FEUDING FAMILIES | GOOD/EVIL |

| PARENT/TEENAGER | MAN/NATURE |

| WOMAN IN MALE DOMINATED SOCIETY |

Structure

The structure of a piece of writing is determined by the parts that it contains and the way they fit together.

Plays have a more obvious structure than novels, because they are often made up of three or five parts, or ACTS. Each act does something different. The last act, for instance, contains the climax and the conclusion. Here is the structure of the original story of Little Red Riding Hood.

PART I	PART II	PART III
Little Red Riding Hood meets wolf in the forest and is questioned by him: he finds out about her grandmother	She arrives at her grand-mother's cottage, but the wolf has got there first. The wolf has already eaten the grandmother and now eats Little Red Riding Hood.	The woodcutter arrives, kills, and cuts open the wolf and both the grandmother and Little Red Riding Hood emerge unscathed
INTRODUCTION	DISASTER	RESCUE

One way of drawing attention to the STRUCTURE of a story is by reducing the story to one sentence. Take the story *Eveline* by James Joyce. Here is a one sentence summary

Eveline, trapped in a boring and frustrating life, meets Frank and decides to elope with him, but her nerve fails at the last minute.

The story falls into three parts:

1. Eveline is bored and frustrated;
2. She meets Frank and decides to elope;
3. Her nerve fails and she does not elope.

With a novel, you might have to stretch to two or three sentences. This is a summary of *Lord of the Flies* by William Golding:

Some schoolboys survive a plane crash on a coral island and begin by organising themselves into hunters and hutmakers. Gradually the hunters become the dominant group, offering both food and protection from the feared imaginary beasts. The group becomes more and more savage-like, two of the boys are murdered, and they set the island on fire before they are rescued.

Activity

Take a short story or complete novel or play that you have read and use the method above to write a summary of the story. Then go on to write about what you liked and disliked about the book. Your review/report should be about 500 words in length.

What's the Point?

Generally stories have a point or 'message'. This may appear obvious in the case of *Little Red Riding Hood* (beware of strangers), or it may be difficult to express, as in the case of *Eveline* (if you are a prisoner too long you lose the will to escape). But when you are writing about a book, always consider – and try to express in a single sentence – the point or message of that book.

Approaches to Different Types of Writing

Unit 3.13 Summary Unit

▶ *See units 3.1–3.12*

What we have looked at in Part 3 of *Do You Read Me?* – plot, setting, characters, conflict, atmosphere, structure and message – are all elements of narrative; together, they make a novel or short story a rounded and satisfying whole. The following table lists and describes these narrative elements in a short novel by George Orwell. (It's a very short novel and would not take you long to read.)

a	story/plot	Animals rebel and take over a farmyard
b	setting	Manor Farm
c	characters	Pigs (Snowball, Napoleon), carthorse (Boxer), etc.
d	conflict	Farmer Jones v animals Pigs v other animals
e	structure	Three parts/chapters
f	atmosphere/mood	First, resentment and frustration, followed by excitement and a sense of triumph, in turn followed by an increasingly fearful, disillusioned mood
g	point	Revolutions do not bring about lasting change

Activity

See if you can identify these narrative ingredients in a story you are reading for your coursework. Record them in the form of a table as above. Then convert and expand these notes into a complete review, along the following lines:

	ANIMAL FARM
Paragraph 1: Type of Book/Plot	*Animal Farm* by George Orwell, subtitled a fairy tale, is apparently just that: a fanciful story in which animals who can talk, rebel and take over a farm. It is, however, an example of an allegory, a story which works on two levels, because the animals represent human revolutionaries and the farm owner a ruler . . .
Paragraph 2: Setting	Most of the action takes place in or around the farmyard, in an unspecified English county.
Paragraph 3: Characters	The chief characters in the story are the pigs, Snowball and Napoleon . . . Snowball is . . .
Paragraph 4: Conflict	There is not simply a conflict between the animals and Farmer Jones, but conflict within the ranks of the animals themselves.
Paragraph 5: Structure	
Paragraph 6: Mood/atmosphere	The mood changes from that of excitement and exhilaration (after the Victory of the Battle of the Cowsheds) to terror (seeing the fierce dogs) to disillusionment (at the end).
Paragraph 7: The point . . .	

Read the following story by the American writer Thomas Wolfe. Then list and describe the narrative elements in it, using the list and review of narrative elements in *Animal Farm* as a model. You will notice the absence of dialogue in this story. Why is there no dialogue?

The Far and the Near

Thomas Wolfe

On the outskirts of a little town upon a rise of land that swept back from the railway there was a tidy little cottage of white boards, trimmed vividly with green blinds. To one side of the house there was a garden neatly patterned with plots of growing vegetables, and an arbor for the grapes which ripened late in August. Before the house there were three mighty oaks which sheltered it in their clean and massive shade in summer, and to the other side there was a border of gay flowers. The whole place had an air of tidiness, thrift, and modest comfort.

Every day, a few minutes after two o'clock in the afternoon, the limited express between two cities passed this spot. At that moment the great train, having halted for a breathing-space at the town near by, was beginning to lengthen evenly into its stroke, but it had not yet reached the full drive of its terrific speed. It swung into view deliberately, swept past with a powerful swaying motion of the engine, a low smooth rumble of its heavy cars upon pressed steel, and then it vanished in the cut.

For a moment the progress of the engine could be marked by heavy bellowing puffs of smoke that burst at spaced intervals above the edges of the meadow grass, and finally nothing could be heard but the solid clacking tempo of the wheels receding into the drowsy stillness of the afternoon.

Every day for more than twenty years, as the train had approached this house, the engineer had blown on the whistle, and every day, as soon as she heard this signal, a woman had appeared on the back porch of the little house and waved to him. At first she had a small child clinging to her skirts, and now this child had grown to full womanhood, and every day she, too, came with her mother to the porch and waved.

The engineer had grown old and gray in service. He had driven his great train, loaded with its weight of lives, across the land ten thousand times. His own children had grown up and married, and four times he had seen before him on the tracks the ghastly dot of tragedy converging like a cannon-ball to its eclipse of horror at the boiler heat – a light spring-wagon filled with children, with its clustered row of small stunned faces; a cheap automobile stalled upon the tracks, set with the wooden figures of people paralyzed with fear; a battered hobo walking by the rail, too deaf and old to hear the whistle's warning; and a form flung past his window with a scream – all this the man had seen and known. He had known all the grief, the joy, the peril and the labor such a man could know; he had grown seamed and weathered in his loyal service, and now, schooled by the qualities of faith and courage and humbleness that attended his labor, he had grown old, and had the grandeur and the wisdom these men have.

But no matter what peril or tragedy he had known, the vision of the little house and the women waving to him with a brave free motion of the arm had become fixed in the mind of the engineer as something beautiful and enduring, something beyond all change and ruin, and something that would always be the same, no matter what mishap, grief or error might break the iron schedule of his days.

The sight of the little house and of these two women gave him the most extraordinary happiness he had ever known. He had seen them in a thousand lights, a hundred weathers. He had seen them through the harsh bare light of wintry gray across the brown and frosted stubble of the earth, and he had seen them again in the green luring sorcery of April.

He felt for them and for the little house in which they lived such tenderness as a man might feel for his own children, and at length the picture of their lives was carved so sharply in his heart that he felt that he knew their lives completely, to every hour and moment of the day, and he resolved that one day, when his years of service should be ended, he would go and find these people and speak at last with them whose lives had been so wrought into his own.

That day came. At last the engineer stepped from a train onto the station platform of the town where these two women lived. His years upon the rail had ended. He was a pensioned servant of his company, with no more work to do. The engineer walked slowly through the station and out into the streets of the town. Everything was as strange to him as if he had never seen this town before. As he walked on, his sense of bewilderment and confusion grew. Could this be the town he had passed ten thousand times? Were these the same houses he had seen so often from the high windows of his cab? It was all as unfamiliar, as disquieting as a city in a dream, and the perplexity of his spirit increased as he went on.

Presently the houses thinned into the straggling outposts of the town, and the street faded into a country road – the one on which the women lived. And the man plodded on slowly in the heat and dust. At length he stood before the house he sought. He knew at once that he had found the proper place. He saw the lordly oaks before the house, the flower beds, the garden and the arbor, and farther off, the glint of rails.

Yes, this was the house he sought, the place he had passed so many times, the destination he had longed for with such happiness. But now that he had found it, now that he was here, why did his hand falter on the gate; why had the town, the road, the earth, the very entrance to this place he loved turned unfamiliar as the landscape of some ugly dreams? Why did he now feel this sense of confusion, doubt, and hopelessness?

At length he entered by the gate, and walked slowly up the path and in a moment more had mounted three short steps that led up to the porch and was knocking at the door. Presently he heard steps in the hall, the door was opened, and a woman stood facing him.

And instantly, with a sense of bitter loss and grief, he was sorry he had come. He knew at once that the woman who stood there looking at him with a mistrustful eye was the same woman who had waved to him so many thousand times. But her face was harsh and pinched and meager; the flesh sagged wearily in sallow folds, and the small eyes peered at him with timid suspicion and uneasy doubt. All the brave freedom, the warmth and the affection that he had read into her gesture, vanished in the moment that he saw her and heard her unfriendly tongue.

And now his own voice sounded unreal and ghastly to him as he tried to explain his presence, to tell her who he was and the reason he had come. But he faltered on, fighting stubbornly against the horror of regret, confusion, disbelief that surged up in his spirit, drowning all his former joy and making his act of hope and tenderness seem shameful to him.

At length the woman invited him almost unwillingly into the house, and called her daughter in a harsh shrill voice. Then, for a brief agony of time, the man sat in an ugly little parlor, and he tried to talk while the two women stared at him with a dull, bewildered hostility, a sullen timorous restraint.

And finally, stammering a crude farewell, he departed. He walked away down the path and then along the road toward town, and suddenly he knew that he was an old man. His heart, which had been brave and confident when it looked along the familiar vista of the rails, was now sick with doubt and horror as it saw the strange and unsuspected visage of an earth which had always been within a stone's throw of him, and which he had never seen or known. And he knew that all the magic of that bright lost way, the vista of that shining line, the imagined corner of that small good universe of hope's desire, was gone forever, could never be got back again.

PART 4: STORY AND GENRE

In this section we return to the subject we introduced in Part 1: genres – different types of writing. Part 4 of *Do You Read Me?* deals with the different types of prose story, as well as the various kinds of poem and playscript. Parts 3 and 4 have prepared you for this by dealing with approaches to different kinds of reading and writing.

Before you go on to look at some of the types of prose narrative, it is worth pointing out that one type of writing you will tackle – personal or autobiographical writing – often counts as story. So stories do not have to be fiction.

Story and Genre

Unit 4.1 The Modern Short Story

Introduction ◆ Reading a Short Story 1 ◆ Reading a Short Story 2

◗ *See units 2.7, 2.8, 4.3, 4.4*

Introduction

The modern written short story, of the kind you will find in glossy magazines or anthologies, is about one hundred years old, and is by far the youngest of the genres we are considering here. Short stories, written by people such as H. G. Wells and Rudyard Kipling, started to appear in the 1890s when magazines stopped serialising novels. A short story is a story that you could probably read in one lesson. Edgar Allan Poe once said that a short story should be read at one sitting.

A 'convention' is the usual way of doing something. Here are some conventions of the traditional short story:

◆ it deals with a single significant incident or situation
◆ it has just two or three main characters
◆ it deals with a conflict of some kind, that is resolved at the end, sometimes in an unexpected way.

Otherwise the short story has all the ingredients of a novel.

◆ a structure
◆ an atmosphere or mood
◆ a point.

Reading a Short Story – 1

Here is a short story by O'Henry – slightly abridged – that illustrates the conventions listed above. It is a good story to read aloud. After you have read the first paragraph pause for a moment and ask yourself how effective the opening is, and how the writer encourages us to read on. Discuss these points with a partner.

In *The Last Leaf* Sue and Johnsy – two women painters – live in an apartment in New York City. Johnsy has caught pneumonia.

The Last Leaf

O'Henry

That is, pneumonia. The trick is that the writer has turned him into a person. (See personification in the language reference section.)

Mr. Pneumonia was not what you would call a chivalric old gentleman. A mite of a little woman with blood thinned by California zephyrs was hardly fair game for the red-fisted, short-breathed old duffer. But Johnsy he smote; and she lay, scarcely moving, on her painted iron bedstead, looking through the small Dutch window-panes at the blank side of the next brick house.

One morning the busy doctor invited Sue into the hallway with a shaggy, gray eyebrow.

"She has one chance in – let us say, ten," he said, as he shook down the mercury in his clinical thermometer. "And that chance is for her to want to live. This way people have of lining-up on the side of the undertaker makes the entire phar-

Pause here for a moment and ask yourself these questions: How effective is the opening? How is the writer encouraging us to read on?

macopoeia look silly. Your little lady has made up her mind that she's not going to get well. Has she anything on her mind?''

"She – she wanted to paint the Bay of Naples some day,'' said Sue.

"Paint? – bosh? Has she anything on her mind worth thinking about twice – a man, for instance?''

"A man?'' said Sue, with a jew's-harp twang in her voice. "Is a man worth – but, no, doctor; there is nothing of the kind.''

"Well, it is the weakness, then,'' said the doctor. "I will do all that science, so far as it may filter through my efforts, can accomplish. But whenever my patient begins to count the carriages in her funeral procession I subtract 50 per cent. from the curative power of medicines. If you will get her to ask one question about the new winter styles in cloak sleeves I will promise you a one-in-five chance for her, instead of one in ten.''

After the doctor had gone Sue went into the workroom and cried a Japanese napkin to a pulp. Then she swaggered into Johnsy's room with her drawing board, whistling ragtime.

Johnsy, lay, scarcely making a ripple under the bedclothes, with her face toward the window. Sue stopped whistling, thinking she was asleep.

She arranged her board and began a pen-and-ink drawing to illustrate a magazine story. Young artists must pave their way to Art by drawing pictures for magazine stories that young authors write to pave their way to Literature.

As Sue was sketching a pair of elegant horseshow riding trousers and a monocle on the figure of the hero, an Idaho cowboy, she heard a low sound, several times repeated. She went quickly to the bedside.

Johnsy's eyes were open wide. She was looking out the window and counting – counting backward.

"Twelve,'' she said, and a little later "eleven''; and then "ten,'' and "nine''; and then "eight'' and "seven'', almost together.

She looked solicitously out of the window. What was there to count? There was only a bare, dreary yard to be seen, and the blank side of the brick house twenty feet away. An old, old, ivy vine, gnarled and decayed at the roots, climbed half way up the brick wall. The cold breath of autumn had stricken its leaves from the vine until its skeleton branches clung, almost bare, to the crumbling bricks.

"What is it, dear?'' asked Sue.

"Six,'' said Johnsy, in almost a whisper. "They're falling faster now. Three days ago there were almost a hundred. It made my head ache to count them. But now it's easy. There goes another one. There are only five left now.''

"Five what, dear. Tell your Sudie.''

"Leaves. On the ivy vine. When the last one falls I must go, too. I've known that for three days. Didn't the doctor tell you?''

"Oh, I never heard of such nonsense,'' complained Sue, with magnificent scorn. "What have old ivy leaves to do with your getting well? And you used to love that vine, so, you naughty girl. Don't be a goosey. Why, the doctor told me this morning that your chances for getting well real soon were – let's see exactly what he said – he said the chances were ten to one! Why, that's almost as good a chance as we have in New York when we ride on the street cars or walk past a new building. Try to take some broth now, and let Sudie go back to her drawing, so she can sell the editor man with it, and buy port wine for her sick child, and pork chops for her greedy self.''

Pause here and discuss:
* what you think will happen next;
* how you think the story will end.

"You needn't get any more wine,'' said Johnsy, keeping her eyes fixed out the window. "There goes another. No, I don't want any broth. That leaves just four. I want to see the last one fall before it gets dark. Then I'll go, too.''

"Johnsy, dear,'' said Sue, bending over her, "will you promise me to keep your eyes closed, and not look out the window until I am done working? I must hand those drawings in by to-morrow. I need the light, or I would draw the shade soon.''

"Couldn't you draw in the other room?'' asked Johnsy, coldly.

"I'd rather be here by you,'' said Sue. "Besides I don't want you to keep looking at those silly ivy leaves.''

"Tell me as soon as you have finished,'' said Johnsy, closing her eyes, and lying white and still as a fallen statue, "because I want to see the last one fall. I'm tired of waiting. I'm tired of thinking. I went to turn loose my hold on everything, and go sailing down, down, just like one of those poor, tired leaves."

"Try to sleep," said Sue. "I must call Behrman up to be my model for the old hermit miner. I'll not be gone a minute. Don't try to move 'til I come back."

Old Behrman was a painter who lived on the ground floor beneath them. He was past sixty and had a Michael Angelo's Moses beard curling down from the head of a satyr along the body of an imp. Behrman was a failure in art. Forty years he had wielded the brush without getting near enough to touch the hem of his Mistress's robe. He had been always about to paint a masterpiece, but had never yet begun it. For several years he had painted nothing except now and then a daub in the line of commerce or advertising. He earned a little by serving as a model to those young artists in the colony who could not pay the price of a professional. He drank gin to excess, and still talked of his coming masterpiece. For the rest he was a fierce little old man, who scoffed terribly at softness in any one, and who regarded himself as especial mastiff-in-waiting to protect the two young artists in the studio above.

Sue found Behrman smelling strongly of juniper berries in his dimly lighted den below. In one corner was a blank canvas on an easel that had been waiting there for twenty-five years to receive the first line of the masterpiece. She told him of Johnsy's fancy, and how she feared she would, indeed, light and fragile as a leaf herself, float away, when her slight hold upon the world grew weaker.

Old Behrman, with his red eyes plainly streaming shouted his contempt and derision for such idiotic imaginings.

"Vass!" he cried. "Is dere people in de world mit der foolishness to die because leafs dey drop off from a confounded vine? I haf not heard of such a thing. No, I will not pose as a model for your fool hermit-dunderhead. Vy do you allow dot silly pusiness to come in der prain of her? Ach, dot poor leetle Miss Yohnsy."

"She is very ill and weak," said Sue, "and the fever has left her mind morbid and full of strange fancies. Very well, Mr Behrman, if you do not care to pose for me, you needn't. But I think you are a horrid old—old flibbertigibbet."

"You are just like a woman!" yelled Behrman. "Who said I will not bose? Go on. I come mit you. For half an hour I haf peen trying to say dot I am ready to bose. Gott! dis is not any blace in which one so goot as Miss Johnsy shall lie sick. Some day I vill baint a masterpiece, and ve shall all go away. Gott! yes."

Johnsy was sleeping when they went upstairs. Sue pulled the shade down to the window-sill, and motioned Behrman into the other room. In there they peered out the window fearfully at the ivy vine. Then they looked at each other for a moment without speaking. A persistent, cold rain was falling, mingled with snow. Behrman, in his old blue shirt, took his seat as the hermit-miner on an upturned kettle for a rock.

When Sue awoke from an hour's sleep the next morning she found Johnsy with dull, wide-open eyes staring at the drawn green shade.

"Pull it up; I want to see," she ordered, in a whisper.

Wearily Sue obeyed.

But, lo! after the beating rain and fierce gusts of wind that had endured through the livelong night, there yet stood out against the brick wall one ivy leaf. It was the last one on the vine. Still dark green near its stem, but with its serrated edges tinted with the yellow of dissolution and decay, it hung bravely from a branch some twenty feet above the ground.

"It is the last one," said Johnsy. "I thought it would surely fall during the night. I heard the wind. It will fall to-day, and I shall die at the same time."

"Dear, dear!" said Sue, leaning her worn face down to the pillow, "think of me, if you won't think of yourself" What would I do?"

But Johnsy did not answer. The lonesomest thing in all the world is a soul when it is making ready to go on its mysterious, far journey. The fancy seemed to possess her more strongly as one by one the ties that bound her to friendship and to earth were loosed.

The day wore away, and even through the twilight they could see the lone ivy leaf clinging to its stem against the wall. And then, with the coming of the night the north wind was again loosed, while the rain still beat against the windows and pattered down from the low Dutch eaves.

When it was light enough Johnsy, the merciless, commanded that the shade be raised.

The ivy leaf was still there.

Johnsy lay for a long time looking at it. And then she called to Sue, who was stirring her chicken broth over the gas stove.

"I've been a bad girl, Sudie," said Johnsy. "Something has made that last leaf stay there to show me how wicked I was. It is a sin to want to die. You may bring me a little broth now, and some milk with a little port in it, and—no; bring me a hand-mirror first, and then pack some pillows about me, and I will sit up and watch you cook."

An hour later she said

"Sudie, some day I hope to paint the Bay of Naples."

The doctor came in the afternoon, and Sue had an excuse to go into the hallway as he left.

"Even chances," said the doctor, taking Sue's thin, shaking hand in his. "With good nursing you'll win. And now I must see another case I have downstairs. Behrman, his name is—some kind of an artist I believe. Pneumonia, too. He is an old, weak man, and the attack is acute. There is no hope for him; but he goes to the hospital to-day to be made more comfortable."

The next day the doctor said to Sue: "She's out of danger. You've won. Nutrition and care now—that's all."

And that afternoon Sue came to the bed where Johnsy lay, contentedly knitting a very blue and very useless woollen shoulder scarf, and put one arm around her, pillows and all.

"I have something to tell you, white mouse," she said. "Mr Behrman died of pneumonia to-day in the hospital. He was ill only two days. The janitor found him on the morning of the first day in his room downstairs helpless with pain. His shoes and clothing were wet through and icy cold. The couldn't imagine where he had been on such a dreadful night. And then they found a lantern, still lighted, and a ladder that had been dragged from its place, and some scattered brushes, and a palette with green and yellow colors mixed on it, and—look out the window, dear, at the last ivy leaf on the wall. Didn't you wonder why it never fluttered or moved when the wind blew? Ah, darling, it's Behrman's masterpiece—he painted it there the night that the last leaf fell."

Questions

1. What is the main incident that the story centres on?
2. How many main characters are there? Who are they?
3. What conflict is there? (Think of the two women.)
4. Look at the structure of the story and divide it into three sections. Describe briefly what each section is about.
5. What is the mood of the story? How do you feel at the end?
6. What is the point of the story?

Activity

Imagine there is an inquest into the death of Old Behrman. Write:
a the doctor's evidence,
b Johnsy's evidence,
c Sue's evidence.

Reading a Short Story – 2

Here is a short story called *There Will Come Soft Rains* by Ray Bradbury. This story is less traditional, and does not keep to all the conventions. Before you read the story, it might be useful to discuss the following questions, in groups.

- What do you think the world will be like in ten years' time? In fifty years time? In a thousand years' time?
- What will be better or worse about the future?

There Will Come Soft Rains

Ray Bradbury

The house was a good house and had been planned and built by the people who were to live in it, in the year 1980. The house was like many another house in that year; it fed and slept and entertained its inhabitants, and made a good life for them. The man and wife and their two children lived at ease there, and lived happily, even while the world trembled. All of the fine things of living, the warm things, music and poetry, books that talked, beds that warmed and made themselves, fires that built themselves in the fireplaces of evenings, were in this house, and living there was a contentment.

And then one day the world shook and there was an explosion followed by ten thousand explosions and red fire in the sky and a ram of ashes and radio-activity, and the happy time was over.

In the living room the voice-clock sang. *Tick-tock, seven A.M. o'clock, time to get up!* as if it were afraid nobody would. The house lay empty. The clock talked on into the empty morning.

The kitchen stove sighed and ejected from its warm interior eight eggs, sunny side up, twelve bacon slices, two coffees, and two cups of hot cocoa. *Seven nine, breakfast time, seven nine.*

'Today is April 28th, 1985,' said a phonograph voice in the kitchen ceiling. 'Today, remember, is Mr. Featherstone's birthday. Insurance, gas, light and water bills are due.'

Somewhere in the walls, relays clocked, memory tapes glided under electric eyes. Recorded voices moved beneath steel needles:

Eight one, run, run, off to school, off to work, run run, ticktock, eight one o'clock!

But no doors slammed, no carpets took the quick tread of rubber heels. Outside, it was raining. The voice of the weather box on the front door sang quietly: 'Rain, rain, go away, rubbers, raincoats for today.' And the rain tapped on the roof.

At eight thirty the eggs were shrivelled. An aluminium wedge scraped them into the sink, where hot water whirled them down a metal throat which digested and flushed them away to the distant sea.

Nine fifteen, sang the clock, time to clean.

Out of the warrens in the wall, tiny mechanical mice darted. The rooms were acrawl with the small cleaning animals, all rubber and metal. They sucked up the hidden dust, and popped back in their burrows.

Ten o'clock. The sun came out from behind the rain. The house stood alone on a street where all the other houses were rubble and ashes. At night the ruined town gave off a radioactive glow which could be seen for miles.

Ten fifteen. The garden sprinkler filled the soft morning air with golden fountains. The water tinkled over the charred west side of the house where it had been scorched evenly free of its white paint. The entire face of the house was black, save for five places. Here the silhouette, in paint, of a man mowing a lawn. Here, a woman bent to pick flowers. Still farther over, their images burned on wood in one titanic instant, a small boy, hands flung in the air – higher up, the image of a thrown ball – and opposite him a girl, her hands raised to catch a ball which never came down.

The five spots of paint – the man, the woman, the boy, the girl, the ball – remained. The rest was a thin layer of charcoal.

The gentle rain of the sprinkler filled the garden with falling light.

Until this day, how well the house had kept its peace. How carefully it had asked, 'Who goes there?' and getting no reply from rains and lonely foxes and whining cats, it had shut up its windows and drawn the shades. If a sparrow brushed a window, the shade snapped up. The bird, startled, flew off! No, not even an evil bird must touch the house.

And inside, the house was like an altar with nine thousand robot attendants, big and small, servicing, attending, singing in choirs, even though the gods had gone away and the ritual was meaningless.

A dog whined, shivering, on the front porch.

The front door recognized the dog voice and opened. The dog padded in wearily, thinned to the bone, covered with sores. It tracked mud on the carpet. Behind it whirred the angry robot mice, angry at having to pick up mud and maple leaves, which, carried to the burrows, were dropped down cellar tubes into an incinerator which sat like an evil Baal in a dark corner.

The dog ran upstairs, hysterically yelping at each door. It pawed the kitchen door wildly.

Behind the door, the stove was making pancakes which filled the whole house with their odour.

The dog frothed, ran insanely, spun in a circle, biting its tail, and died.

It lay in the living room for an hour.

One o'clock.

Delicately sensing decay, the regiments of mice hummed out of the walls, soft as brown leaves, their electric eyes blowing.

One fifteen.

The dog was gone.

The cellar incinerator glowed suddenly and a whirl of sparks leaped up the flue.

Two thirty-five.

Bridge tables sprouted from the patio walls. Playing cards fluttered onto pads in a shower of pips. Martinis appeared on an oaken bench.

But the tables were silent, the cards untouched.

At four-thirty the tables folded back into the walls.

Five o'clock. The bathtubs filled with clear hot water. A safety razor dropped into a wall-mould, ready.

Six, seven, eight, nine o'clock.

Dinner made, ignored, and flushed away; dishes washed; and in the study, the tobacco stand produced a cigar, half an inch of gray ash on it, smoking, waiting. The hearth fire bloomed up all by itself, out of nothing.

Nine o'clock. The beds began to warm their hidden circuits, for the night was cool.

The gentle clock in the study wall. A voice spoke from above the crackling fireplace:

'Mrs McClellan, what poem would you like to hear this evening?'

The house was silent.

The voice said, 'Since you express no preference, I'll pick a poem at random.' Quiet music rose behind the voice. 'Sara Teasdale. A favourite of yours, as I recall.'

> There will come soft rains and the smell of the ground
> And swallows circling with their shimmering sound;
>
> And frogs in the pools singing at night,
> And wild plum-trees in tremulous white.
>
> Robins will wear their feathery fire
> Whistling their whims on a low fence-wire;
>
> And not one will know of the war, not one
> Will care at last when it is done.
>
> Not one would mind, neither bird nor tree!
> If mankind perished utterly:
>
> And Spring herself, when she woke at dawn,
> Would scarcely know that we were gone.'

The voice finished the poem. The empty chairs faced each other between the silent walls, and the music played.

At ten o'clock, the house began to die.

The wind blew. The bough of a falling tree smashed the kitchen window. Cleaning solvent, bottled, crashed on the stove.

'Fire!' screamed voices. 'Fire!' Water pumps shot down water from the ceilings. But the solvent spread under the doors, making fire as it went, while other voices took up the alarm in chorus.

The windows broke with heat and the wind blew in to help the fire. Scurrying water rats, their copper wheel spinning, squeaked from the walls, squirted their water, ran for more.

Too late! Somewhere, a pump stopped. The ceiling sprays stopped raining. The reserve water supply, which had filled baths and washed dishes for many silent days, was gone.

The fire crackled upstairs, ate paintings, lay hungrily in the beds! It devoured every room.

The house was shuddering, oak bone on bone, the bared skeleton cringing from the heat, all the wires revealed as if a surgeon had torn the skin off to let the red veins quiver in scalded air. Voices screamed, *'Help, help, fire, run!'* Windows snapped open and shut, like mouths, undecided. *Fire, run!* the voices wailed a tragic nursery rhyme, and the silly Greek chorus faded as the sound-wires popped their sheathings. Ten dozen high, shrieking voices died, as emergency batteries melted.

In other parts of the house, in the last instant under the fire avalanche, other choruses could be heard announcing the time, the weather, appointments, diets; playing music, reading poetry in the fiery study, while doors opened and slammed and umbrellas appeared at the doors and put themselves away – a thousand things happening, like the interior of a clock shop at night, all clocks striking, a merry-go-round of squeaking, whispering, rushing, until all the film spools were burned and fell, and all the wires withered and the circuits cracked.

In the kitchen, an instant before the final collapse, the stove, hysterically hissing, could be seen making breakfasts at a psychopathic rate, ten dozen pancakes, six dozen loaves of toast.

The crash! The attic smashing kitchen down into cellar and subcellar. Deepfreeze, armchairs, filmtapes, beds, were thrown in a cluttered mound deep under.

Smoke and silence.

Dawn shone faintly in the east. In the ruins, one wall stood alone. Within the wall, a voice said, over and over again and again, even as the sun rose to shine upon the heaped rubble and steam:'Today is April 29th, 1985. Today is April 29th, 1985. Today is . . .'

Questions

1. What has happened in this story?
2. Why is there a poem in the story? What bearing does it have on the whole story?
3. Who is telling the story?
4. What is unusual about the dialogue – the spoken words – in this story?

Activity

Write a description of the interior of this house (before it collapses) as if you were an estate agent, describing it for a would-be buyer. You could begin: 'This is a modern house, built in 1980. It consists of living room, kitchen . . .'.

Commentary on 'There Will Come Soft Rains'

Despite the date (April 28th, 1985) this is a short story set in the future, after a nuclear war has destroyed the world. Technology briefly outlives man. The house carries on functioning after the occupants have been erased. There is a bubbly, cheerful opening paragraph, and the jolly mood is sustained by the stupid phonograph voice that goes on issuing cheerful instructions even though the family are all dead. The pace is swift, the collapse of the house sudden and the stream of activity matched by the succession of short paragraphs. The poem, with apt comment on the insignificance of man to nature:

'Not one would mind, not bird or tree
If mankind perished utterly.'

offers a brief pause before the house finally begins to fall apart – a process triggered, ironically, by that self-same indifferent tree.

Questions

1. Comment on this commentary. Is it clear? Would it make you want to read the story?
2. Does *There Will Come Soft Rains* seem to have any of the qualities of the traditional short story or is it just not telling a story at all?
3. Is there any point in a story without people or without a surprise ending? (Read *Eveline* by James Joyce.)
4. Compare *The Last Leaf* with *There Will Come Soft Rains*. To structure your comparison, write notes on the differences/similarities between the two stories under the following headings:

CHARACTERS   SETTING   FEELING   TYPE OF STORY

MESSAGE   EVENTS

Write a draft and final version of your comparison.

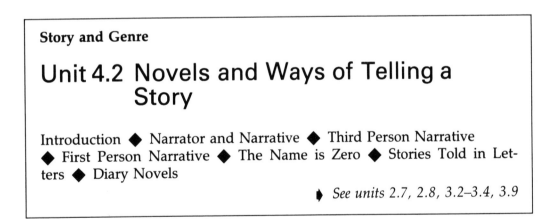

Story and Genre

Unit 4.2 Novels and Ways of Telling a Story

Introduction ◆ Narrator and Narrative ◆ Third Person Narrative ◆ First Person Narrative ◆ The Name is Zero ◆ Stories Told in Letters ◆ Diary Novels

◆ *See units 2.7, 2.8, 3.2–3.4, 3.9*

Introduction

In this section we will concentrate on novels. A conventional novel is a long prose story, which, although fictional, pretends to describe real events. Novels are several times longer than short stories, usually focus on characters and come in many forms. We will consider some of these types – horror, romantic and detective stories – a little later on.

Compared to poems and plays, novels do not have a long history. Novels started to become popular about 250 years ago, particularly among rich women who had plenty of spare time in which to read. At the time, some people regarded novels in the same way that some people regard space invader machines today – as a waste of time and damaging to the mind.

Activities

In groups, discuss the following:

1. How do you spend your leisure time?
2. Do you find it hard to fill up your spare time or do you have plenty to do?
3. Does it matter how you spend your leisure time?

Narrator and Narrative

Novelists have stories to tell and these stories can be presented in a number of ways. Unit 3.11 introduced you to some of the ways in which novelists can tell their stories. You will remember that in some novels you (the reader) are not aware of who is telling the story (the narrator) and in some you are.

Third Person Narrative

Third person narrative is the type of story in which you are not aware of who is telling the story. The narrator stands outside the story, but appears to know everything that is going on. This is how Susan Cooper begins her long fantasy trilogy *The Dark is Rising*. Despite what is to come later, the opening is very ordinary.

| **The Dark is Rising**

Susan Cooper | "Where is he?"
  Barney hopped from one foot to the other as he clambered down from the train peering in vain through the white-faced crowds flooding eagerly to the St. Austell ticket barrier.
  "Oh, I can't see him. Is he there?"
  "Of course he's there," Simon said, struggling to clutch the long canvas | bundle of his father's fishing rods. "He said he'd meet us. With a car."
  Behind them, the big diesel locomotive hooted like a giant owl, and the train began to move out.
  "Stay where you are a minute," Father said, from a barricade of suitcases. "Merry won't vanish. Let people get clear." |

Activity

Write a story in which one of the following fantastic elements appears:

POLTERGEIST   GHOST   TIME TRAVELLING

Write your story in the third person and start it off in a very ordinary way. It should be set in a place you know well.

First Person Narrative

Sometimes we are aware of the storyteller, who, as in this example, is telling the story of what happened to him or her. This is the opening of a novel called *Herland* by Charlotte Perkins Gilman, in which a group of men, deep in the Amazonian jungle, stumble accidentally on an all-female community, where, to quote the blurb, 'generations of women live in peace and harmony – and have learnt to reproduce without men'. The novelist is a woman but she tells the story from the point of view of a group of men.

Herland

Charlotte Perkins Gilman

This is written from memory, unfortunately. If I could have brought with me the material I so carefully prepared, this would be a very different story. Whole books full of notes, carefully copied records, firsthand decipherings, and the pictures – that's the worst loss. We had some bird's eyes of the cities and parks; a lot of lovely views of streets, of buildings, outside and in and some of those gorgeous gardens, and most important of all, of the women themselves.

Questions

1. How has the author made it sound as if these events really happened?
2. This is an example of a genre called Utopian fiction. Can you think of any examples of stories where explorers discover unusual communities?
3. In *Herland* the women live without men and have learnt to reproduce without men. What would be the advantages of an all-woman society? What might be the disadvantages? Discuss this in mixed sex groups. Then you could read the novel.

The Name is Zero

Here is a further example of a first person narrative. The storyteller is actually a character within the story: an insider.

The Name is Zero

Lorna Reed

My first excited thought was that this guy of about forty, in a leather jacket and jeans, must be from a record company. He was about to offer us a recording contract – yes, that was it! I'd heard of this happening. Unknowns were suddenly 'discovered' and, after that, fame and fortune followed fast.

But it wasn't to be; not yet.

'My name's John Hamers. I work for an agency responsible for booking acts into hotels and clubs. I spend half my evenings popping along to gigs to see if there are any promising newcomers. You lot . . . you're a bit raw, but the punters like girls in a band. Now, if you could tart yourselves up a bit – you know, tight dresses, nice plunging tops – '

'Either our music's good enough without all that rubbish, or it isn't,' Joss snapped in frosty tones.

I felt a sudden stab of foreboding. If Joss was going to allow her feminist beliefs to come before our musical career, then I could see we wouldn't get very far. Surely, at this stage, we needed to take everything we were offered, both for the experience and the money?

The man shrugged, said, 'Well, it's your decision,' and was about to leave when I spoke up.

'Just a minute . . . give us a moment to talk this over, could you?'

'There's nothing to talk over,' Joss said threateningly.

It was about time I stood up to her, I decided. Obviously Rob wasn't going to say anything, and Pip would certainly back Joss up.

The man sidled out into the corridor, and I went over and shut the door. 'He's offering us work and we can't turn it down,' I stated emphatically. 'Anyway, lots of people make an effort to look good when they're on stage or TV. Why shouldn't we? It wouldn't hurt us, would it, just for one night?'

'Don't you understand anything?' Pip exploded. 'I think it's time we educated her,' she said to Joss. 'Where have you been for the last few years? Reading Barbara Cartland romances? We women have been fighting for years not to be looked on as sex objects, and to be accepted on equal terms with men, and here you are, trying to turn the clock back to the bad old days. You'll be telling me in a minute that you think women should be slaves to their husbands, and spend all day at the hairdresser's and the beauty parlour, and never read anything more improving than Woman and Home!'

Now she'd really made me angry. I

wasn't going to let myself be insulted and talked down to like this! 'I know perfectly well what women's lib is all about and I agree with it wholeheartedly. But getting somewhere in life is a matter of compromise and tactics, not just following your beliefs blindly' I said heatedly. 'I think you and Joss should swallow your pride, just for one night. I'm prepared to do it –'

'And I'm willing to wear false eyelashes and a frock if it would help,' Rob said, and I had to choke back a chuckle.

Activity

In groups re-read the extract from *The Name is Zero*. Joss and Pip are against the idea of glamourising themselves, but Ireka (the narrator) and Rob are prepared to compromise their principles in the hope of a lucky break. Are the girls Joss and Pip right to make a stand on this? Does the fact that the narrator holds one view make you (the reader) see her view only?

Stories Told in Letters

To create the illusion that the story they had made up was real, many early novelists told the story in the form of a series of letters. An 'epistle' is an old word for a letter, so these were called 'epistolary novels'. The first example is from an eighteenth century novel called *Pamela* by Samuel Richardson. Pamela, a servant girl, writes regular letters to her parents, complaining of how Mr. B. (her employer) pesters her.

Pamela

Samuel Richardson

O let me, my dear parents, take up my complaint, and say, Never was poor creature so barbarously used, as your Pamela! Indeed, my dear father and mother, my heart is just broken! I can neither write as I should do, nor let it alone; for to whom but to you can I vent my griefs, and keep my heart from bursting! Wicked, wicked man! I have no patience when I think of him! But yet, don't be frightened–for–I hope–I am honest! But if my head and my heart will let me, you shall hear all.

The epistolary form is not used very much today, but we do find it in Alice Walker's *The Color Purple*, and, as you see below, *French Letters*, a story told in the form of a series of letters from a girl to a friend in the North:

Activity

Imagine you are the central character in one of the following situations.

YOU ARE LIVING AMONG STRANGERS: YOU'VE LOST YOUR MEMORY BUT HAVE AN ADDRESS TO WRITE TO THAT VAGUELY RINGS A BELL	YOU ARE IN THE MIDDLE OF A WAR BETWEEN THE NORTH AND SOUTH OF ENGLAND

YOU HAVE STARTED WORK FOR A FIRM THAT IS BREAKING THE LAW

YOU ARE IN A PRISON FOR A CRIME YOU DID NOT COMMIT	YOU ARE HELD ON BOARD A HIJACKED PLANE FOR TWO WEEKS

French letters

Eileen
Fairweather

Harrisons's Betting Shop
c/o 96 Sheraton Road
London N8

August 21st

Dear Jean,

It's like this. I've been worrying all night about our bet and no offence but it *isn't* moral. When it comes to being the first to get a real boyfriend, you've got a head start. You live above a pub *and* you have a brother AND you'll soon be going to a mixed school. All I've got is a sister, a school that might as well be a convent, and a dad in a useless job. Well he might enjoy helping old ladies with their shopping trolleys, but what chance have I got of meeting anyone rich and famous on a bus?

What I'm getting at is that I don't think it should be like you said, with a flat prize of a fiver no matter *who* wins. Seeing as I've got all these handicaps and you've got all these advantages, I think we should have different odds on winning, like dogs do. So – if you're the first you should win at two-to-one, i.e. get two quid from me. But if I'm the first I should come in at five to one, i.e. get five quid off you.

I hope you think this arrangement is fair. I think it is. Today I miss you more than ever.

luv,
Max

PS: In case your Maths is as bad as ever, this assumes our stake's a quid.

Hornsey
London N8

August 28th

Dear Jean,

What do you mean, I'm not being FAIR??!! I was going to increase the odds in my favour even more, seeing as I'm fatter than you. But then being the kind person I am I thought it wouldn't be nice to bankrupt a friend. Fat chance I've got of that, being ten stone four.

So all right, it's probably my own fault that you're eight stone and I'm not. So all right, I'm probably weak willed and pathetic and eat too many chocolate bars. BUT – it is not my fault if my dad's a bus conductor while yours is a publican. Pubs are good for meeting boys. On the buses, all a girl can meet are old people and the unemployed. Those are well-known Facts.

It's bad enough you leaving me to cope with Haringey Girls on my own. Denying your advantages now you're going mixed is just about the last straw.

Two quid if you win, four quid if I do. That's my final offer.

Max

Write a series of five or six letters that describe what happens to you in this situation. The letters need not all be written from the viewpoint of the hero/heroine. Some of the letters could be written by other characters involved in the situation. Before you start to write, you will need to consider the following:

*PLOT	What is going to happen – what story are you going to tell through your sequence of letters?
*POINT OF VIEW	Will all the letters be written by the central character in the story, or will some be written by others? Having letters written by different people is a good way of putting across different points of view.
*CHARACTERS	How will you describe the characters in your story? (Remember the way a person writes says things about his/her character.)
*REGISTER	What sort of people are the central characters? How would they write? Think carefully about who they are writing to, and how they would express themselves.

Here is an example of how you could use a series of letters to tell a story about a firm breaking the law:

LETTER	CONTENT	PLOT FUNCTION
1	From new employee to his girlfriend, saying he's found out that the firm is breaking the law	Sets up the story
2	From girlfriend to employee saying perhaps you've made a mistake and please don't try to be a hero	Creates emotional interest
3	From hero to girlfriend saying he's going to the police	Next stage of plot
4	From bent Sales Manager to Head of Crime Syndicate saying we've been found out and what can we do about it	New and sinister angle on events
5	From Head of Crime Syndicate to Sales Manager saying 'rub him out'	Climax of plot
6	From girlfriend to hero saying why haven't you been in touch . . . I'm worried about you	Makes reader tense
7	From hero's mother to girlfriend saying hero has disappeared . . .	Sinister and alarming ending

You may wish to practise using this outline. You could write the letters outlined above and ask a friend to read them and make comments. Then make up your own story and write your own letters. Make sure that the title you choose for your story clearly describes the situation.

Diary Novels

Another way of making a novel seem more realistic is to tell the story in the form of a diary or journal. This is particularly suitable if you are telling the story of someone who is on his or her own for a period of time.

In this diary novel the diarist believes she is the sole survivor of a nuclear war. These are the opening paragraphs of the novel.

Z for Zachariah

Robert C. O'Brien

I am afraid.

Someone is coming.

That is, I think someone is coming, though I am not sure, and I pray that I am wrong. I went into the church and prayed all this morning. I sprinkled water in front of the altar, and put some flowers on it, violets and dogwood.

But, there is smoke. For three days there has been smoke, not like the time before. That time, last year, it rose in a great cloud a long way away, and stayed in the sky for two weeks. A forest fire in the dead woods, and then it rained and the smoke stopped. But this time it is a thin column, like a pole, not very high.

Activities

1. Continue this story. For more information go back to Unit 2.8 'Openings' where you can find out more about the story.

2. Probably the best known 'diary' novels today are the two Adrian Mole books. We have not included material from them in this book as they are so well known, but before you start this activity, remind yourself of these books. If you do not know them, read one of them. The titles are *The Secret Diary of Adrian Mole* and *The Growing Pains of Adrian Mole*, both by Sue Townsend, published by Methuen.

   Imagine you are another person, such as your brother, sister, father, mother, teacher, a friend or even yourself five years ago. Write diary entries for five days in this person's life.

   You will need to think carefully about the lifestyle of your chosen person. Include in your diary entries details of the person's daily routine and any interesting or significant events that occur. You should also include the person's reactions to these events, and possibly some general reflections on life.

   For a real challenge, try to write a diary from the point of view of someone of the opposite sex, as Sue Townsend did in *The Diary of Adrian Mole*.

3. Write a diary for a week of your present life in which a fantastic day is followed by a terrible day which is followed by another fantastic day and so on for the rest of the week. Emphasise the swings of mood.

Story and Genre

Unit 4.3 Popular Romantic Fiction

Introduction: The two Rs ◆ A Popular Genre ◆ Conventions of
Romantic Fiction ◆ A Dream World ◆ Romantic or Real?
◆ Romantic writing and advertising   ◗ *See units 4.1, 4.4*

Novels are a type – or genre – of prose, which is itself one of the main genres
of writing. But novels themselves have a number of different sub-genres. In
the following units we shall consider just two of them:

      ROMANTIC GENRE   HORROR GENRE

There are many more genres of novel which we are not considering here.

To grasp the idea of genres of novel, it may help you to think of films, and the
different kinds of films you can see at the cinema and on television. There are –
amongst others – adventure films, spy films, comedy films and horror films. The
ingredients of these different types of film do not usually mix. You would not
expect to see a cowboy in a space film. The different types – genres – of film stick
to certain conventions. We will concentrate on conventions as we look at two
different types of novel.

Introduction: The Two Rs

The word ROMANTIC has two distinct meanings. Perhaps the easiest way
to remember them is to think of 'Romantic with a big R' and 'romantic with a
small r'.

1. Romantic with a big 'R' refers to two related types of writing:

   a Novels written two hundred years ago that sought to arouse strong
   feelings in the reader by unfolding atmospheric tales of adventure set in
   wild landscapes peopled with terror-stricken heroines and sinister villains;
   b poetry written by poets such as Keats, Byron and Wordsworth, who were
   preoccupied with nature and death and are called 'The Romantics'.

2. Romantic with a small 'r' means to do with idealised love of an escapist,
   fantasy kind.

A Popular Genre

The type of romantic stories we are going to look at here are romantic with a
small 'r'. Read the following passage silently and jot down your reactions.

| **Dancing in the Dark**

Carolyn Ross | That night, as I lay in bed, my head whirled with thoughts of Eric's kisses. I relived the moment at least a hundred times in my mind. I had to let him know | that I wanted to be much more than a dance partner, that I did want him to kiss me again – if he wanted to. |

Commentary

Whether this makes you go 'Yuk' or 'Aaah', there is no denying that romantic fiction is one of the most popular genres. Go into a bookshop and you will see how many books of this kind are on sale there, especially in bus and railway station newsagents. Why? Look at the list of best selling books in Unit 2.7. Many of these are examples of romantic fiction. How many people from your class will admit to having read a romantic novel?

Activity

Why are romantic novels so popular? Discuss the following possible reasons.

> GIRLS READ MORE THAN BOYS,
> AND THEY ARE MORE ROMANTIC

> LIFE IS DULL –
> THESE STORIES ARE A FORM OF ESCAPE

> YOU KNOW THE STORY
> WILL END HAPPILY

Conventions of Romantic Fiction

Here is an extract from a romantic story published by Mills and Boon, who sell millions of such novels every year. Mills and Boon actually advertise a tape for would-be writers of romantic fiction. On this tape a voice tells the writer what ingredients a love story should contain. We will try to identify the conventions for ourselves.

| **Cage of Ice**

Sally Wentworth | They could only kiss avidly, their desire in no way abated despite the frenzied passion of their embrace.

But then suddenly Ace put his hands on her arms and pushed her away from him, holding her there, his breathing ragged and uneven. The snow fell softly, settling on their hair, melting on their skin, their grasping breath sending it whirling into the night. 'Oh hell!' he muttered forcefully, his mouth twisted as if he were in pain. 'I knew that you meant trouble from the first moment I set eyes on you.'

'What?' Still dazed by desire, Domino looked at him without understanding. She wanted to be held in his arms again, for him to go on kissing her. Every nerve end was on fire and her body ached for his touch, so much that it was like a physical pain. 'Ace' she breathed yearningly. |

Response

The first things we notice are the names. 'Ace' and 'Domino' are not ordinary names, so we can guess that they are the main characters. The setting is romantic: it is night and it is snowing ('The snow fell softly, settling on their hair, melting on their skin . . .') But the most noticeable thing about this passage is the emphasis on emotion – extreme emotion. "Every nerve end was on fire and her body ached for his touch . . . 'Ace' she breathed yearningly."

A Dream World

Does romantic fantasy encourage people to live in a dream world and expect to meet handsome strangers in real life?

Consider this extract from a popular romantic novelist.

Secrets Danielle Steele	She curled up in her bed that night, thinking of him. There was so much about him that she liked, and he was so different now, so much warmer and more open. And the next morning when he picked her up, there was a long-stemmed pink rose on her seat, tied with a white ribbon. "For you, mademoiselle." He held it out to her, and she took it, pleased. It was a lovely way to start the day.

Activities

1. Look at the following ingredients of popular romances and make notes on each of them, using the questions as a prompt.
   * Glamorous setting – What is a glamorous setting?
   * Central Female Character – Why is a woman usually the central character?
   * Handsome Hero – What makes a man handsome?
   * Emotional Involvement
   * Emotional Problem
   * Happy ending – What is a happy ending?
2. In pairs, choose a short romantic story from the 'Sweet Dreams', 'Heartline', or 'Mills and Boon' series, and read it carefully. Next, divide a piece of paper into six columns – one for each of the ingredients in Activity 1 – and list the details of these ingredients in the story you have chosen.

Romantic or Real?

Here is a story – told alternatively in 'romantic' and 'realistic' versions. As you read the stories, try to identify the following conventions:

* Beautiful heroine
* Romantic setting
* Passionate emotion
* Happy ending

Jane Rogers

True Romance

First Look

1. *At last, across the crowded room, he managed to catch her eye. She gazed back at him, arrested, beautiful and unselfconscious as a wild creature facing a man; curious, but entirely other. She was lovely, and he knew then he must have her. It was love at first sight.*

2. I really can't remember.

First Kiss

1. *She looked forward to Sunday all week, and time passed so slowly it seemed more like a year. But like all good things, it proved a day well worth waiting for. There was a gusty, fitful wind and brave silvery sunshine, with fleecy little clouds racing across the great bare sky. He was waiting for her at the gate, as he said he would be, and his stern tanned face broke into a wide smile as he saw her battling against the wind towards him. He helped her over the gate and they walked together along the clean-washed beach, leaning forward into the wind, breathless and laughing. There was no need to talk – they were together. He reached for her hand, and she allowed his to brush hers, then teasingly drew it away. He glanced at her, her eyes were sparkling with delight. Light as a leaf in the wind she spun away from him across the sand, her laughter tinkling behind her – and danced down to the sea's edge. He started to move after her, then froze for a moment as his heart lurched to a sudden love for her, as she ran, abandoned as a child, towards the sea, her blonde hair streaming out behind her. As he watched she reached the water's edge and stopped, a tiny fearless figure facing the great blue ocean, as if unaware of, or defying, the dangers and terrors those deeps held. He yearned to protect that fearlessness, to guard that innocent trust; to stand with her, to face together that great hazardous sea.*

With a sense of passionate urgency he ran towards her, and as he approached she seemed to sense him and she turned to meet him. He grasped her violently in his arms and bent his lips to hers in a kiss that ran through her lips and body like a fire, melting her to him, fusing them together, man and woman, one being, in the promise of love.

2. On Sunday we were supposed to be going for a walk. It was very windy. I didn't want to go, when it came to it; it looked cold, and I was sure we would run out of conversation. We couldn't agree on where to go, I knew the wind would be terrible on the beach, coming straight off the sea, and I wanted to go along the valley which was at least reasonably well sheltered. But he wanted the beach. Which is where we went in the end. I was right, the wind was fierce, the spray spattered on us like rain. He was very jokey and talkative to begin with, talking about a film he'd seen last night (on his own?) and making jokes about English summers. But going along that beach was hard work. You had to keep your head down and your eyes half closed to stop the sand getting in; lean at a forty-five degree angle forwards into the wind; and shout at the top of your voice if you wanted to be heard above the roaring and crashing. I was wearing my anorak and it blew up with air so that I must have looked like a walking Michelin man. I just couldn't think of anything to say. Every now and then I could feel he was looking at me, so I'd look back at him and he'd give a smile or else look away quickly, so in the end I felt awkward and didn't know where to look.

After a bit he started talking, asking me things, I could hardly hear a word and had to keep screaming 'What?' and pointing to my ears to show I couldn't hear. He was asking me about my family and how long we'd lived here. Deliberately thinking of things to keep a conversation going. I wanted to say, if he must talk, why not go up further over the sand dunes so we'd be more protected? But I felt embarrassed to suggest it – couples go in the dunes – and anyway it would have meant we'd *have* to talk. When he gave up for a minute I ran off in front of him, partly to escape the next 'what?', partly because I was beginning to feel such a lump, plodding along. It would look as if I was enjoying it. I was, in a way, but it felt so awkward. I could have cheerfully run on, away, at full speed. He came running after me so I really put a spurt on, but he caught up with me in the end – grabbed my arm and I fell over on the sand. He leant over close to pull me up but instead of letting myself be pulled up I grabbed at his hands and pulled him sideways, so that he stumbled and fell heavily. I got up and stood laughing at him. But I felt awkward. I'd been too violent. I must have seemed like a silly kid – horse play. Was he trying to pull me towards him? I felt completely embarrassed, and started walking on. He caught up with me but didn't say anything. We walked back most of the way in silence. When we got to where the track meets the beach he stopped, poking a shell around with his toe in the sand. Then he picked it up again and said, 'Look.' I went to take it from him and he grabbed my hand. 'What?' I said, feeling foolish. I wished he'd get on with it, I could feel myself going red. He pulled me near and kissed my mouth, then he let go my hand and put his arm round my neck. He was pressing my head to him. He didn't just kiss me, he kept his mouth there, I couldn't breathe. I pushed at his chest and he drew back looking at me in surprise. I laughed, to excuse myself, and ducked under his arm and started to run up the beach. He would think I was stupid, I didn't know what to do. I wanted him to kiss me – I suppose I did – but not – I didn't know what I was supposed to do. Should I have taken my mouth away to breathe then kissed him back? I thought it would look as if I was too eager. I couldn't bear him to know no one had kissed me before.

Every time I thought of it afterwards I went hot with embarrassment; he would think I was a kid.

First Morning

1. *He bent over her sleeping head and whispered, 'I love you.' She stirred softly, and reached out her arms. Then she opened her eyes slowly and smiled at him. They embraced again.*

'I'm so happy,' she said.

'You look like a fluffy little bird,' he whispered, stroking his hand over her rumpled curls. 'My little nest bird!' Gently, he kissed her lips, her eyes, her cheeks, pulled her tight to him again. 'I could stay here forever.' She turned her bright head away from him suddenly – 'Look! It's snowed!' He raised his head to look. Excited as a lovely child she jumped out of bed and ran to the window and clapped her hands.

'It's deep! It's perfectly white everywhere – oh look!'

Rapt, she stared out. He gazed at her profile, pure as a marble statue in the reflected snow light. She turned to him. 'It's for us,' she said. He looked puzzled. 'It's like a new world – everything clean and beautiful, all the dirt and ugliness is covered up, a beautiful white sparkling world – a world for lovers – our new world!' Moved, he got up and went to stand by her. Together they looked out at the dazzling unfamiliar scene.

'We must go out!' she exclaimed. Turning to him, pleading as she saw his expression. 'Just for a little, just to run around and make some footprints. To show we know it's for us!' What a creature of impulse she was! She would be lovely in the snow, but standing here warm beside him, she was even lovelier. He pulled her more closely to him. 'Come back to bed first,' he breathed, in a voice thick with desire. With a mysterious little smile playing at the corners of her mouth, she tilted back her head and surveyed him. She was Cleopatra, mistress of love's secrets, artful. Then as suddenly she was close to him again, surrendered, loving, abandoned in her generosity. He carried her to the bed, watching her precious, familiar ever-new face, entranced; she was all women; like a beautifully cut diamond her many magical sides sparkled and complimented each other. This everchanging love could never end. Burying his face in her hair, he said softly, 'I love you. I love you.' Raising his head thoughtfully for a moment, speaking almost despite himself, he whispered to the white snow-lit room, 'It's the real thing.'

2. It didn't seem as if I'd slept but I must have done because I opened my eyes and it was very light in the room – it was white. The light seemed unnatural, glaring. My eyes were watering like an old woman's. I turned my head and I could see his shoulder and hair. Carefully, I lifted up the bedclothes and got out of bed. He didn't move. I felt as if I would crack when I moved my legs apart. Very quietly I opened the door and went to the bathroom. The first thing I did was look in the mirror. I half expected – I don't know – to see a different face. At least to see that it had registered somewhere. I expected to look sensual, or experienced, or something. But the same blank face faced me. All its expressions were peeled off and it didn't tell me a thing. It didn't look secretive either. I went to the toilet and then I noticed the blood on my thigh, a thick black smear, dried. My stomach went tight. I started

rubbing at it, then I wet some toilet paper and rubbed and scrubbed till it had gone, leaving a red scratched patch on my leg. I filled the sink and washed myself between the legs. It was sore.

When I'd finished I sat on the edge of the bath with the towel around me, I was cold but I didn't want to move. I felt as if I couldn't do anything. I wanted a mother or someone like that to take charge. What happens next? What when he wakes up? I wanted to be alone. I couldn't bear him to look at me till I knew what I was. I was like someone who's had an accident; they don't feel anything for a while, they're numb. I tried to think about it. But I felt nothing. I told myself, 'You've done it at last, you're like everyone else now. The barrier's down.' I tried to laugh at that, but my stone face refused to move. I didn't want to think over the details of it. 'You were glad when it was finished,' I told myself. That must be wrong. I didn't like it. It seemed like nothing.

I remembered I'd read about a custom in a tribe somewhere – in Africa, I expect. Just before a girl is married they keep her away from all the men, in a hut with her mother and all women relatives, and they prepare her. The night before the wedding they have a great feast and dance, with masks and music, a great ritual, the bride dances among the women and the music gets more and more frenzied, beating and beating, and at the climax the headman – with them all watching – he does it to her with a stick, a special kind of stick. And they all sing and celebrate when he shows the blood. They all rejoice. Then her women take her back and clean her and help her, and she meets her husband the next day, without that awful virginity between them. When I read it, it revolted me. Now I wish it had happened to me. Now I wish it had happened to me. It wouldn't be like nothing then; it would really be something.

I noticed the whitish light again and knelt on the toilet seat and lifted up the mucky net curtain to look out. It had snowed – everywhere was covered in white. I started to cry. It was utterly still out there, everything buried under thick snow, and the sky seemed low, deep grey; nothing moved. The whole world had changed in the night. I didn't want to be alone there. I thought we would be together. I did feel pleased in a way, that I'd done it – just because I had, like smoking your first cigarette. But it should be more than that. I was ashamed of my thought, because it made me even more separate from him. The tears kept rolling down my cheeks. I could keep them going, it was soothing. I stopped suddenly. I could see myself. *Wanting* to feel sad. I wasn't sad. I didn't feel anything.

I stay very still now, kneeling, looking out. My head is empty, I stare at the white snow and think nothing and feel nothing except the stillness.

I stare at it till my eyes are full of whiteness, my head is full of whiteness like a million empty pages; it doesn't matter, it hasn't even happened. Nobody knows it's happened except me, maybe it didn't even happen. What would make it real? Nobody knows, it's nothing. Nothing can matter; nothing matters to me. I am snow.

But I imagine him. The ice cracks. I see what he might see. Wondering where I am, coming quietly to the door and listening, then pushing it open slightly. Seeing me kneeling there with the towel round me looking out at the snow. I can see the picture he would see, the narrow brown shoulders and slipping towel and pink feet sticking out soles upwards. The separate captive creature staring out. His heart would melt. He'd come and put his arms around me. He would love my singleness. Yes!

I am posing.

When I went back to the bedroom I was nearly blue with cold but I felt fairly controlled. It was as if I'd put a great distance or age between myself and it. But he was still asleep! I could hardly believe that, it seemed to deny that I existed. I got dressed.

As I was putting my shoes on he woke up. 'Are you up already?'

'Yes.'

'Oh.' I stood for a moment waiting as if my feet were touching a crack in the ice. Say 'Come here', say 'I love you', say 'Are you all right?' He didn't say anything. I went to the window quickly, but my face was burning because he watched me walk.

'It's snowed.'

'Has it?'

'Yes.' Silence. Suddenly he sat up violently and said: 'I'm starving, it always makes me hungry. Let's go and buy some stuff to cook a big breakfast. Pass my jeans – on that chair.'

I couldn't believe it. 'It always makes me hungry.' While he got dressed I kept looking out the window. But he didn't even notice. He went to the door. 'Are you coming?' He started to go downstairs. He was behaving as if nothing had happened. Well? Nothing had happened.

But I felt frightened, as if I'd thrown something away without knowing its value. I remembered that he'd never even said 'I love you'. I'd been cheated.

Activity

In this story the romantic is placed alongside the realistic. Choose an incident in your life when things went sadly wrong. Describe this in an honest, realistic way. Then write another version, in which things happen as you wished they had.

Romantic writing and advertising

This story appeared in national newspapers like *The Times* as a full-page advertisement for Volvo cars.

We hadn't been back to Skye since our honeymoon, but nothing had changed.

Lochalsh was just as breathtaking, Helen just as lovely.

"You're still an admirer, then?" she said, indicating the Volvo.

"More than ever," I replied fervently, and it was quite clear that I didn't mean the car.

Which was a little awkward, considering we'd been divorced for nearly three years.

The timely arrival of the ferry saved me from further confusion and we were across the lock and heading for Harlosh before Helen asked the inevitable questions.

"So what are you doing here? A sentimental journey?"

"Not at all," I replied a little too quickly. "I had some business in Inverness and, well, it's a chance to try out the car. I only took delivery on Monday."

Helen must have caught a note of pride in my voice, for she snuggled deeper into the leather seats and looked up impishly at me.

"A little extravagant for you, isn't it?"

"It cost £19,800 excluding number plates and delivery." I said mildly.

"For that I get a 2.3 litre, turbocharged, fuel-injected engine, capable of speeds far in excess of anything I need these days, but pleasing all the same."

"It's extremely comfortable, as you may have noticed, very reliable and it has a hint of luxury that I not only like, but feel I've earned."

The smile faded from Helen's face.

"Were we part of the price?"

There was no answer to that, so I didn't attempt one. To give myself a breathing space, I slipped a tape into the player and filled the car with Thelonious Monk.

For the next few miles, Helen seemed lost in the music, whilst I was pleasantly absorbed in noting how effortlessly the 760's new suspension coped with the bumpy, twisting mountain road.

And then, inevitably, the nearer we got to Harlosh, the farther back my thoughts drifted.

Thirteen years ago, I had driven down this same road, in the same make of car, with the same girl in the passenger seat.

My first love, my first car. I'd no idea what happened to the Volvo, but Helen and I had followed a well-trodden path.

We hadn't so much drifted apart as sailed full steam in opposite directions, both of us so busy building our separate careers that one day we found we'd made separate lives as well.

"Richard?"

Her voice cut through the Monk and the memories and I looked across at her.

"Were you surprised to see me at the ferry?"

I nearly choked.

Surprised? Just because I drive into a remote Scottish port that I haven't visited for thirteen years and find my ex-wife waiting at the dockside, calmly asking for a lift to the hotel where we'd spent our honeymoon?

"Not at all, I always keep in touch with old friends this way." I said flippantly, and instantly regretted it when I caught the flash of pain in her eyes.

"I came up here to do some research for the rag," she volunteered, "and I suppose the fact that it would have been our anniversary put the idea into my head."

"Anyway, when I saw the Volvo drive up, I thought God, wouldn't it be funny if it was Richard and then when you got out . . ."

"It wasn't so funny after all," I finished for her.

"Something like that."

There was an odd note in her voice and I waited, wondering what was coming next.

"Do you remember that old Volvo we had?"

I thought of the battered snapshot in my wallet and said nothing.

"No electric sun-roof," she continued, "no electronic climate control, no electronic anything, but it was a sweet little car."

Ahead of me the lights of Harlosh flickered in the gathering gloom, and I slowed, searching for the turning to the hotel.

"What do you think happened to it, Richard?"

"Knowing Volvos," I said casually, "it's probably still going strong."

"Unlike us," murmured Helen in a voice so low I could barely catch it.

I counted silently to three, took a deep breath and plunged.

"We should be there in time for dinner, if you'd care to join me?"

"For old time's sake?" she asked. I shook my head and thought, oh well, in for a penny, etc.

"They say the average life of a Volvo is about twenty-one years," I said carefully.

Helen merely looked at me.

"It occurred to me." I went on, "that if you're not doing anything for the next decade or so, we could put this one to the test."

Then she said quietly, "Don't you trade your car in every three years or so?"

"Usually," I replied and noticed I was gripping the wheel a little too firmly.

"But just lately I've learnt that some things become even more valuable, the longer you hold on to them."

"I am," said Helen slowly, "quite remarkably hungry."

The new Volvo 760 Turbo

Activities

1. Explain why this is a romantic story. Look at
   a   the setting
   b   the situation
   c   the language
   d   the characters
   e   the ending.
2. Write a paragraph explaining what we learn about Volvos from this story.
3. Write a short story in the same style, to advertise the Honda Prelude. Include the following information:

> Honda Prelude Sports Car
> 4 wheel steering system
> 4 wheel suspension
> 4 wheel anti-lock braking
> 2.6 litre engine
> 16 valve engine
> Racing car bonnet shape
> Wide glass area

Introduction

The second genre of story we shall look at is the horror story. You may think that they are a very modern sort of story, but some of the earliest novels in English were horror stories (they developed, in fact, from those atmospheric novels mentioned in Unit 4.3). The original *Frankenstein* was written by Mary Shelley in 1816. Bram Stoker's *Dracula* is probably the most celebrated of all horror stories. We can tell something about the genre just by looking at the covers of some paperback books. Horror stories clearly promise to be terrifying. They deal with the stuff of which nightmares are made.

Activities

1. In pairs discuss the following:
   - ◆ Fear: Why do people pay to be frightened at fairgrounds, in cinemas and in novels?
   - ◆ Dreams and nightmares: find out whether your partner
     a   dreams often or rarely,
     b   has vivid, memorable or recurring dreams,
     c   thinks dreams mean anything important,
     d   can describe a particularly striking dream or nightmare.
   Jot down your ideas and report to the class.

2. Next, write a description of a dream weekend, followed by an account of a nightmare weekend.

The Conventions of Horror

Most horror novels deal with the supernatural, that is, events which appear to be beyond ('super') what is normal ('natural'). They deal with vampires, zombies, ghouls, werewolves, living corpses, poltergeists, satanic possession, ghosts, monsters – and the counter-forces of good, usually symbolised by the crucifix. Horror novels are usually very 'moral', and end with the triumph of good over evil. The setting is frequently a remote isolated place – a moor, a deserted house or an island.

Here are some of the conventions of the horror story:

- ◆ A deceptively calm, quiet opening,
- ◆ A strong, good central character,
- ◆ A supernatural element (usually evil or threatening),
- ◆ A victim or series of victims,
- ◆ A series of setbacks,
- ◆ The ultimate triumph of Good over Evil.

Some horror stories may not have all these conventions – or they may include different ones. The above are the most common ones.

The Language of Horror

As you read the following extracts, concentrate on the words the writers use to create an atmosphere of fear and horror. The first passage describes a vampire attacking his prey, the second a black mass. . .

Salem's Lot

Stephen King

"Come, false priest. Learn of a true religion. Take my communion."

"No! Don't . . . don't –"

But the hands were implacable. His head was drawn forward, forward, forward.

"Now priest," Barlow whispered.

And Callahan's mouth was pressed against the reeking flesh of the vampire's cold throat, where an open vein pulsed. He held his breath for what seemed like aeons, twisting his head wildly and to no avail, smearing the blood across his cheeks and forehead and chin like war-paint.

Yet at last he drank.

Commentary

In this extract, Barlow, who has become a vampire, overpowers a priest who has lost his religious faith. The language reinforces the horror. Understanding comes to Callahan 'in a ghastly flood'. The vampire has 'reeking flesh' and a 'cold throat', but the real horror comes from the significance of the situation: we know that if Callahan submits he too will become a vampire, so when we read 'yet at last he drank' we know that he is doomed.

Here is an extract from a Dennis Wheatley novel *The Devil Rides Out*, in which a girl, Tanith, is watching a Black Magic ritual.

The Devil Rides Out

Dennis Wheatley

'They are mad, mad, mad,' she found herself saying over and over again, as she rocked to and fro where she stood, weeping bitterly, beating her hands together and her teeth chattering in the icy wind.

The dance ceased on a high wail of those discordant instruments and then the whole of that ghastly ghoul-like crew sank down together in a tangled heap before the Satanic throne. Tanith wondered for a second what was about to happen next, even as she made a fresh effort to drag herself away. Then Simon was led out from among the rest and she knew all too soon that the time of baptism was at hand. As she realised it, a new menace came upon her. Without her own volition, her feet began to move.

In a panic of fear she found herself setting one before the other and advancing slowly down the hill. She tried to scream, but her voice would not come. She tried to throw herself backward, but her body was held rigid, and an irresistible suction dragged at each of her feet in turn, lifting it a few inches from the ground and pulling it forward, so that, despite her uttermost effort of will to resist the evil force, she was being drawn slowly but surely to receive her own baptism.

The weird unearthly music had ceased. An utter silence filled the valley. She was no more than ten yards from the nearest of those debased creatures who hovered gibbering about the throne. Suddenly she whimpered with fright for, although she was still hidden by the darkness, the great horned head of the Goat turned and its fiery eyes became fixed upon her.

She knew then that there was no escape. The warnings from Rex and her mother had come too late. Those powers which she had sought to suborn now held her in their grip and she must submit to this loathsome ritual despite shrinking of her heart.

Commentary

The author here carefully chooses words which have disturbing associations, in order to increase the tension and feeling of horror. The girl, Tanith, starts by repeating the word 'mad' and weeps 'bitterly, beating her hands together'. The 'icy wind' adds to her discomfort. As well as the weather and the sight of the 'ghastly ghoul-like crew', the sounds too are discordant: the instruments make a 'high wail' and 'weird unearthly music'.

The tension increases and the attention turns to the girl. She is in a state of panic, tries to scream, 'but her body was held rigid' and as she feels the evil forces pulling her towards them she 'whimpers with fright'. She realises that she 'must submit to this loathsome ritual'. Just as in the Stephen King extract, evil seems to be triumphing over good. We need the reassurance of a happy ending otherwise we would go mad!

Activities

Jot down the three things that most frightened you when you were young (or still do!). These might include:

| SPIDERS | SCENE FROM A FILM, VIDEO OR TV PROGRAMME | THE DARK |

Build on this to write a short story that conveys fear and terror. It does not have to involve lots of blood; look at how Dennis Wheatley achieves those effects. Decide whether you are going to tell the story from your point of view. You may include as many of the conventions of the horror story as you wish.

Ghost Stories: Assignment

A related, but slightly less horrific genre is that of the Ghost Story. Here is an assignment, based on *The Birthday Present* by Marjorie Darke. It is meant to be done in class as a piece written under controlled conditions.

Instructions

For question one, you will be asked to make notes under three headings and then use your notes in a continuous piece of writing. You may find it useful to draw up the chart below for your notes.

1. As readers we expect certain things of a ghost story. These features might be typical characters, setting, objects, atmosphere and feelings.

   a Before you read Marjorie Darke's story, jot down some typical features of ghost stories.
   b After you have read the story,
     i) jot down examples of the features you expected to find;
     ii) jot down some of the things which surprised you about the story and which you did not expect to find.

BEFORE READING	AFTER READING	
Typical features	What I expected	What I did not expect

Now use your notes to answer the following question:
Is *The Birthday Present* a typical ghost story? Give reasons for your answer and support what you say with examples from the story.

Make sure you include all the points and examples from your notes. Use the three headings to help you structure your answer. Write at least three paragraphs. (35 marks)

A Ghost Story

from *The Birthday Present*

by Marjorie Darke

Kevin has just managed to escape from his mother, Mam, and an old neighbour, Fatty Scrimshaw. Fatty has been going on about the blitz. Kevin's mother does not approve of his skateboard, a birthday present from his brother, Dave; she calls skateboards 'Old Lady Killers'. And she certainly doesn't like him going out on a Saturday night when his team has been playing Spurs . . .

I didn't waste any more time. Reckoning that the tea-making would take about five minutes, I pulled my skateboard from behind our Dave's old cardboard box, where he keeps his motorbike spares, buzzed out of the flat and was three flights down before I heard Mam calling:

5 'Kev . . . Kevin!'

I kept going. It would mean a belting when I got back, but it was worth it. There were two routes to the place where I was heading. The long way is all streets, but there's a short cut through the cemetery. It's a bit weird when it gets dark. Orange light from the naphtha lamps on the main road, drips through the trees and makes

10 these spidery shapes which grab at you when the wind gets up. There was a stiff breeze now, but I risked it. After all I'd had to hang about long enough already. By this time it was getting pretty dark and the gravestones stood up like giants' mossy teeth – huge and gappy. The breeze made the trees dip and scratch with knotted twig fingers. They aren't too well looked after – the trees I mean – and they hang

15 down low. So you can imagine what I felt like when one combed my hair for me! I did this Olympic jump about six miles high. There was a smell too. I tried to think what it reminded me of, but was in too much of a tearing rush to work out. I was glad to get shot of the place and reach the jetty, I can tell you! Gave me the creeps it did.

20 Galloping across the waste ground at the end of the jetty, I arrived at the main road which circles our town. Part of this road is up on stilts with other roads crossing beneath. There's a subway tunnel as well, for people on foot. It forks at the far end – left to the station and right to Jakes Road. Skateboarding isn't allowed, but lots of kids do. It's okay so long as you keep your eyes peeled for nosy parkers

25 who'll tell on you.

It was really dark when I got there. A queer purplish sort of gloom that reached towards the subway, but got cut off by the bright strip lighting. I could hear traffic zooming along the main road. The usual weekend stream of cars making for the pubs. One or two people in their Saturday gear were walking through the subway –

30 no one that mattered. I put my skateboard down. A couple of left-foot pushes and I was on my way, doing this knockout slalom loop round a bloke in cowboy boots and a black velvet suit. Then curving sharp left so as to miss an Indian woman pushing a pram.

There are moments when you feel as if everything has dropped together. Balance,

35 timing, confidence . . . the lot. This was one of those times. All the creepy quakes I'd experienced coming through the cemetery, vanished. I felt terrific. I *was* terrific, as I stood, squatted, leaned and snaked from side to side. Fantastic! But I knew it was going to be seventy million times better coming back. Picking up my skateboard, I started up the slope.

40 That's when I first saw him. Up at the top he was. A skinny bit of a kid, standing on skates that were much too big. They looked really weird on the end of his matchstick legs. I couldn't help wondering where he'd found them – at a jumble sale by the look. His eyes were out on stalks in this pinched-up face as he watched me. He didn't look a little kid somehow. His face had a queer sort of old-young look that

45 made it difficult to guess what age he was. But he wore short trousers – which seemed odd on such a cold November night. Huge hands he had too. Hanging off spindly wrists that were sticking out of a sweater ten miles too short. I must admit I felt a bit narked. He'd better not get in the way, I thought, putting my board down

again. I was planning this spectacular nose-wheelie sequence and didn't fancy
50 tangling with a shrimp on rollers out of the ark.

Slap Slap with my right foot and I was whooshing along. Both feet on now. Doing
a ton across the mouth of the tunnel. Timing perfect as I balanced first on four
wheels then on two. I was Boy Skateboard Wonder. Olympic Gold Medal variety!

But I wasn't alone. That kid was just behind. For a minute I felt mad. The nit . . .
55 what did he thing he was doing? But I couldn't stay furious. If I was terrific, he was
out of this world! There was nothing he couldn't do on those mouldy old skates –
turns, spins, figures of eight. I tell you I felt quite jealous!

We swooped up towards the station. I grinned in admiration. I just couldn't help
it. And he grinned back. Then, without having to say a word, we set off like one
60 man, as if we'd been practising for weeks. Weaving, turning, cutting across each
other with split second precision. It was fabulous! Up at the Jakes Road end I
stopped to get my breath. He was just behind and I could see him watching me.
There was a kind of hungry look in his eyes and I knew exactly what he wanted.

'Like a go?' I asked – casually, so he wouldn't guess I was itching to try his skates.
65 He nodded and his pinched white face seemed almost to glow.

'Down and back twice then. Give us your skates.'

We did the swop and I started to buckle on the old skates. I was hearing these
queer echoing crashing sounds at the same time, like voices and thunder crackling
inside seventy-six empty oil drums. I tried shaking my head and the noise dulled
70 down, but didn't go away. It was a bit rattling. To cover up, I fiddled with the skate
straps some more, asking him what he was called.

'Stan.'

The name was in my ears. I wasn't looking straight at him (I was still hunched
over my feet) but I could've sworn his mouth didn't move. He stroked my
75 skateboard as if it was a favourite pet cat, then put it down and shoved off just as
though he'd been doing it all his life.

'Hang on!' I shouted, standing up and staggering like a drunk, as I aimed for the
subway entrance where he'd been heading.

'Wait for me!' I felt a right nana, I can tell you. Twice I nearly hit the deck. On my
80 feet his almost magical skates turned into awkward lumbering booby-traps. I
lurched forward a few paces. Tipped dangerously. Righted myself – only to find he
wasn't there. The noises which had sunk into the background came back, though.
Real noises this time. A bunch of yobs in scarves and bobble hats, with football
favours pinned to their anoraks, were surging towards me. Most were waving cans
85 of beer. Not their first by the yodels and ear-splitting catcalls that echoed through
the subway.

Too late I thought of all Mam's blood-curdling Hooligan tales, as they spotted me
and started calling out:

'Here, look what we've found . . .'
90 'It's Popeye . . .'

'No it ain't . . .'

'Yer it is . . . before he ate his spinach!'

'Give us a go on yer skates, kid . . .'

I wanted to run, but there was no chance with my feet going in all directions. If
95 I'd had my board I might have escaped. In a daft sort of way I half turned, looking
for some bolt-hole, and saw Stan at the mouth of the subway. He was on my board
– my beautiful skateboard.

The yobs saw too. 'Gerroff that skateboard, Skinny!

'Beat it, Stan,' I yelled. 'Scram . . . quick!'
100 The next thing I knew was that one of the yobs had hurled a can at me which
caught my shin and made me hop and curse. Then, of course, I lost my balance and
fell against one of his mates, who shoved me into one of the others, who shoved me
back . . . It got a bit rougher each time. They were laughing, but I felt pretty scared.
The hairs on the back of my neck prickled, and a strong yearning to be in front of
105 our telly watching that crummy film, hit me. Anywhere would be better than here! I
don't know how long they might have gone on tackling and passing me like a
human football, but midway from one to another I caught sight of something

hurtling towards us. Straight and swift as a bullet it came.

Stan. On my skateboard.

110 The yobs had seen him as well. They panicked and tried to get out of the way, but everything was happening too fast and there was nowhere to go. I couldn't move. It was just as if the old skates had grown roots and were keeping me plonk in the middle of the subway. In spite of all the racket and jostle, I felt as alone as if I'd been standing on the moon. I was picturing the chaos to come. There'd be a heap of
115 sprawling bodies, and underneath . . . shattered wreckage of plastic, wood and steel.

But it didn't happen like that.

One of the yobs lunged out, meaning to grab Stan and pull him off the board, but froze where he stood and the look on his face could've curdled ten gallons of milk!

120 For Stan travelled through the lot of us! Yes, through! Like a power-boat slicing water. Even now I don't know how it happened. All I remember of the actual moment is a terrible icy cold, deafening silence that cut off the world, and this strong nostril-tingling smell of mildewed biscuits. How long it lasted is another mystery. A second? A year. It seemed like both. Then noises came back. Noises
125 made by running feet as the yobs scattered, scared to death, leaving me stunned and really alone.

No. That's not true. I wasn't quite alone. My skateboard was lodged against the wall at the far end of the tunnel. No Stan. No skates either I realised as I began to run towards it.

130 Scooping up the skateboard I went on running, my feet taking me across the waste ground and through the cemetery. Running . . . running . . . not noticing eerie naphtha light or bony tree fingers or mossy gravestone teeth this time. I had one goal – HOME!

When I got there, old Fatty Scrimshaw was still in the kitchen. He hadn't got off
135 his favourite subject.

'Wiped out,' he was saying. 'Every man jack, would you believe.' He shook his bald head.

Our Mam was nodding, eyes glued to his face as if this was the very first time she'd ever heard the story. Quivery though I still was, I couldn't help marvelling at
140 the way she could act. She deserved an Oscar!

Old Fatty brought out a large checked hanky and blew his nose. 'Every man jack . . . except the youngest Dreefe lad. They never did find him. Mind you, a lot went missing that night. Funny lad he was. Quiet. Thin as a piece of string, with great big hands.'

145 A queer feeling started under my ears and worked down my neck. Like seventy-eight spiders doing a war dance. There was something I wanted to ask, but the question stuck to my teeth.

'Where'd he gone?' our Mam shouted.

A sigh escaped old Fatty and he shrugged his mountain shoulders. 'Out on them
150 old skates his brother give him of course. You couldn't keep him off 'em. Mind you, nobody saw him go. But I reckon that's what happened. He was really taken with them roller skates. Could've gone on the Halls he was that good.' He leaned towards Mam, and under the kitchen light his eyes showed up damp. 'Time and again he used to go to the top of our street, come whizzing down, turn a figure of
155 eight and stop dead at the front door, neat as you please. I tell you, Mrs. Hollins, if I had one of them new-fangled fifty pences for every time I've seen him do that, I'd be a rich man now.'

Our Mam seemed wrapped in the story. She hadn't spotted me. 'He can't just've vanished.'

160 Old Fatty sighed again. 'There were a lot o' bombs fell that night.'

'You mean they didn't find so much as a hair of his head?'

'Not one. Not even a wheel off his skates.'

All this time I'd been standing still as a goal-post, but he looked away from our Mam and straight at me. Little sparks of light flicked off the damp in his eyes, but
165 he wheezed out a laugh and the wobble ran from his chins into the crinkling skin. 'You don't get skates for your birthday and not use 'em, eh, Kevin?'

170   Our Mam swivelled round in her chair. She was frowning and I started to quake all over again. I heard her say:'Skating . . .' in her centipede-skewering voice. Then she paused and gave a little snort, staring at me. I saw her grim face relax, and her voice came out sort of croaky: 'You've skated on some pretty thin ice tonight, me lad!' Picking up the biscuit tin, she held it out. She was almost smiling.

175   I took a Jammy Dodger and bit it. The smell was oat-sweet, gooey, biscuity. Then I remembered, and there wasn't any need for my question. That was it – biscuits . . . mouldy biscuits. The graveyard smell. I knew. The whole story nearly spilled out of me then and there, specially with old Fatty still damp around the eyes. Maybe it would help if I told? But something held me back. Our Mam got up to put the keetle on again and I slopped into my bedroom, shutting the door.

    'That's two I owe you, Stan,' I said, quiet like so no one else would hear. 'Thanks!'

180   After all, how am I to know when I might need saving again?

2. Imagine you are one of the football fans. In the safety of the pub, you tell your mates what happened in the subway. Re-read that part of the extract so that you can include appropriate details. Write down what the fan told his friends. Write in a way a fan would talk. (25 marks)

3. Study the following extract from a personal essay by Marjorie Darke.

Not a single work can be written without the vital IDEA. Ideas can arrive from anywhere at any time – at a bus stop, watching TV, from conversation, reading books, newspapers – but sometimes they seem to take a mean delight in nipping just out of reach of the sweating writer!

The idea for *The Birthday Present* played this trick, until one day, walking to town through a complex subway system where several paths travelled downhill and met, a boy on a skateboard came sailing past me. His skill was effortless, superb. As he swooped by, a childhood memory was triggered. Myself, enviously watching another boy swooping along the pavement on his new roller skates which had shining steel wheels. From there it was a short step to wondering what these two, present day and wartime boys, would think of each other's skates and skills. It was an even shorter step into imagining them meeting. In fact they could have met, but the wartime boy would be middle-aged. I wanted the immediacy of each boy seeing the other, and that could only be through the medium of a ghost story. Precisely what I wanted to write!

What kind of boys were they, I wondered? Why had the wartime boy died young? It could have been an accident, but more likely in this war-torn city it would have been because of an air raid. In my mind's eye I saw the awful picture of bombs exploding, reducing a row of houses, homes of many families, into heaps of rubble that sprawled across the road. Screaming and thunder of more bombs. Great jets of water from shattered mains, fountained into the air. Then, from beneath a pile of bricks and broken furniture, came a boy. Thin, wearing a tatty version of the splendid metal roller skates I had envied all those years ago, he seemed unhurt, though was curiously pale.

"Thanks, Stan," I said.

Why Stan? I don't know. He was always Stan from that moment? Perhaps he told me.

Who knows?

Write another story in which Kevin and Stan meet up. You may want to build the idea for your story out of Marjorie Darke's comments; you may want to give Kevin and Stan a chance to talk to each other about their lives; Stan may be rescuing Kevin from another tricky situation . . . (40 marks)

Story and Genre

Unit 4.5 Stage Plays

Introduction ◆ Gregory's Girl ◆ Dialogue, Setting, Sound Effects and Characters ◆ Scenes and Movement

◆ *See units 1.4, 3.6*

Introduction

A play is a form of literature that is meant to be performed by actors, whether on stage, in the television studio or on the film set.

In this unit we will concentrate on stage plays, leaving film scripts until Unit 4.10. Plays make prominent use of dialogue, which is supported by stage directions, character notes, sound effects and scene-setting details. Here is the opening of *Androcles and the Lion* by George Bernard Shaw, which shows these features. It is set in Roman times, in the days when Christians were thrown to the lions. Androcles is a Christian. Despite its grim subject it is a comic play.

Androcles and the Lion

A Fable Play

George Bernard Shaw

Setting

Character Notes

PROLOGUE

Overture: forest sounds, roaring of lions, Christian hymn faintly.   Sound effects

[*A jungle path.* *A lion's roar, a melancholy suffering roar, comes from the jungle. It is repeated nearer. The lion limps from the jungle on three legs, holding up his right forepaw, in which a huge thorn sticks. He sits down and contemplates it. He licks it. He shakes it. He tries to extract it by scraping it along the ground, and hurts himself worse. He roars piteously. He licks it again. Tears drop from his eyes. He limps painfully off the path and lies down under the trees, exhausted with pain. Heaving a long sigh, like wind in a trombone, he goes to sleep.*   Stage directions
Androcles and his wife, Megaera come along the path. He is a small, thin, ridiculous little man who might be any age from thirty to fifty-five. He has sandy hair, watery compassionate blue eyes, sensitive nostrils, and a very presentable forehead; but his good points go no further: his arms and legs and back, though wiry of their kind, look shrivelled and starved. He carries a big bundle, is very poorly clad, and seems tired and hungry.
His wife is a rather handsome pampered slattern, well fed and in the prime of life. She has nothing to carry, and has a stout stick to help her along.]

MEGAERA   [*suddenly throwing down her stick*] I won't do another step.   Dialogue
ANDROCLES   [*pleading wearily*] Oh, not again, dear. What's the good of stopping every two miles and saying you won't go another step? We must get on to the next village before night. There are wild beasts in this wood: lions, they say.

MEGAERA   I don't believe a word of it. You are always threatening me with wild beasts to make me walk the very soul out of my body when I can hardly drag one foot before another. We haven't seen a single lion yet.

ANDROCLES	Well, dear, do you want to see one?
MEGAERA	[*tearing the bundle from his back*] You cruel brute, you dont care how tired I am, or what becomes of me [*she throws the bundle on the ground*]: always thinking of yourself. Self! Self! always yourself! [*she sits down on the bundle*].
ANDROCLES	[*sitting down sadly on the ground with his elbows on his knees and his head in his hands*] We all have to think of ourselves occasionally, dear.
MEGAERA	A man ought to think of his wife sometimes.

Activity

The lion in the play has a thorn in its paw. Can you predict what is going to happen next? What do you think would happen after that?

Gregory's Girl

This more modern example is *Gregory's Girl* by Bill Forsyth. The story tells how Gregory, a fourth year boy in a Scottish school, falls for the girl who takes his place in the school football team, Dorothy.

Gregory's Girl

by Bill Forsyth

Scene 6 The cookery class

[*CAROL, LIZ, SUSAN, ANN and others set up the Home Economics room. They are making pastry.*]   — STAGE DIRECTION

CAROL	Did you hear about the trial?
LIZ	Trial?
CAROL	Football trial. Dorothy joined it.
LIZ	And about time too.
SUSAN	Why is it boys are such a physical disaster?
CAROL	Apparently Phil wouldn't let her play.
SUSAN	Too much to lose I expect.
CAROL	Well, she stuck it out and showed him up something rotten.
ANN	Oh God, not pastry. I hate pastry and it hates me. Give me a goulash anyday. It doesn't fight back.
CAROL	She scored three times with him in goal.
SUSAN	Poor Phil.
LIZ	Have you see his moustache?
CAROL	Anyway he's got to pick her now.
LIZ	Men's hair fascinates me. It's so temporary.
ANN	Equal parts of Trex and lard. Isn't that it?

DIALOGUE Short sharp sentences. Often one or two words

DIALOGUE Several people talking at cross purposes

[*The boys are coming in for the lesson. It is a mixed lesson. STEVE is in first. He is a professional. Already he has his bench organised.*]   — STAGE DIRECTION

STEVE   Anyone seen Gregory? He's meant to be working with me . . . oh dear Lizzie, not the hands. Lay off the hands till the last possible minute.

[*GREGORY is late and makes his way through the girls. He is trying to be both charming and surreptitious.*]   — STAGE DIRECTION

GREGORY	Sorry I'm late.
STEVE	Where've you been?
GREGORY	Football.
STEVE	Playing?
GREGORY	No . . . watching from afar.
STEVE	Hands!

Note the short sentences, characteristic of genuine speech

[*Gregory shows him his hands. It is a routine inspection*] STAGE DIRECTION

GREGORY That's just paint there.
STEVE I've got the biscuit mix started, you get on with the sponge and put the oven on, four hundred and fifty degrees.
GREGORY Yes, boss.

[*SUSAN approaches STEVE. She is wearing a worried look and a grotty apron.*]

SUSAN Steve, can you help me out with the pastry mix thing?
GREGORY Hello, Susan.

[*GREGORY is ignored.*]

STEVE Pastry? What pastry? There's more than one kind you know. *What does this reveal?*
Is it rough puff, short crust . . . flaky . . . suet?

[*SUSAN's face is a blank.*]

STEVE Just tell me, what are you making?
SUSAN A meat pie. Margaret's doing the Strudel Soup, and I'm doing the pie. It's the eggs for the pastry that I'm not sure of . . .
STEVE Strudel Soup eh? I'd like to try some of that. It's NOODLE *Which of the exchanges do you find amusing?*
soup, and what eggs? You don't put eggs in a pastry. It's 8 ounces flour, 4 ounces margarine . . .
GREGORY . . . a pinch of salt . . .
STEVE . . . some salt, mix it up, into the oven, fifteen minutes . . . and that's it, okay? No eggs, no strudels, nothing.
SUSAN Is that all? That's *simple*, really easy. [*She wanders off.*]
STEVE To think there are five guys in fifth year crying themselves to *Notice how the speeches become longer here. Why should this be?*
sleep over that.
GREGORY Six, if you count the music teacher.
STEVE Watch your mixing, it goes stiff if you overdo it, thirty seconds is enough. Give me the sugar.
GREGORY It's time you were in love. Take your mind off all this for a while . . .
STEVE Plenty of time for love. I'm going to be a sex maniac first. Start this summer. Get rid of my apron and let my hair down, put love potions in my biscuits. Anyway I want to be rich first, so that I can love something really . . . expensive.
GREGORY You're daft. You should try it. Love's great.
STEVE Who told you?
GREGORY I'm in love. [*He means it. He is abstractedly stirring the sponge *Note the contrast between what STEVE says and what GREGORY SAYS*
mix with his finger.*] I can't eat, I'm awake half the night, when I think about it I feel dizzy. I'm restless . . . it's wonderful.
STEVE That sounds more like indigestion.
GREGORY I'm serious.
STEVE Or maybe you're pregnant, science is making such progress . . . [*STEVE extracts GREGORY's finger from the mixing bowl and starts to wipe it clean.*] Come on, who is it? Is it a mature woman? Did you do anything dirty? Did you wash your hands?
GREGORY Don't be crude.
STEVE Come on! Who is it?
GREGORY You'll just laugh, and tell people.
STEVE Give us a clue.
GREGORY [*Reluctantly*] It's somebody in the football team.
STEVE [*Silent for a moment*] Hey, that's really something. Have you mentioned this to anyone else? Listen, it's probably just a phase . . . is it Andy, no, no . . . is it Pete?

| GREGORY | Come on! I mean Dorothy, she came into the team last week. She's in 4A . . . she's a wonderful player, she's a girl. She goes around with Carol and Susan, she's got long lovely hair, she always looks really clean and fresh, and she smells mmm . . . lovely. Even if you just pass her in the corridor she smells, mmm, gorgeous . . . She's got teeth, lovely teeth, lovely white, white teeth . . . | *GREGORY has come to dominate this scene. Why? What is the purpose of this scene?* |
| STEVE | Oh, that Dorothy, the hair . . . the smell . . . the teeth . . . *that* Dorothy. | |

Questions

1. What kind of person is (a) Steve? (b) Dorothy? Give evidence to support your answer.
2. What do we learn about Susan? Do we learn this from the girls or from someone else?
3. *Gregory's Girl* is a mixture of comedy and seriousness. Find an example of each in this scene.
4. Why do you think the author makes Steve the best cook?
5. Does this conversation sound realistic? Give reasons for your answer.

Activity

1. In small groups, read or perform this scene. Try to visualise the characters, concentrating in particular on the differences between them. Then decide how you could make them sound different. Decide what props you might need. Present the scene to the class. Add your own stage directions.
2. Write a scene in which Dorothy is interviewed for the local paper about what it is like to be a girl in a boys' football team. Write it as a play with, for example, a reporter who asks stupid questions which Dorothy handles very well.

Gregory's Girl was originally written as a screenplay by Bill Forsyth. The film was directed by Bill Forsyth himself and produced by Clive Parsons and Davina Belling for Lake Film Productions. A novel from the film script has been written by Gerald Cole. Andrew Bethell has adapted the screenplay script for the ACT NOW series. He has divided the story into fourteen scenes, avoiding the frequent changes of location and fragmentary pieces of dialogue which are intrinsic to a film script. The play is suitable for reading in class or performance.

Dialogue, Setting, Sound Effects and Characters

Plays can be published in book form, and also in comic book form. Here is an extract from a cartoon version of *Macbeth*. Macbeth has just murdered Duncan, King of Scotland. He returns to find his wife still carrying the murder weapon. Focus your attention on the words – the DIALOGUE, but notice the setting (NIGHT) and sound effects (KNOCKING).

Questions

1. How does Shakespeare create a feeling of horror and fear by:
   a the situation in this scene
   b the words the characters use?
2. What sort of relationship do Macbeth and Lady Macbeth seem to have? Who is the stronger of the two in this scene?

Scenes and Movement

In this example, a photo story has been adapted to illustrate an extract from a play by Edward Albee, called *Who's Afraid of Virginia Woolf!* The rowing couple are meant to be middle-aged, but there is nothing wrong with using a bit of artistic licence. In Edward Albee's play the man is called George, the woman Martha, and this is the start of one of their many bitter arguments:

MARTHA: Well you can go on like that as long as you want to. And when you've done . . .

GEORGE: Have you ever listened to your sentences? Have you ever listened to the way you talk?

In a picture story it looks like this:

Activities

1. Armed with a camera and a playscript, take a series of photographs to illustrate the different stages of one of the scenes above. Mount the photographs on card and attach the appropriate speech balloons.

2. Use the characters in a photo story, or photographs from a colour supplement, to make your own illustrated version of a play. Cut out the word balloons, arrange (or rearrange) the pictures and insert the words from a play you are studying. You will need a good supply of photo stories to do this activity!

   You could, if you wish, draw your own pictures, or cartoons to create your illustrated version. And you do not have to reproduce a scene from a famous play; you could even write your own dialogue.

   Perform the scene and discuss the differences between performance and picture version. (Compare, for example, the 'frozen' moments we see in pictures with the continuous section we see in performance.)

See units 2.2, 2.3

Story and Genre

Unit 4.6 Screenplays and Scripts

Introduction ◆ Reading for Information ◆ The Television Script

Introduction

When we are in the cinema watching a film, listening to the radio, or watching a television programme, whether it is news, documentary or comedy, we are listening to something that has been scripted. Here is an example: the screenplay of the television film of *Sons and Lovers*, a novel by D. H. Lawrence, which tells the story of a mining family. In this scene the body of the eldest son, William Morel, is brought home after his death in London.

Sons and Lovers

Screenplay by Trevor Griffiths

SCENE 67

Interior. Bestwood house, front room. Night.

Down the middle of the cleared front room, six chairs, face to face. In the window, against the lace curtains, Arthur holds up a lighted candle. By the open door, against the night, Annie holds another, the brass candlestick glittering.

SCENE 68

Interior. Bestwood house, kitchen. Night.

Morel stands by the table, staring at his wife. Paul stands by the open back door, holding a lighted candle. Mrs. Morel sits in her chair to the side of the grate. Her face is frighteningly empty. Morel is frightened by it. Morel moves to the front room.

SCENE 69

Interior. Bestwood house, front room. Night.

Morel stares at the chairs.

MOREL   [*To no one*] You niver seed such a length as he is.
ANNIE   [*Leaning out to see better*] Father!
Sounds of wheels in the blackness.
MOREL   He's here.

SCENE 70

Exterior. Bestwood house. Night.
A lamp on the vehicle uncertainly reveals a few thin, pale faces; there are some grunts. Morel goes out to join them. Mrs. Morel comes out from the kitchen. Paul, candle in hand, watches over her shoulder.
Morel's voice: Steady!
Morel and the first of the other men, miners, heave into the candlelight with their gleaming coffin-end. They stagger, taking the steepish step; the dark weight sways. Annie whimpers. Arthur watches, grim, fascinated.
MOREL   Steady! Steady! Now then.
MRS.MOREL   [*Soft singing*] O my son! O my son! o my son, my son, my son!
Paul puts his arm round her waist.
PAUL   Mother! Mother!
MRS. MOREL   O my son, my son, my son!

SCENE 71

Interior. Bestwood house, front room. Night.

The miners inch their heavy way into the parlour. Furniture budges, to let them through. Sweat falls from brows and chins. The coffin is tiltingly lowered onto the chairs. Sweat plops onto it from Morel's face.

MINER [*Very quiet*] My word, he's a weight.

Morel eases the men out roughly. The door is closed. The family is alone in the parlour with the great polished box. Mrs. Morel strokes and strokes the polished lid.

Compare this with the novel's version of the same scene. Look at what is in one that is not in the other.

Sons and Lovers

D. H. Lawrence

At ten o'clock Morel called: He's here!'

Everyone started. There was a noise of unbarring and unlocking the front door, which opened straight from the night into the room.

'Bring another candle,' called Morel.

Annie and Arthur went. Paul followed with his mother. He stood with his arm round her waist in the inner doorway. Down the middle of the cleared room waited six chairs, face to face. In the window, against the lace curtains, Arthur held up one candle, and by the open door, against the night, Annie stood leaning forward, her brass candlestick glittering.

There was the noise of wheels. Outside in the darkness of the street below Paul could see horses and a black vehicle, one lamp and a few pale faces; then some men, miners, all in their shirtsleeves, seemed to struggle in the obscurity. Presently two men appeared, bowed beneath a great weight. It was Morel and his neighbour.

'Steady!' called Morel, out of breath.

He and his fellow mounted the steep garden step, heaved into the candlelight with their gleaming coffin-end. Limbs of other men were seen struggling behind. Morel and Burns, in front, staggered; the great dark weight swayed.

'Steady, steady!' cried Morel, as if in pain.

All the six bearers were up in the small garden, holding the great coffin aloft. There were three more steps to the door. The yellow lamp of the carriage shone alone down in the black road.

'Now then!' said Morel.

The coffin swayed, the men began to mount the three steps, with their load. Annie's candle flickered, and she whimpered as the first men appeared, and the limbs and bowed heads of six men struggled to climb into the room, bearing the coffin that rode like sorrow on their living flesh.

'Oh, my son – my son!' Mrs. Morel sang softly, and each time the coffin swung to the unequal climbing of the men: 'Oh, my son – my son – my son!'

'Mother!' Paul whimpered, his hand round her waist. 'Mother!'

She did not hear.

'Oh, my son – my son!' she repeated.

Paul saw drops of sweat fall from his father's brow. Six men were in the room – six coatless men, with yielding, struggling limbs, filling the room and knocking against the furniture. The coffin veered, and was gently lowered on to the chairs. The sweat fell from Morel's face on its boards.

'My word, he's a weight!' said a man, and the five miners sighed, bowed, and, trembling with the struggle, descended the steps again, closing the door behind them.

The family was alone in the parlour with the great polished box. William, when laid out, was six feet four inches long. Like a monument lay the bright brown, ponderous coffin. Paul thought it would never be got out of the room again. His mother was stroking the polished wood.

Activities

1. First make notes on the differences between the two versions. You could list the differences on a table, like this:

DIFFERENCES IN DIALOGUE	DIFFERENCES IN ACTION/MOVEMENTS	DIFFERENCES IN WHAT IS DESCRIBED

2. Imagine you are Ursula Weekley, D. H. Lawrence's step-daughter. Write a letter to Trevor Griffiths, the writer of the TV version of *Sons and Lovers*, arguing that the play is a travesty of the original. Then write Griffith's reply, stressing the similarities between the two versions.

Reading for Information

Making a film for television

David Leland

Film making is a hazardous and unpredictable process. Even though a film may begin with the words of one person, the writer, ultimately it is the product of many people all involved in a process in which no single individual has complete control. Film making is a communal art. The best way to find out about it, film or video, is to do it yourself.

It may surprise some people when I refer to *Flying into the Wind* as a 'film', and this raises an important point about how television programmes are made. Everything we see on television is recorded on either video tape or film. The same holds true for television drama. Some dramas are recorded on video tape, some on film, and some are a combination of the two mediums.

Watch any television news report and you will soon discover that the visual quality of video (newsreader in the studio) is different from that of film (on location news reports). People differ in their preference between the two mediums, often choosing to work in one rather than the other. My purpose here is not to make comparisons of merit between the two but to explain how video and film are used in the production of television drama, and how a television company prepares and makes television film drama.

In the main, dramas recorded on video tape are shot in studios with specially constructed sets.

The principle of recording drama on video tape is the same as the broadcast of a football match on *Match of the Day*. The action is covered from different angles by several cameras, and a Vision Mixer cuts from one camera viewpoint to another. What the viewer sees is an instant edited selection of several possible images. The finished result is what we see when watching a live television broadcast of a football match.

Unlike a football match, drama is rehearsed and therefore it is easier to control what happens in front of the cameras. In the studio, whole sequences are rehearsed by the actors, camera positions are fixed, and then the scene is recorded onto a master tape, each camera shot being cut together at the push of a button by the Vision Mixer from the control panel.

Anyone who has seen an outside broadcast unit in action will know that the video equipment – cameras, cables and mobile recording units – takes up a lot of space. Like a travelling circus, it's very large and difficult to move. This presents relatively few problems if the action is confined to one location (such as a concert hall or a tennis court), but with a drama where the action is usually spread across several locations, then the practical problems tend to multiply. However, as new video equipment comes into use, exciting possibilities as to how we use video are presented and are waiting to be explored.

Drama shot on film for television tends to be shot almost exclusively on location, i.e. it uses real places to locate the action as opposed to artificially constructed sets. This is not a rule and there are many exceptions – I am merely pointing out the major areas of division.

Film dramas are usually shot using only one camera. The film camera is adaptable and can be fixed to different kinds of equipment to produce different kinds of shot. It can be mounted on a tripod, on wheels, on tracks, carried by hand or mounted on giant cranes or hoists.

Film is recorded one shot at a time. For example: a wide shot will give a general, overall picture of the action rehearsed and performed by the actors; then, perhaps, close-ups of each character's actions and reactions will be shot, and so on. This means that scenes must be enacted by the performers not once but many times. It is often a long, painstaking and meticulous process, taking hours to shoot very short sequences. It requires tremendous concentration and skill from the actors and technicians to produce the required effect.

Unlike video, which has instant playback, when a sequence of action has been recorded on film, the film has to be processed – just like holiday snaps – before the results can be seen.

Sound is recorded separately but technically synchronised so that the dialogue and other sounds can be matched to the visual action of the film. This is the purpose of the clapperboard. Apart from giving a visual record of the scene and shot numbers, the actual clapper marks a visual and sound starting point to which sound and vision can be synchronised to play back in the viewing studio.

If all the shots (or rushes) of a particular sequence are strung together, what one sees is a disjointed sequence of actions, often with some of the sequence repeated several times, which makes no clear sense.

It is not until the film is literally cut up and joined together with sellotape that the action begins to make some kind of sense and resemble what we expect to see on the screen. This process is called editing and often takes up more time than the actual shooting of the film. What this process entails can easily be discovered by anybody using a Super 8 camera and simple editing equipment.

Birth of a Nation, Flying into the Wind, Rhino and *Made in Britain* were shot entirely on film and on location.

The making of a film has several basic stages of production: writing the script, pre-production, shooting the film, editing, promotion and presentation. Once a script has been written and the company makes a commitment to produce the film (in other words, is prepared to spend its money), then the film goes into pre-production.

Pre-production is an intensive period of time during which all the departments involved in the making of the film prepare for the most intensive period of all – shooting the film. The departments involved include: production department (which includes writer, director and producer, plus the location manager whose job it is to find the locations to shoot the film); the camera and sound departments; the art department, responsible for the design of the film; the wardrobe, make-up and hairdressing departments; and editing, accounts, publicity, electricians, props, construction, transport and (most important) catering. Actors are interviewed and contracted to play the parts in the script.

Shooting a film is a failsafe mission – once you start there is no going back. Each day has been carefully scheduled, each scene has only a limited period of time in which to be rehearsed and shot. Any delay costs money. Big delays may result in whole sequences having to be cut from the script or rewritten in order to fit into a new schedule. If the film is being shot outside then everybody prays for the weather to be kind.

Once a film is shot most of the crew disperse, moving on to other work, while the editor and the director get on with cutting the film. The producer and the writer often collaborate in this process; and the lighting cameraman or woman comes in to grade the colour and visual quality of the final print of the film. Then the film is ready for presentation. On average the time between the finished scripts and presentation – when the public sees the film – is one year.

As can be seen from this brief account of film production, a completed script is only a beginning. Having written the script, some writers want nothing to do with production, preferring to move on to new projects. Some writers would prefer to be involved in the production but are excluded or gently elbowed out of the process by the company. Other writers, having spent a lot of time researching and writing the script, wish to be part of the making of the film and are considered an essential part of the production team. Many directors and writers work closely together, interpreting, changing and rewriting the script as the shooting of the film progresses, which is, in the main, how I worked on these four films.

Questions

1. What does the writer mean when he says 'Film making is a communal art'?
2. What is the difference between film and video? (The differences are suggested in a number of places in the passage.) Make a list of the differences.
3. What do the following terms mean:
   a on location
   b rushes
   c clapperboard
   d editing?
4. What are the various stages in making a film? Make a list of them.
5. What can happen if the weather is bad?
6. Do script writers have much control over the filming?

Activities

1. If you wanted to present this information in the form of a television programme, how would you do it? Write the script!
2. Using information from the passage, but in your own words, write a short article for a Media Studies booklet. Call the article 'How a Television Play is Filmed'. Write between 300 and 400 words.

The Television Script

As we have just seen, some scripts are written with film or television in mind, and then published in book form. (*Gregory's Girl* is an example.) The television or film actors would not have had a book, but a series of loose sheets, probably stapled together.

Here is an extract from 'Yosser's Story' (which was originally a television play, but was later adapted as a playscript), in the series *Boys from the Blackstuff*. This is an extract from the playscript, not the original television script. Yosser Hughes is unemployed and desperate. There is no work in Liverpool, and the authorities are trying to take his three children away from him. He goes to see a priest in the confessional box.

Yosser's Story

from
Boys from the Blackstuff

Alan Bleasdale

Yosser is still sobbing. The priest goes again to take hold of the curtain, but stops. He talks over Yosser's sobs.

PRIEST: A trouble shared in a place of peace my son. A haven. I'm Father Thomas, 'Doubting' for short!

He opens the curtain again as he repeats the 'joke'.

Doubting Thomas.

Yosser has his head resting against the grille, his hands clasped together, knuckles white.

Daniel Thomas. I'm here to help you, Yosser Hughes. Daniel. Don't worry about the 'father'.

YOSSER: I'm desperate, father.

Yosser looks up at the priest, then closes his eyes

PRIEST: Call me Dan. Dan.

YOSSER: I'm desperate, Dan.

Yosser looks up at the priest again. There is a fraction of a manic glance and he tries to laugh. Then he stops instantly. He seems to be screaming silently as he leans back and then brings his head forward to butt the wooden frame surrounding the wire grille. The crucifix above drops down and hits him as he then butts and butts and butts the wire grille.

Questions

1. Do you think that this is meant to be funny?
2. Could this be performed on a stage or in the classroom? What additional information would you need to include if this was written as a television script?

Story and Genre: Talking, Reading and Writing

Unit 4.7 The Elements of Drama: Action, Dialogue and Writing a Script

Introduction ◆ Couples and Conflict ◆ First Couple ◆ Second Couple ◆ Third Couple ◆ Fourth Couple ◆ Writing Your Own Script ◆ Making a Radio Script

◗   *See units 1.4, 2.3, 3.6, 3.11, 3.12*

Introduction

As far as we know, drama originates from ancient ritual and ceremony. If you think about it, modern rituals like weddings and funerals are situations in which we act a part, but – unlike ancient Greek rituals – they involve more speech than action.

In stage plays, movement and positioning on the stage can be a very important part of the spectacle.

Action holds our attention: a film drama such as *Raiders of the Lost Ark* is nearly all action!

Activities

1. Watch a television drama and list the different sorts of action. Identify slow action and fast-moving action. Focus on scenes where there is very little, or no, dialogue.

2. In pairs roleplay a situation in which one person has power and high statu
and the other person low status. Use no words, but suggest status throug
expression, gesture and movement.

Couples and Conflict

You may remember the photostory in Unit 4.5 showing a couple arguing. We
shall use this theme of conflict to look at some of the other elements of drama
namely

- Dialogue
- Scenes
- Movement
- Set

First Couple: Jo and Boy

Here is a conversation between a named girl, Jo, and an unnamed boy.

A Taste of Honey Shelagh Delaney	BOY: JO: BOY: JO: BOY: JO: BOY: JO: BOY: JO: BOY: JO: BOY: JO: BOY: JO: BOY: JO: BOY: JO: BOY: JO: BOY: JO: BOY: JO: BOY: JO: 	Listen, I'm going to ask you something. I'm a man of few words. Will you marry me? Well, I'm a girl of few words. I won't marry you but you've talked me into it. How old are you? Nearly eighteen. And you really will marry me? I said so, didn't I? You shouldn't have asked me if you were only kidding me up. [*She starts to go*] Hey! I wasn't kidding. I thought you were. Do you really mean it? You will marry me? I love you. How do you know? I don't know why I love you but I do. I adore you. [*Swinging her through the air*] So do I. I can't resist myself. I've got something for you. What is it? A ring? This morning in the shop I couldn't remember what sort of hands you had, long hands, small hands, or what. I stood there like a damn fool trying to remember what they felt like. [*He puts the ring on and kisses her hand*] What will your mother say? She'll probably laugh — Doesn't she care who her daughter marries? She's not marrying you, I am. It's got nothing to do with her. She hasn't seen me. And when she does? She'll see a coloured boy. No, whatever else she might be, she isn't prejudiced against colour. You're not worried about it, are you? So long as you like it. You know I do. Well, that's all that matters. When shall we get married? My next leave? It's a long time, six months. It'll give us a chance to save a bit of money. Here, see . . . this ring . . . it's too big; look, it slides about . . . And I couldn't wear it for school anyway. I might lose it. Let's go all romantic. Have you got a bit of string?

BOY: What for?

JO: I'm going to tie it round my neck. Come on, turn your pockets out. Three handkerchiefs, a safety pin, a screw! Did that drop out of your head? Elastic bands! Don't little boys carry some trash. And what's this?

BOY: Nothing.

JO: A toy car! Does it go?

BOY: Hm hm!

JO: Can I try it? [*she does*]

BOY: She doesn't even know how it works. Lord, not like that. [*He makes it go fast*]

JO: I like that. Can I keep it?

BOY: Yes, take it, my soul and all, everything.

JO: Thanks. I know, I can use my hair ribbon for my ring. Do it up for me.

BOY: Pretty neck you've got.

JO: Glad you like it. It's my schoolgirl complexion. I'd better tuck this out of sight. I don't want my mother to see it. She'd only laugh. Did I tell you, when I leave school this week I start a part-time job. I'm leaving Helen and starting up in a room somewhere.

BOY: I wish I wasn't in the Navy.

JO: Why?

BOY: We won't have much time together.

JO: Well, we can't be together all the time and all the time there is wouldn't be enough.

BOY: It's a sad story, Jo. Once I was a happy young man, not a care in the world. Now! I'm trapped into a barbaric cult …

JO: What's that? Mau-Mau?

BOY: Matrimony.

JO: Trapped! I like that! You almost begged me to marry you.

BOY: You led me on. I'm a trusting soul.

Questions

1. What are they talking about?
2. How old is the girl?
3. What do we learn about (a) the boy and (b) the girl?
4. Why does the boy ask 'What will your mother say?'?
5. Read this in pairs. Is it reasonably easy to read? Do either of you want to make changes to make the dialogue flow more easily? Is this natural speech? Give reasons for your answer.

Second Couple: Rita and Frank

Plays are made up of dialogue: exchanges, arguments, speeches – spoken language. In this extract from *Educating Rita*, by Willie Russell, Rita, a hairdresser, meets her Open University tutor. The dialogue in this scene is fast moving, witty and in short sentences.

Educating Rita	FRANK	Will you have another drink? [*He goes to the small table*]
	RITA	[*shaking her head*] If I'd got some other tutor I wouldn't have stayed.
	FRANK	[*pouring himself a drink*] What sort of other tutor?
Willy Russell	RITA	Y'know, someone who objected to swearin'
	FRANK	How did you know I wouldn't object?
	RITA	I didn't. I was just testin' y'.
	FRANK	[*coming back to the desk and looking at her*] Yes. You're doing rather a lot of that, aren't you?
	RITA	That's what I do. Y'know, when I'm nervous.
	FRANK	[*sitting in the swivel chair*] And how am I scoring so far?

RITA   Very good, ten out of ten go to the top of the class an' collect a gold star. I love this room. I love that window. Do you like it?

FRANK   What?

RITA   The window.

FRANK   I don't often consider it actually. I sometimes get an urge to throw something through it.

RITA   What?

FRANK   A student usually.

RITA   [*smiling*] You're bleedin' mad you, aren't y'?

FRANK   Probably.
        Pause

RITA   Aren't you supposed to be interviewin' me?

FRANK   [*looking at the drink*] Do I need to?

RITA   I talk too much, don't I? I know I talk a lot. I don't at home. I hardly every talk when I'm there. But I don't often get the chance to talk to someone like you; to talk at you. D' y' mind?

FRANK   Would you be at all bothered if I did?
        She shakes her head and then turns it into a nod.
        I don't mind. [*He takes a sip of his drink*]

RITA   What does assonance mean?

FRANK   [*half spluttering*] What? [*He gives a short laugh*]

RITA   Don't laugh at me.

FRANK   No. Erm – assonance. Well, it's a form of rhyme. What's a – what's an example – erm -? Do you know Yeats?

RITA   The wine lodge?

FRANK   Yeats the poet.

RITA   No.

FRANK   Oh. Well – there's a Yeats poem, called 'The Wild Swans at Coole'. In it he rhymes the word 'swan' with the word 'stone'. There, you see, an example of assonance.

RITA   Oh. It means gettin' the rhyme wrong.

FRANK   [*looking at her and laughing*] I've never really looked at it like that. But yes, yes you could say it means getting the rhyme wrong; but purposefully, in order to achieve a certain effect.

RITA   Oh. [*There is a pause and she wanders round*] There's loads I don't know.

FRANK   And you want to know everything?

RITA   Yeh
        FRANK nods and then takes her admission paper from his desk and looks at it.

FRANK   What's your name?

RITA   [*moving towards the bookcase*] Rita.

FRANK   [*looking at the paper*] Rita. Mm. It says here Mrs. S. White.
        RITA goes to the right of FRANK, takes a pencil, leans over and scratches out the initial 'S'.

RITA   That's 'S' for Susan. It's just me real name. I've changed it to Rita, though. I'm not a Susan anymore. I've called meself Rita – y'know, after Rita Mae Brown.

FRANK   Who?

RITA   Y'know, Rita Mae Brown who wrote *Rubyfruit Jungle*? Haven't y' read it? It's a fantastic book. D' y' wanna lend it?

FRANK   I'd – erm – I'd be very interested.

RITA   All right.
        RITA gets a copy of 'Rubyfruit Jungle' from her bag and gives it to FRANK. He turns it over and reads the blurb on the back cover.
        What's your name?

FRANK   Frank.

RITA   Oh. Not after Frank Harris?

FRANK   Not after Frank anyone.

RITA   Maybe y' parents named y' after the quality. [*She sits in the chair by the desk*]
        FRANK puts down 'Rubyfruit Jungle'

RITA   Y'know Frank, Frank Ness, Elliot's brother.

FRANK   What?
RITA   I'm sorry – it was a joke. Y'know, Frank Ness, Elliot's brother.
FRANK   [*bemused*] Ah.
RITA   You've still not got it, have y'? Elliot Ness – y' know, the famous Chicago copper who caught Al Capone.
FRANK   Ah. When you said Elliot I assumed you meant T. S. Eliot.
RITA   Have you read his stuff?
FRANK   Yes.
RITA   All of it?
FRANK   Every last syllable.
RITA   [*impressed*] Honest? I couldn't even get through one poem. I tried to read this thing he wrote called 'J. Arthur Prufrock'; I couldn't finish it.
FRANK   'J. Alfred'.
RITA   What?
FRANK   I think you'll find it was 'J. Alfred Prufrock', Rita. J. Arthur is something else altogether.
RITA   Oh yeh. I never thought of that. I've not half got a lot to learn, haven't I?
FRANK   [*looking at her paper*] You're a ladies' hairdresser?
RITA   Yeh.
FRANK   Are you good at it?
RITA   [*getting up and wandering around*] I am when I wanna be. Most of the time I don't want to though. They get on me nerves.
FRANK   Who?
RITA   The women. They never tell y' things that matter. Like, y' know, doin' a perm, well y' can't use a strong perm lotion on a head that's been bleached with certain sorts of cheap bleach. It makes all the hair break off. But at least once a month I'll get a customer in for a perm who'll swear to God that she's not had any bleach on; an' I can tell, I mean I can see it. So y' go ahead an' do the perm an' she comes out the drier with half an inch of stubble.
FRANK   And what do you do about it?
RITA   Try and sell them a wig.
FRANK   My God.
RITA   Women who want their hair doin', they won't stop at anythin', y' know. Even the pensioners are like that, y'know; a pensioner'll come in an' she won't tell y' that she's got a hearing aid: so y' start cuttin' don't y'? Next thing – snip – another granny deaf for a fortnight. I'm always cuttin' hearin' aid cords. An' ear lobes.
FRANK   You sound like something of a liability.
RITA   I am. But they expect too much. They walk in the hairdresser's an' an hour later they wanna walk out a different person. I tell them there's a fad on, y' know like Farrah Fawcett Majors.
FRANK   Who?
RITA   Far-rah Fawcett Majors. Y'know, she used to be with Charlie's Angels.
         FRANK remains blank
RITA   It's a telly programme on ITV.
FRANK   AH.
RITA   [*wandering towards the door*] You wouldn't watch ITV though, would y'? It's all BBC with you, isn't it?
FRANK   Well, I must confess . . .
RITA   It's all right, I know. Soon as I walked in here I said to meself, 'Y' can tell he's a Flora man'.
FRANK   A what?
RITA   A Flora man.

Questions

1. What do we learn about (a) Rita and (b) Frank in this scene?
2. Pick out any sentences and statements which you think are revealing about Rita and Frank and help you imagine their characters.
3. At this point in the play Rita and Frank are virtual strangers. What kind of relationship is developing between them? How well are they getting on with each other? How well are they communicating?

Activity

With a partner, read through the scene again, and prepare a performance of it. You will need to decide how you are going to play the characters and what movements and actions you are going to include.

Third Couple: George and Martha

Who's Afraid of Virginia Woolf?

Edward Albee

GEORGE: There is no moment . . . there is no moment any more when we could . . . come together.

MARTHA: [*Armed again*] Well, maybe you're right, baby. You can't come together with nothing, and you're nothing! SNAP! It went snap tonight at Daddy's party. [*Dripping contempt, but there is a fury and loss under it*] I sat there at Daddy's party, and I watched you . . . I watched you sitting there, and I watched the younger men around you, the men who were going to go somewhere. And I sat there and I watched you, and you weren't there! And it snapped! It finally snapped! And I'm going to howl it out, and I'm not going to give a damn what I do, and I'm going to make the damned biggest explosion you ever heard.

GEORGE: [*Very pointedly*] You try it and I'll beat you at your own game.

MARTHA: [*Hopefully*] Is that a threat, George? Huh?

GEORGE: That's a threat, Martha.

MARTHA: [*Fake spits at him*] You're going to get it, baby.

GEORGE: Be careful, Martha . . . I'll rip you to pieces.

MARTHA: You aren't man enough . . . you haven't got the guts.

GEORGE: Total war?

MARTHA: Total.

[*Silence. They both seem relieved . . . elated. Nick re-enters*]

Questions

1. What reason does Martha give for hating George?
2. Which words convey the extreme emotion being expressed here?

Activity

Write a scene in which a person has a terrific row with someone else. First set the scene and describe the characters. Write about 500 words. Here are some suggestions for your confrontation.

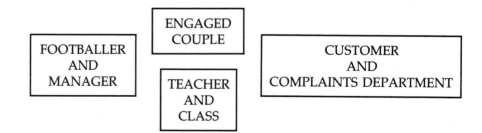

Fourth Couple: Macbeth and Lady Macbeth

In this scene from *Macbeth*, it is the middle of the night and Macbeth has just murdered Duncan, the King of Scotland.

Macbeth

William Shakespeare

[*Enter Macbeth*]

MACBETH: I have done the deed. Didst thou not hear a noise?

LADY MACBETH: I heard the owl scream and the crickets cry. Did not you speak?

MACBETH: When?

LADY MACBETH: Now.

MACBETH: As I descended?

LADY MACBETH: Ay.

MACBETH: Hark! Who lies i' the second chamber?

LADY MACBETH: Donalbain.

MACBETH: This is a sorry sight. [*Looking at his hands*]

LADY MACBETH: A foolish thought, to say a sorry sight.

MACBETH: There's one did laugh in's sleep, and one cried 'Murder!' That they did wake each other: I stood and heard them: but they did say their prayers, and address'd them again to sleep.

LADY MACBETH: There are two lodg'd together.

Question

In this scene, how does Shakespeare create a feeling of tension and fear through the dialogue?

Activities

1. Perform each of these scenes.
2. In pairs, make a tape-recording of the complete conversation in each scene. Choose appropriate background music if you wish.
3. Choose any one of the four extracts involving couples, and copy the dialogue into a box in the middle of a sheet of paper. Next, imagine you are going to direct the scene, and consider all the aspects of performance other than dialogue, as follows:

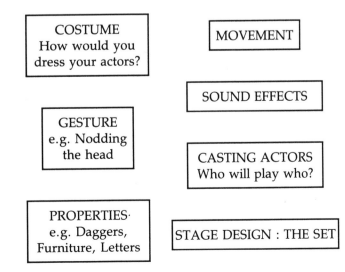

COSTUME
How would you
dress your actors?

MOVEMENT

SOUND EFFECTS

GESTURE
e.g. Nodding
the head

CASTING ACTORS
Who will play who?

PROPERTIES·
e.g. Daggers,
Furniture, Letters

STAGE DESIGN : THE SET

Around your dialogue box, make annotations giving details of all the above aspects in the extract. You could do this by underlining the relevant parts of the dialogue in different coloured pens and drawing lines to boxes containing the appropriate information. So you might, for example, have a line going from the character name LADY MACBETH to a box with the information 'Costume: Long black cloak' in it.

4. Read and then compare three plays or books which explore the subject of love in a divided society where the parents might not want their child to have anything to do with a person from a particular group of people. Here are some suggestions:

Across the Barricades by Joan Lingard
Romeo and Juliet by William Shakespeare
West Side Story (the film script)
Three Minute Heroes by Leslie Stewart
Huckleberry Finn (Chapters 17 and 18) by Mark Twain
Wednesday's Child by Tony Higgins

Some of Nadime Gordimer's books or short stories would be appropriate for this activity as well. Choose at least one play and one short story or novel. This is a longer piece of coursework and you should try to write about 1,000 words for it.

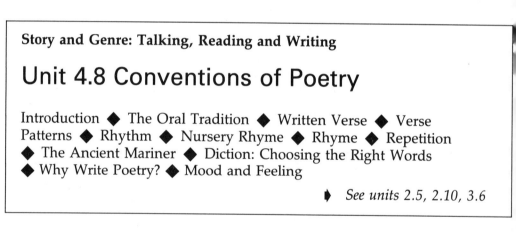

Story and Genre: Talking, Reading and Writing

Unit 4.8 Conventions of Poetry

Introduction ◆ The Oral Tradition ◆ Written Verse ◆ Verse Patterns ◆ Rhythm ◆ Nursery Rhyme ◆ Rhyme ◆ Repetition ◆ The Ancient Mariner ◆ Diction: Choosing the Right Words ◆ Why Write Poetry? ◆ Mood and Feeling

◗   *See units 2.5, 2.10, 3.6*

Introduction

Many of the activities in this unit encourage you to write poems of your own. Grouped together a number of these poems will constitute a coursework unit. Remember what was said at the beginning of this book about drafting. Successful poems are often the product of several drafts.

In Part I (Unit 1) poetry was identified as one of the three main literary genres. But, what is poetry? Here is one explanation from *A Dictionary of Literary Terms* by Martin Gray; 'Verse is discriminated from prose because it contains some element which is repeated, creating a sense of pattern.'

The Oral Tradition

Much good verse is meant to be spoken or sung. Ballads are for singing; rapping is a form of talking verse. Here are two examples: two songs – one from the West

Indies, the other from the USA, both by black artists. They are written down, but, as you read them, remember that they are meant to be heard, not read silently.

African

Don't care where you come from
As long as you're a black man, you're an
  African
No min' your nationality
You have got the identity of an African.
Cos if you come from Clarendon, you
  are an African
And if you come from Portland, you are
  an African
And if you come from Westmoreland,
  you are an African
Don't care etc.
Cos if you come from Trinidad, you are
  an African
And if you come from Nassau, you are
  an African
And if you come from Cuba, you are an
  African
So don't care etc.
No min' your complexion
There is no rejection, you are an African
Cos if you 'plexion high, high, high
If your 'plexion low, low, low
And if your 'plexion in between
You are an African
So don't care etc.
No min' denomination
That is only segregation, you are an
  African
Cos if you go to the Catholic, you are an
  African
Or if you go to the Methodist, you are
  an African
And if you go to the Church of God,
  you are an African
So don't care etc.
Cos if you come from Brixton, you are
  an African
And if you come from Neasden, you are
  an African
And if etc. (with Willesden, Bronx,
  Brooklyn, Queens,
Manhattan, Canada, Miami,
  Switzerland, Germany, Russia,
Taiwan – Fade)

Peter Tosh

The Harder They Come

O they tell me of a pie up in the sky
Waiting for me when I die
They never seem to hear you when you
  cry
So as sure as the sun will shine
I'm goona get my share now, what's
  mine
And then the harder they come, the
  harder they fall
One and all
Ooh the harder they come, the harder
  they fall
One and all.
Well the oppressors are trying to keep
  me down
Trying to drive me underground
And they think that they have got the
  battle won
I say forgive them, Lord they know not
  what they've done
Because as sure as the sun will shine
  etc.
And I keep on fighting for the things I
  want
Though I know that when you're dead
  you can't
But I'd rather be a free man in my grave
Than living as a puppet or a slave
So as sure as the sun will shine etc.

Jimmy Cliff

Traditional folk songs and songs like these which grow out of a particular culture often reveal the many varieties of English that differ from what we call Standard English. Reggae songs, Liverpudlian songs and Yorkshire songs – to name but a few – may be written in a special type of English.

Questions

1. Which of these two songs differs most noticeably from the English used by newsreaders, and how could you show this?
2. Which of the two struck you most obviously as being a song, even though it is in print? What is it that made you think this?

Written Verse

Earlier on in this unit we quoted a definition of poetry which described it as being different from prose 'because it contains some element which is repeated, creating a sense of pattern'. Let us look more closely at the elements in poetry which create this sense of pattern.

Verse Patterns

Verse has a form or shape that can most easily be seen by looking at the physical appearance of a poem or a page of a printed book. At a glance we see that many poems are presented in blocks which we call verses or stanzas, and that verse two is shaped like verse one and verses three, four and five. There is a regularity about the verses, and if the verses are not regular we want to know why, just as we want to know why a church is a different shape and size to a house.

If we examine the rhythm we shall probably find that this, too, follows a pattern, and the rhyme too, may have a pattern. All these structural patterns reflect the pattern of thought and feeling behind the poem.

In the following two poems both blocks of lines (verses) and sounds (rhymes) are repeated.

Roger the Dog

Ted Hughes

What is the rhyme here?

Asleep he wheezes at his ease.
He only wakes to scratch his fleas.

Dog starts asleep

He hogs the fire, he bakes his head
As if it were a loaf of bread.

He's just a sack of snoring dog.
You can lug him like a log.

Description of dog

You can roll him with your foot,
He'll stay snoring where he's put.

I take him out for exercise,
He rolls in cowclap up to his eyes.

Dog goes out. Is he awake? Or is it a flash-back?

He will not race, he will not romp,
He saves his strength for gobble and chomp.

He'll work as hard as you could wish
Emptying his dinner dish.

Then flops flat, and digs down deep,
Like a miner, into sleep.

Dog ends asleep

**The Song of
the Whale**

Kit Wright

Heaving mountain in the sea,
Whale, I heard you
Grieving.

Great whale, crying for your life,
Crying for your kind, I knew
How we would use
Your dying:

Lipstick for our painted faces,
Polish for our shoes.

Tumbling mountain in the sea,
Whale, I heard you
Calling.

Bird-high notes, keening, soaring:
At their edge a tiny drum
Like a heartbeat.

We would make you Dumb.

In the forest of the sea,
Whale, I heard you
Singing,

Singing to your kind,
We'll never let you be.
Instead of life we choose

Lipstick for our painted faces,
Polish for our shoes.

Activities

1. Copy out the verses of these two poems and annotate them as follows:

   ◆ Colour code any words or sounds that rhyme or are repeated. You will need a set of highlighter pens to do this. Your colour coding of the two verses of 'Roger The Dog' should look like this:

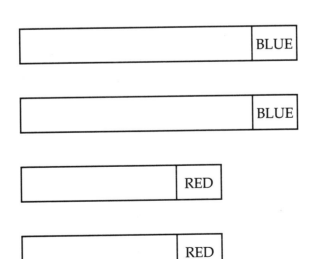

   ◆ Write comments next to each verse, describing the number of lines and the pattern of rhyme or repetition.

Rhythm

Music has rhythm – a good beat is something we all recognise. The beat that forms the rhythm is a repeatedly stressed sound. It is the same with poetry.

The beat can be in the form of a rhythmical pattern, best appreciated when the poem is read aloud. Here is part of a poem about post carried by train. The rhythm of the poem recreates the rhythm of a moving train. The poem was written as part of the soundtrack for a film – so it goes with visual images, too. To 'feel' the rhythm, try reading the poem aloud.

Night Mail

W. H. Auden

Letters of thanks, letters from banks,
Letters of joy from girl and boy,
Receipted bills and invitations
To inspect new stock or visit relations,
And applications for situations
And timid lovers' declarations
And gossip, gossip from all the nations,
News circumstantial, news financial,
Letters with holiday snaps to enlarge in,
Letters with faces scrawled in the margin,
Letters from uncles, cousins and aunts,
Letters from Scotland and the south of France

Activities

1. Continue this poem in a similar style: like this, for example:

    > Letters from Fred, letters from Ted,
    > Letters that will end up under the bed.
    > Letters from cranks and the recently crying
    > Notes about money and the world of buying
    > The trying, the sighing and the endlessly prying . . .

2. Write a poem that matches the rhythm of the sea, a pneumatic drill or a milk float. Think of the sound and the movements of each – the surge and fall of the sea, the bursts of the drill, the whine and then silence of the milk float. Try to make the length of the lines match these 'bursts' of sound.

Nursery Rhyme

Rhyme is part of everyone's childhood. A recent newspaper article suggested that children who had regular contact with nursery rhymes such as *Little Jack Horner*, *Hey Diddle Diddle* and *Jack and Jill*, have a greater feel for language; they can spell and read more easily than those who did not.

> The power of Humpty Dumpty, Jack Horner and the rest of the nursery rhyme gallery lies not in their venerable pedigree but in the fact that they introduce young children to rhyme. And there is increasing evidence from the researchers that a grasp of rhyme and alliteration – in effect, what happens to words when you juggle the old familiar combinations like 'wall' and 'fall', 'Jill' and 'hill', and the hilarious 'jelly, welly, belly' games that small children delight

in, is essential to later progress with language learning.

"It is now very clear that young children who come to school with a good appreciation of rhyme and alliteration – all the things which nursery rhymes and word games give them – are going to have an advantage in learning to read and spell," Dr. Bradley said. "But just as important is the knowledge that for those who don't have those advantages, there are ways helping them to catch up".

Alliteration means using words that start with the same letter (for instance, *the furrow followed free*).

The Nursery Rhyme is a simple form of poem. Here is a well-known nursery rhyme and a limerick – a nonsense poem. Look at the rhyme patterns in each of them.

Jack and Jill
Went up the hill
To fetch a pail of water
Jack fell down
And broke his crown
And Jill came tumbling after.

(Rhyme pattern aa b cc b)

There was a young lady from Ryde
Who swallowed some apples and died.
The apples fermented
Inside the lamented
And made cider inside her inside.

(Rhyme pattern aa bb a)

Activity

Read *Jack and Jill* again and then, working in groups, make up a Nursery Rhyme about a different boy-girl pairing. You might, for example, choose to write about Sue and Lee. Next, brainstorm some words that rhyme with the second of the names you chose, eg:

FEE   AGREE   SEE   THREE   SAFETY

Then write your Nursery Rhyme, using the same pattern of rhythm and rhyme as *Jack and Jill*.

Rhyme

Rhyme, as mentioned in earlier unit, has a number of functions in poetry. It can create humour, or, as in the following extract from Auden's *Night Mail*, help to emphasise the sense of relentless forward movement created by the rhythm.

Night Mail

W.H. Auden

This is the night mail crossing the border,
Bringing the cheque, and the postal order,
Letters for the rich, letters for the poor,
The shop at the corner, and the girl next door.

But do not become a slave to rhyme when you write poetry. Above all, do not force the rhyme!

Traditional	Roses are red Violets are blue Most poems rhyme This one doesn't

There are plenty of other devices you can use to create striking effects in your poems.

Activity

Write a poem with the simple rhyme pattern of *Roger the Dog* on p220.

Repetition

Poetry uses repetition in a number of ways:

- in the rhyme (as in the Nursery Rhymes above),
- in the sounds at the beginnings of the words, as in 'round the rugged rocks the ragged rascal ran' (called Alliteration),
- in the vowels sounds *within* the words, as in 'A host of golden daffodils' (called Internal Rhyme or Assonance).

Repetition can contribute to rhythm. But repetition and rhyme may simply be used by the poet to draw attention to, and emphasise certain words. Always ask yourself 'Why has the poet repeated this?'

The Ancient Mariner

In the following extract from Coleridge's *Rime of the Ancient Mariner*, the poet uses repetition, rhyme and changes of rhythm to create certain striking effects. The Mariner has just shot the albatross that has been travelling with the ship, and the thick fog that had enveloped the vessel has miraculously lifted.

| **The Rime of the Ancient Mariner**

Samuel Taylor Coleridge

Internal rhyme

Inverted repetition | Nor dim nor red, like God's own head,
The glorious Sun uprist:
Then all averred, I had killed the bird
That brought the fog and mist.
'Twas right, said they, such birds to slay
That bring the fog and mist.

The fair breeze blew, the white foam flew
The furrow followed free
We were the first that ever burst
Into that silent sea.

Down dropt the breeze, the sails dropt down,
'Twas sad as sad could be;
And we did speak only to break
The silence of the sea! | *Internal rhyme*

Repetition

Alliteration
Rhythm suggests speed

Rhythm suddenly slows down here |

	All in a hot and copper sky, The bloody Sun at noon, Right up above the mast did stand, No bigger than the Moon.	*Assonance in this verse. Vowel sounds that nearly rhyme*
Repetition gives idea of slow passing of time. *Simile*	Day after day, day after day, We stuck, nor breath nor motion; As idle as a painted ship Upon a painted ocean.	
Rhythm and repetition creates idea of complete lack of movement	Water, water, everywhere, And all the boards did shrink; Water, water, everywhere, Nor any drop to drink.	*Creates impression of breathlessness and thirst*

Activity

Copy out the table below and list all the examples of repetition, rhyme and of fast and slow rhythm you can find in the extract above.

	Repeated words and phrases	Rhyming words	Rhythm: fast or slow – with examples
Verse 1			
Verse 2			

Diction: Choosing the Right Words

Here is the first verse of John Keats's *Ode to Autumn*. Some of the words have been left out. When you have read the poem several times, discuss in pairs which words you would select to fill in the gaps. Work out the rhyme scheme – this will help with two of the gaps. For the other gaps consider words which are in keeping with the rhythm, the sense and the atmosphere.

Ode to Autumn John Keats	Season of mists and mellow fruitfulness, Close bosom-friend of the maturing sun; Conspiring with him how to load and bless With fruit the vines that round the thatch-eaves run; To with apples the moss'd cottage-trees, And fill all fruit with ripeness to the ; To swell the gourd, and the hazel shells With a sweet kernel; to set budding more, And still more, later flowers for the bees, Until they think warm days will never , For Summer has o'erbrimm'd their cells.

Read the rest of this poem. (You will find it in most traditional anthologies.)

Why Write Poetry?

An answer to the question could be arrived at by comparing two treatments of the same subject – one in prose, one in poetry. The subject we are going to look at is the way teenagers are told off.

PROSE EXAMPLE

My Mother and my teacher and my sisters are always ordering me about. I'd run away if there was somewhere to go. I wish more people were kind and considerate like my gran.

VERSE EXAMPLE

Orders of the Day

John Cunliffe

Get up!
Get washed!
Eat your breakfast!
That's my mum,
Going on and on and on and on
    and on . . .

Sit down!
Shut up!
Get on with your work!
That's my teacher,
Going on and on and on and on
    and on . . .

Come here!
Give me that!
Go away!
That's my big sister,
Going on and on and on and on
    and on . . .

Get off!
Stop it!
Carry me!
That's my little sister,
Going on and on and on and on
    and on . . .

Boss
Boss
Boss
They do it all day
Sometimes I think I'll run away,
But I don't know
Where to go.

The only one who doesn't do it,
Is my old gran.
She says,
'Would you like to get washed?'
Or,
'Would you like to sit on this chair?'

People say she spoils me,
And that she's old-fashioned.
I think it's the others that spoil;
Spoil every day.
And I wish more people were
    old-fashioned
. . . like my gran.

Questions

1. How does the poet use language to convey his feelings? What strikes the eye and ear in this poem?
2. Compare the poem with the prose example, noting the differences.

Mood and Feeling

A poem should make you *feel* something. It is a waste of time analysing a poem if it does not move you in some way. Poems frequently create a mood which we can identify and respond to. Here are three moods: sad, cheerful and comic.

In Memoriam (Easter 1915)

Edward Thomas

The flowers left thick at nightfall in the wood
This Eastertide call into mind the men,
Now far from home, who, with their sweethearts, should
Have gathered them and will do never again.

Little Fish	The tiny fish enjoy themselves
	in the sea
D. H. Lawrence	Quick little splinters of life
	their little lives are fun to them
	in the sea.

Mad Gardener's Song	He thought he saw an Elephant
	That practised on a fife
	He looked again, and found it was
	A letter from his wife.
Edward Lear	'At length I realise ' he said
	'The bitterness of life!'

Question

What mood would you be in if you

- failed your driving test?
- saw a baby being born?
- were lying in a warm, comfortable bed on a freezing cold day?
- were waiting to see the doctor?
- were returning to your home town after being away?
- had just had a very expensive haircut?
- noticed from your bedroom window that it had been snowing.

Activities

1. Write a poem about a place where people gather. It could be a shop, telephone box, library, launderette or bus station. To prepare yourself, visit the place you have chosen, soak up the atmosphere and mood, and jot down your impressions as soon as you return home.
2. Read the following poem and discuss its mood. Look at how the mood is created through words and ideas.
   - It might help you recreate the mood if you imagine yourself to be the poet's father talking about his wife. Write what you think he would say about her.
   - What does the last stanza mean?

Long Distance	Though my mother was already two years dead
	Dad kept her slippers warming by the gas,
Tony Harrison	put hot water bottles her side of the bed
	and still went to renew her transport pass.
	You couldn't just drop in. You had to phone.
	He'd put you off an hour to give him time
	to clear away her things and look alone
	as though his still raw love were such a crime.
	He couldn't risk my blight of disbelief
	though sure that very soon he'd hear her key
	scrape in the rusted lock and end his grief.
	He knew she'd just popped out to get the tea.
	I believe life ends with death, and that is all.
	You haven't both gone shopping; just the same,
	in my new black leather phone book there's your name
	and the disconnected number I still call.

PART 5:
LANGUAGE REFERENCE SECTION

When we talk about the English language we are being slightly inaccurate. Such is the diversity of different types of English, we really ought to talk about the English languages. There are numerous varieties of spoken English (called dialects) used in different parts of the country, as well as different types of written English, ranging from the novels of Jane Austen to the graffiti you find in the lavatory. It is all language, but it is all so different!

One of the most prestigious forms of English is the dialect called Standard English. This is the form of English that you will need to use when you are at a job interview, or if you are writing a formal letter, such as a job application. Standard English uses the spelling you will find in a dictionary, and conventions of word order and punctuation that, if you are unfamiliar with them, will put you at a disadvantage.

The best way to learn about language is to look at your own writing, and the writing produced by other students in your group.

Language Reference Section

Unit 5.1   A-Z of Useful Terms

The terms listed and explained in this section are worth getting to know because they will help you to think more carefully about language and to talk more easily about your own writing.

Accent
Regional pronunciation. Everyone in Britain has an accent of some kind. Liverpool (Scouse), Tyneside (Geordie), Glaswegian and Cockney are some of the best-known British accents.
The word accent also means the stress placed on a syllable within a word:
   Ri'chard   Sa'lly   Ela'ine

Allegory
A story in which the episodes and characters have symbolic meaning as well as literal meaning. *The Pilgrim's Progress* and *Animal Farm* are well-known examples of allegories. In *Animal Farm* the takeover of a farm by the animals that live on it and the subsequent conflict between the animals themselves once they have taken control, are symbols of revolution, anarchy and repression on the human level. An allegory is a story that works on two levels.

Alliteration
Repetition of a consonant sound, usually the consonant sound at the beginning of words. Alliteration is a device frequently used by poets:
   The fair breeze blew, the white foam flew,
   The furrow followed free . . . (Coleridge)
but you will also find it in tongue-twisters and advertising jingles:
   Peter Piper picked a peck of pickled pepper;
   Pick up a Penguin.
See **Assonance**.

Ambiguity
A statement that can have two different meanings, such as:
   Toilet out of order – please use floor below;
   Police found drunk in shop window.

Antithesis
A contrast between words, or between ideas. For example:
   To err is human, to forgive divine.
   Many are called, but few are chosen.
   God creates, man destroys.

Archaic
An archaic word is one that has fallen out of use. When an archaic word is used, it is often for effect.
See also **Dated words**.

Assonance
Use of the same or a similar vowel sound in nearby words to create a rhyming effect. For example:
   The cat sat napping;
   A gloomy tomb.

Assonance is sometimes called Internal Rhyme. Like **Alliteration**, assonance is found in poetry, tongue-twisters and in advertising jingles:

Milk has got a lot of bottle.

Circumlocution

A long-winded or round-about way of saying something. For example:

'After an earnest colloquy with the custodian of the vehicle it was agreed that our transportation should be accomplished for the sum of one pound'

is a circumlocution. In straightforward English we would say 'We spoke to the taxi-driver and agreed on a fare of one pound.'

Cliché

A phrase that has become stale or hackneyed because it has been used so often. 'Nice one', 'Go for it', and 'loony left' are all examples of clichés.

Colloquialism

A word or phrase used in ordinary speech, but not used in STANDARD ENGLISH. Words like 'bloke' or 'naff', and expressions like 'to be browned off', or 'to be stony broke' are all colloquialisms.

Dated Words

These are words that have gone or are beginning to go out of fashion. (They should not be confused with **Archaic** or obsolete words which are words that have fallen into disuse and are only found in the writing of earlier centuries.) Most dated words, although they sound old-fashioned, are recognisable to us. They refer to things that we now call by different names. Here are some examples:

DATED	Wireless	Omnibus	LP	Thou
NOW	Radio	Bus	Album	You

Dialect

Regional variety of English with its own words, expressions and usage. Some dialect words and expressions have become well-known outside the regions they originally come from. Examples include the Scottish word 'bairn', meaning child, and 'wee' meaning little. In Lincolnshire dialect 'while' means 'until', which caused considerable problems when British Rail put up the sign 'Wait while the red lights flash'!

Here are some examples of regional dialect usage with their equivalents in Standard English.

NON-STANDARD DIALECT	STANDARD ENGLISH
I looked out the window.	I looked out of the window.
We got off of the bus.	We got off the bus.
She asked the two on us.	She asked the two of us.

It is important to be aware that dialect words and expressions are different from Standard English, because there are occasions – applying for a job, for instance – when you will be expected to use Standard English rather than dialect.

Dialect should not be confused with **Accent**, which refers to the way words are pronounced.

Dialogue

A conversation between two people.
See also **Monologue**.

Diction

The choice or range of words used by a writer or speaker.

Doggerel
Poor quality poetry. For example:
> Our hero then travelled far
> Till he got to Africa
> Where he made a famous name
> Shooting all sorts of big game.

Elegy
A poem with a serious or reflective mood, usually one written on the death of someone. Examples include Shelley's *Adonaïs* (mourning the death of his fellow poet Keats), and Tennyson's *In Memoriam* (mourning Arthur Hallam). Thomas Gray's *Elegy in a Country Churchyard* is perhaps the most famous example of the genre.

Epigram
A short, witty saying, such as:
> I can resist anything except temptation.

Epilogue
A speech at the end of a play, which provides a commentary on the events of the play, for instance, Prospero's speech at the end of *The Tempest*.

Euphemism
A statement or word that expresses something unpleasant in a gentle or more discreet way. For instance:
> She has passed away. = She has died.
> Powder one's nose. = Go to the toilet.
> He's helping police with their enquiries. = He has been arrested.

Grammar
The study of language and the way that it seems to conform to certain rules.

Homonyms
Words which are spelt in the same way but have different meanings, such as:

fair { blonde / just / good (of weather)

port { drink / harbour

Homophones
Words which sound the same, but are spelt differently, such as:
> maize\maze   right\write\rite   fair\fare   rain\reign

Hyperbole
Deliberate use of exaggeration, as in:
> I ate tons of cake
> I've been waiting for ages

Imagery
Pictures created by a writer in order to put across an idea in visual form, or to describe somebody or something in a particular (often a vivid) way. For instance:
> Time like an ever rolling stream bears all its sons away.

is an image that conveys forcefully the inexorable passing of time and the transience of human life.

The following image helps the writer make her description vivid and grotesquely humorous:

His face is overripe
  Wensleydale
Going blue at the edges (Wendy Cope)
See also **Metaphor** and **Simile**

Irony

The deliberate use by a speaker or writer of words whose literal meaning is the opposite of the meaning the speaker or writer intends. Sarcasm is a form of irony intended to be wounding or hurtful, as when you say 'well done' to a goalkeeper who has let in ten goals in a football match. Just as we use sarcasm in everyday speech to criticise or attack a person, so writers use irony to criticise or ridicule something or someone they disapprove of.

Jargon

Specialist language used by a particular profession or group of people, such as lawyers, sociologists or computer programmers. Some words start off as jargon, and eventually work their way into the mainstream of the language. Here is an example of jargon from the world of hi-fi:

PHILIPS\PYE 2A CHASSIS (CTV)

In cases of mains fuse blowing and a low resistance reading between the collector and emitter of BUT11, check that capacitor C2264 has not gone s\c. If it has, replace D6664 as well.

Lyric

A poem expressing personal feelings.
LYRICS are the words of a song.

Malapropism

Use of the wrong word (usually because it sounds similar to the word really intended). The word comes from Mrs Malaprop, a character in Sheridan's play *The Rivals*, who frequently uses malapropisms. Particularly ludicrous examples include:
  . . . an allegory (alligator) by the banks of the Nile;
  . . . the pineapple (pinnacle) of perfection.

Metaphor

A figure of speech in which a thing\person is described as being something\somebody else that it resembles in some way, as in:
  He is a cunning fox.
Writers make frequent use of metaphor to make their descriptions more vivid or to convey ideas in an arresting way. Metaphors can be short:
  The sands of time are running out;
  Life is not a bed of roses
or extended to form a whole poem, as in Brian Patten's *The Projectionist's Nightmare* (p 73), or even a whole novel, as in George Orwell's *Animal Farm*. But metaphors aren't just found in writing; they are all around us – particularly in the nicknames we give to people because of their personalities or their physical appearance. Mrs Thatcher's determination and grit has earned her the title of 'Iron Lady'; Joel Garner – a six foot ten inch West Indian fast bowler – is known as the 'Big Bird'.
We use **metaphorical** language (language involving metaphors) every day of our lives. Look at the following sentences that are not literally true, but use metaphors to describe an action more vividly and excitingly:
  He bulldozed his way through the crowd.
  She was rooted to the spot.
  He drove his sister up the wall.
See also **Imagery** and **Simile**.

Monologue
Speech in a play spoken by one person to himself\herself.
See **Dialogue**.

Neologism
A new word or expression, such as:
   yuppie   greenhouse effect
Once a word is no longer new, it stops being a neologism! Forty years ago the word television was a neologism.

Onomatopoeia
The imitation of sounds in words. This can include individual words like 'bang' or 'plop' which imitate the actual sound they designate, or groups of words arranged so as to imitate a particular sound, as in:
   The stuttering rifles rapid rattle . . . (Wilfred Owen)
   . . . the long ripple washing through the reeds. (Tennyson)

Paradox
A statement which appears to be contradictory, such as:
   More haste, less speed
   The child is father to the man.

Parody
A piece of writing which imitates in an exaggerated and humorous way the style of a particular writer.

Personification
The representation of an idea as a person, as in:
   Old father time;
   I met murder on the way . . . (Shelley)

Phrase
A group of words that do not make up a complete sentence.

Prologue
An introduction to a play or poem.

Proverb
A saying which expresses an idea in a brief, memorable way. For example:
   Too many cooks spoil the broth
   Still waters run deep.

Register
The type of language appropriate to a particular situation or context. When applying for a job you would write in a formal register, when talking to a friend at a party you would talk in an informal register. We use different registers to talk to diferent people. There are an enormous number of different registers. Think of the different types of language used in a weather forecast, a bedtime story, a formal report, or in the classroom, the playground, in church, at home, on the football field or in the doctor's surgery.

Simile
A figure of speech in which somebody\something is compared to some-body\something else. For instance:
   She is as good as gold;
   He is as deaf as a post.
Stale similes like these are also *Clichés*. But similes can be strikingly original and make a description vivid and exciting, as in the following:
   Cranes like tall drunks hang
     over the railway . . . (Alan Ross)

Sonnet
A poem of fourteen lines, consisting of a first part eight lines in length (the octet), and a second part six lines in length (the sestet).

Synonyms
Words with (virtually) the same meaning and use, such as:
   wed\marry   child\infant   holiday\vacation
Synonyms are not to be confused with HOMONYMS.

Syntax
The way in which words are ordered in sentences. If words are put in an unusual order – if the syntax is non-standard – it can make the meaning less clear. The following sentence has unusual and confusing syntax:
   Please follow on the packet the instructions given.
Vocabulary (sometimes called *Lexis*) is words – the component parts of the language; syntax is the way in which these words are put together to make meaningful sentences.
See **Vocabulary**.

Tautology
Use of words that express the same thing or repeat the same ideas. For instance:
   Henry II was a medieval king who ruled in the middle ages.
   This unique book is the only one of this kind.

Tense
The tense of a verb indicates when an action happens.

Tone
The character of something that is said or written. The tone of a piece could be angry, light, bitter, satirical etc.

Vocabulary
The words which make up a language. The technical term for vocabulary is *Lexis*.

Language Reference Section

Unit 5.2   Units of thought: the building blocks of writing

Words and spelling ◆ Parts of speech ◆ Sentences ◆ Punctuation ◆ The paragraph

---

Words and spelling

The simplest unit of thought is the word: DOG, ARCHITECTURE, SEX, DOOR, INSINCERITY, PIG etc. Whether the thought is a physical object or an abstract idea, there is a word for it. All the words we use have a standard spelling recorded in the dictionary, although over a period of a hundred years or so a word can change its form. If you find spelling difficult it is not a major crime; indeed, spelling mistakes rarely get in the way of communication. But poor spelling can create an unfavourable impression in the outside world because many people (ordinary people, not just teachers and professors!) consider good spelling very important. For this reason it is worth trying to get the spelling of words absolutely right. This can be done by checking words in a dictionary, asking someone else to check them for you, and by learning those common words that you frequently misspell (or is it mispell?).

Activity

Here are two passages full of words that students often misspell. Working in pairs, one person dictate the passage and the other write it down. Then swap roles. Mark each other's work, checking the correct spelling of the words in a dictionary. (The words that are frequently misspelt are in italics.)

a There was common *agreement*. The *appearance* of the *accommodation* was *disappointing*. Worse, there was *continuous* noise, and the mood of the landlord was *changeable*, there was no *separate* bathroom, and any *independent*, intelligent, reasonable person's verdict would admit that it was the most *monotonous* town on the south coast. What a place to hold a *psychology* conference. If *attendance* were not *compulsory*, he would have left *immediately*. It was no *exaggeration* to say that it was a complete *disaster*.

b It was *definitely* a *catastrophe*. The professor went out for a walk, leaving the *crescent* far behind him, wandering until his body *ached*, covering acre after acre of field. He stumbled across a *laboratory*, *apparently* part of an *efficiently* run *factory*, and was passing a pleasant moment trying to *interpret* the *emergency* regulations, when, much to his *embarrassment*, a security guard appeared. In trying to interpret his mood, he found himself waffling on about how much of a *privilege* it was to visit Mugsborough, a place famous for its *justice*, its space *programme* and its *delicious* pasties. It was a place, he heard himself saying, free from *rogues* and *tragedy*, free from attacks and *violence*, where the *residents* were *straight* and *respectable*, *unsuspicious* and *sympathetic*, *discerning* and *brilliant*. He loved the shops, full of *cameras* and *vegetables*. His *anxiety* turned him into an actor as he praised the *cleanliness* of the town, the *fluorescent* lights, the *mysterious beauties* standing on the *yachts*, the *skilful disguises* used by the police and *lawyers*. He found himself raving like a madman, telling the *security guard* of other towns he had visited where there was *disease* and *weird behaviour*, where *columns* of police *exercised* daily and the lawyers were *corrupt*, where even the *innocent* were *condemned* to stay in collapsing prisons, the walls running with *moisture*, patrolled by *foreign* warders who *quarrelled* with the prisoners and warned them to be utterly *obedient*. The guard stood *fascinated*, as this strange man told him of the *heiress* he was engaged to and the punishment he would *receive* if he was not back in his lodgings by ten o'clock.

Parts of speech

Words do different things in a sentence, and can be defined according to their function.

Technical Term	Function	Examples	Notes
NOUN	To name something.	**Door**	Nouns do not have to be physical objects that you can touch. They include 'abstract' things like 'joy' and 'politics' as well.
VERB	To express an action.	The door **opened**.	'Am', 'is', 'are', 'was', and 'were' are parts of the basic verb 'to be'. This is a basic verb that students often neglect.
ADJECTIVE	To describe a noun.	The **old** door opened.	Colours like red and green are also adjectives.
ADVERB	To describe the action expressed by the verb.	The old door opened **slowly**.	Adverbs don't all end in '-ly', but the majority do. (Words like 'soon' and 'ever' are also adverbs.)
PREPOSITION	To show the relationship between one thing and another.	A tall woman walked **through** the door.	'Above', 'below', 'in', 'out of' and 'up' are all prepositions. Many prepositions express the idea of position or movement.
CONJUNCTION	To join together different parts of a sentence.	The door opened **and** a tall woman walked in.	Other conjunctions include 'so', 'but', 'while' and 'because'.
PRONOUN	To stand instead of a noun when the noun has already appeared in the sentence or in a previous sentence.	The door creaked and I watched as **it** opened slowly.	Pronouns include 'I', 'you', 'he', 'she', 'it', 'we' and 'they'.

Note also:
- The definite article = THE
- The indefinite article = A
- Interjections = exclamations such as 'Oh!' and 'Ah!'

Sentences

A sentence is a statement that makes sense on its own. It begins with a capital letter and ends with a full stop, a question mark or an exclamation mark. In order to be complete, a sentence should usually contain a subject and a verb. A sentence can be very short, consisting only of a subject and a verb:

> He wept.

or rather longer, consisting not only of the elements above, but also of other phrases which describe, expand or qualify;

> He wept bitterly.
> He wept bitterly because his wife had left him.
> He wept bitterly because his wife, who he loved dearly, had left him.

One way of learning more about how sentences are put together is to practise joining short statements to make a more fluent piece of writing.

Activity

Combine each of the following series of statements into a single, whole sentence. Try to avoid using the word 'and'. You can leave out or add a word or two where necessary.

a He did not succeed. He was too lazy.
b Mr Nash was walking down the High Street. He saw a magnificent red pullover. It was exhibited in the window of Newstyle Ltd.
c Susan will go. Jane goes too. She likes company.
d The hikers were tired. They had walked many miles. They came at last to a Youth Hostel. The Hostel stood in spacious grounds.

Punctuation

This is the name we give to the marks put in writing to indicate the sense breaks. Punctuation helps writer structure texts to give meaning, and the messages of punctuation help readers to decode that meaning. Punctuating correctly is a way of avoiding confusion in our writing. Punctuation tells the reader how to read the text.

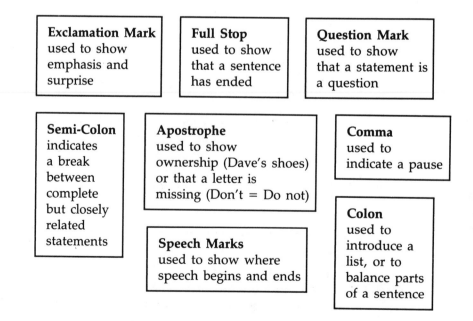

Exclamation Mark used to show emphasis and surprise

Full Stop used to show that a sentence has ended

Question Mark used to show that a statement is a question

Semi-Colon indicates a break between complete but closely related statements

Apostrophe used to show ownership (Dave's shoes) or that a letter is missing (Don't = Do not)

Comma used to indicate a pause

Colon used to introduce a list, or to balance parts of a sentence

Speech Marks used to show where speech begins and ends

In addition to these marks above, don't forget the DASH – which separates – and the HYPHEN (safety-catch) which joins, and the brackets (like these) which enclose.

When you are reading, examine the punctuation. There may be nothing remarkable about it, but there may be a noticeable use of the exclamation mark, the semi-colon, brackets or dashes. Here are three extracts in which the punctuation is noticeable.

> "Phew!" said Julian, mopping his wet forehead. "What a day! Let's go and live at the Equator – it would be cool compared to this!"
>
> He stood leaning on his bicycle, out of breath with a long steep ride up a hill. Dick grinned at him. "You're out of training, Ju!" he said. "Let's sit down for a bit and look at the view. We're pretty high up!"
>
> They leaned their bicycles against a nearby gate and sat down, their backs against the lower bars. Below them spread the Dorset countryside, shimmering in the heat of the day, the distance almost lost in a blue haze. A small breeze came wandering round, and Julian sighed in relief.
>
> "I'd never have come on this biking trip if I'd guessed it was going to be as hot as this!" he said. "Good thing Anne didn't come – she'd have given up on the first day."

> My next care was some ammunition and arms; there were two very good fowling-pieces in the great cabin, and two pistols; these I secured first, with some powder-horns, and a small bag of shot, and two old rusty swords. I knew there were three barrels of powder in the ship, but knew not where our gunner had stowed them; but with much search I found them, two of them dry and good, the third had taken water; those two I got to my raft with the arms. And now I thought myself pretty well freighted, and began to think how I should get to shore with them, having neither sail, oar, or rudder; and the least capful of wind would have overset all my navigation.

> "Heads, heads – take care of your heads!" cried the loquacious stranger, as they came out under the low archway, which in those days formed the entrance to the coach-yard. "Terrible place – dangerous work – other day – five children – mother – tall lady, eating sandwiches – forgot the arch – crash – knock – children look round – mother's head off – sandwich in her hand – no mouth to put it in – head of a family off – shocking, shocking!"

Activity   Punctuate the following, and add capital letters where necessary:

a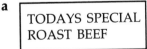

| TODAYS SPECIAL ROAST BEEF | WANT A GOOD BUY FOR SALE HONDA 500 RING 8659 | STOP CHEAP POTATOES | CUT PRICE EX SOLDIERS UNIFORMS |

b 25 armada terrace suntown the personnel manager heinz foods limited bristol dear mr knott thank you for your letter I will be pleased to attend the interview on monday 1st january yours sincerely robert elam c oh i cried stop him its black dog i dont care two coppers who he is cried silver but he hasnt paid his score harry run and catch him one of the others who was nearest the door leaped up and started in pursuit if he were admiral hawke he shall pay his score cried siler and then relinquishing my hand who did you say he was he asked black what dog sir said i has mr trelawney not told you of the buccaneers he was one of them

The paragraph

Writing is less random and more organised than speech, where we often falter, repeat ourselves and talk in incomplete sentences, sprinkled with 'erms', 'sort ofs', 'rights' and 'you knows', as in:

'I was walking down the road, right? when I saw this man, right? And he was acting, like, you know, really strangely . . .'

We can write this in a more fluent and controlled way, removing the redundant 'rights' and 'you knows'.

'I was walking down the road when I saw a man acting really strangely.'

Another way we can organise our writing is by putting groups of sentences into paragraphs. This helps the reader by breaking the text up into manageable units, and signalling to him or her that we have moved on to a new topic.

Activity

In the following piece of writing, see if you can identify the topic being explored in each paragraph.

PRESSURES ON TEENAGERS

Ever since teenagers were first identified as a recognisable group they have been under pressure: people complained about their hairstyles, their clothes, their loud music, their aggressiveness and their casual attitude to sex. Now they are still under pressure as they smoke, drink and experiment with drugs more than older age groups.

Teenage girls have become a major target for cigarette manufacturers', and in most schools and colleges it is the girls rather than the boys who, after an hour's lesson, are dying for a smoke. The brand of cigarettes called Kim advertised in girls' magazines and sponsored the tennis champion Martina Navratilova who wore their distinctive logo whenever she played championship tennis, a game watched by many teenage girls.

Another problem for teenagers is the pressure on them to drink. Many teenagers get very drunk indeed and this is not surprising since discos make most of their money not from the admission charges but from the drinks sold at the bar. If teenagers are unemployed, as many of them are, one way of passing an otherwise intolerably boring day is to spend it drinking from bottles, or cans in the town centre with their friends.

Continue this essay dealing with the following topics in separate paragraphs: a drugs; b AIDS; c unemployment. Round off the essay with a concluding paragraph in which you discuss *the future*.

Postscript: How Do You Read Me?

The last item in this book is an extract from *White Boy Running* by Christopher Hope. This is what the jacket blurb says about the book:

When the award-winning novelist Christopher Hope went back to South Africa in 1987 it was for his first real visit in twelve years, a journey to take him back into his own past and right into the heart of the present. The stimulus for the visit was the all-white election of May 1987, which confirmed Afrikaner Nationalist rule in South Africa.

This is a book about a childhood in South Africa, about growing up in an asylum which the inmates have been running for years. It's about an Irish grandfather, papist republican in the midst of red-hot Afrikaner Calvinists. It's about a journey which finds the traveller caught in a riot in Johannesburg one day and on the beach at Natal another – in South Africa even the sand is segregated. From Balfour to Pretoria, from Capetown to Soweto he criss-crosses the country, tracing and retracing his own footsteps through the cruel absurdities of a world in disarray.

In the following extract, the author describes his visit to an arts centre in Soweto, to talk about his work. During the evening, he comes to see that 'a work is capable of two very different readings' according to the cultural, political, racial and literary background of its audience.

As you read the extract, try out the reading strategies you have discovered in *Do You Read Me?*. What genre is the extract? Does the meaning work at more than one level? How? Who is the audience? What does Christopher Hope say about audiences?

White Boy Running

Christopher Hope

An invitation to read something of my work to a group in Soweto; it is to be an informal, private gathering of writers and readers. There is also to be some dancing, though its theme and nature are not revealed. Like the rest of the arrangements for the evening, they are left strategically vague.

I travel into the township at nightfall and find the arts centre where the reading is to take place already busily preparing for the night ahead. The place works hard for a living, every corner is used to offer space to dancers, actors, musicians, writers, playwrights; leotards hanging behind the door; someone practising a sax next door, the notes a smooth growl deep in the brass throat.

The seats in the small amphitheatre are taken by about seven o'clock and my audience is varied: young children, middle-aged women, and a good number of brooding young men who exude a sense of scepticism, even hostility, which their courteous attention to my opening remarks cannot disguise.

We are all aware of the strangeness of the situation. I am, in the first place, a White South African and these days Whties are not much given to visiting Soweto and sitting around with people, in any capacity. As the young playwright who introduces me explains – it seems as if there is an invisible barrier between Soweto and the City of Johannesburg which Whites will not cross. Then, too, I am a South African writer who lives a long way away and while this is, I suppose, somewhat reassuring, since it presupposes certain disagreements on my part with the way things are done in South Africa, it also means that I am going to be out of touch with the important details of everyday life, the crucial nuances which only those directly involved in the tremendous struggle now taking place can comprehend. The fact that I live abroad is double-edged; in the first place it means I am removed from direct involvement in the machinery of oppression that has put troops and armoured cars on the streets of Soweto; yet I am a White South African so my complicity is also quite apparent. But then strangeness is not something that is going to bother very many of us because it is second nature to us, in a sense we expect to be strange to each other, at odds, out of tune, out of touch, familiar gulfs and hard-won misunderstandings loom between us, and it would be very strange, after nearly half a century of policies aimed at preventing fraternisation between the races, if they did not.

The audience sit in two blocks of seats on either side of me and I sit in the corner of the room upon a low stage or dais. I begin by reading a poem, a kind of soliloquy called 'In the Middle of Nowhere', in which a speaker whom I suppose would be best described as a refined and more articulate version of the man I met in the Balfour bar, Philip of the beautiful Greek ears, who believed himself and his right-wing friends to be the future . . . The poem mimics the sense of injured benevolence and blind good sense found among many Whites who resent the rejection of their best efforts to help Blacks, to lend a hand, to supply medicines, to teach better methods of farming, and encounter the growing resentment of Black people to these charitable enterprises and their unshakeable desire to repudiate Whites and all their works and even to dream of driving them into the sea. The poem concludes with a line which might be either threat or promise: 'Dying will be the last thing we do for them'.

I never get as far as the last line. Just ten lines into the poem and I am interrupted by a suspicious questioner in the front row, a man with woolly bangs and angry eyes. He wants to know who is speaking in the poem. I sketch as best I can in outline the creature of refined paternalism, backed by the kind of murderous self-certainty that allows some people to kill, if they believe this is the only thing that will do the victim any good. But why, the questioner persists, write a poem about such a creature? So there it goes – out of the window – my poem along with what I had hoped were

carefully controlled ironies, nuances; the detached, musing tone of the speaker, and gone too was any notion that I could disclaim responsibility for the attitudes of the speaker in the poem. I had written it, had I not? There were murmurs of approval to this challenge. After all writing was a way of showing where one stood and from where the audience stood, the speaker in my poem did not deserve a line, he was the enemy, and that was the end of it.

I put the poem aside unfinished. I get the point. This is the front line and it will not do to read to front-line troops subtle analyses of the psychological perversions of the enemy.

I contemplate the rest of the reading with foreboding, this is not the usual literary evening. I move swiftly on to my novel, *The Hottentot Room*. I choose a section which describes the flight of the informer, Caleb Looper, to Berlin with the ashes of his elderly friend, Frau Katie, in a cardboard tub concealed in a shopping bag. Before I begin reading I explain very carefully where Berlin is and the way in which the city is divided by a wall into an eastern and western sector; how the eastern sector is controlled by the Russians and the western sector by the forces of Britain, France and the USA.

I remark on Looper's observation, as they drive into East Berlin with the official guide pointing out the architectural achievements of the socialist state, that he feels the place to be very like South Africa, quite uncannily like home. Immediately I am challenged again. What do I mean – like home? After all this is South Africa, and Looper is in the German Democratic Republic – surely there is no comparison? I explain that these are personal reactions and that my feeling when I visited East Germany was that the bureaucracy and tone of the party line which I encountered reminded me so much of South Africa that I felt positively homesick. A very pretty girl who does not look more than fifteen, with a severe and aggressive manner, demands to know whether perhaps the Wall is not a good thing in that it protects the integrity of East Germany. I respond by saying that I dislike intensely people who support walls, build them, or encourage their use. I say that there is no difference in the intensity of my dislike, whether measured against the monstrosity in Berlin or its little brother down the road in their own backyard, and I jerk a thumb over my shoulder. Again a ripple of laughter and I get the chance to press on with the story. I tell how Looper arrives amid a snow storm at the memorial to the Russian dead, one of the stops on the trip, and how he is confronted by someone who had been pursuing him throughout the book and whom he was sure he had escaped, a large, enigmatic Zulu who has been ordered by his masters in the South African Government to get Looper home at all costs, and in any condition.

There is consternation at the mention of the Zulu, mixed with close interest. Why is he a Zulu? What is he wearing? Why is he working for the South African Government? The mention of the Zulu in this company raised a real issue, one that I did not envisage in such sharpness. I used the Zulu because Zulus are an ambiguous force today in South Africa; at once the largest of all the Black groups, they outnumber all others and uncertainty about their precise political status in the struggle for freedom, symbolised in the ambiguous position of their leader Chief Mangosuthu Buthelezi, is of enormous concern and interest to Black radicals, and to many others. In this company the huge, urbane, anonymous, beautifully groomed Zulu who hunts the renegade White agent Looper takes on an importance never intended in the novel, but then, as I discovered earlier with my poem, a work is capable of two very different readings – one which is merely literary and the other which is felt in the flesh. More than that, what is happening here is that my novel is being written by the audience, a task in which I am invited to join by way of speculating on the reasons behind the Zulu's treachery, on what action might be taken against him and how Looper might outsmart his pursuer. My novel becomes more novel by the minute. A more conventional audience would not put these questions. A more pedantic author might reply loftily; 'What I have written, I have written!' But this is no place for pedantry.

Again I take the chance offered to continue the story and read the sections in which Looper does find a last, desperate way to escape the indefatigable Zulu, and how he dies in the snow, but not before scattering the ashes of his old friend, Frau Katie, upon German soil. In doing so he carries out a solemn promise, finally but imperfectly. The German Jewess has come back to Berlin.

Again a challenge: home is home and a promise is a promise. If Looper has not found the very spot where Frau Katie once lived before the German madness set in, then he has failed in this promise. I reply that he has done his best; Looper feels that Frau Katie will have understood why he was unable to fulfil his vow to the letter. But how could he *know* she would understand since Frau Katie is dead? Because the old lady had been through something very similar herself, as a Jew hunted by the Gestapo, and had predicted that Looper would one day be confronted by his pursuers and would have to find a way of escaping them. But Looper was dead, wasn't he? Yes, Looper was dead, but he was also free; he had outwitted and outsmarted his pursuers by taking the only road he knew they could not follow him down. And he had come as close as possible to returning his friend to her home.

So then Looper was not in the end a traitor? demands the brooding young man who had challenged me earlier. No, perhaps not. Now the photographer puts down his camera and becomes one of the audience. Had I perhaps recognised the African connotations of my book, particularly in the relationship between Looper and Frau Katie, because his understanding of her, even after her death, suggested a kind of ancestral loyalty? No, I confess that this has not occurred to me but I am grateful for the comparison; although my book is set a long way away, in England and Germany, it is, I hope, an African novel. But what would have happened if Looper had escaped? asks the nurse; what sort of end would I have imagined for him then? Was there any chance of reconciliation with the Zulu? After all, it was not enmity but solidarity which one prayed for. Certainly it was, but I was unable to imagine any end for Looper other than the one I had written.

Though I feel unable to do so, this does not stop members of the audience, now that they have a firm, even an obsessive, grip on the story, from suggesting a variety of other resolutions to the novel which has never occurred to me. I thank these other writers of a book other than mine for their suggestions, grateful that the mood of the evening has changed from hostility and impatience to a far more cordial encounter, the price for this being that my listeners have taken over, my novel is no longer my property.

What more could a writer ask? I do not think I have experienced as much pleasure, or trepidation, since I managed to amuse and intrigue my friends thirty years before, in my hostel days, when getting people who believed that reading was bad for the eyes, or grew hair on their hands, to pick their way through twenty lines of closely worked rhyming couplets, not because they cared a hoot for something called poetry, or even because they enjoyed seeing justice done to themselves and vengeance wreaked upon enemies and considered themselves the only appropriate judges of such pleasures and rewards, but because they appreciated an accurate depiction of themselves and their world.

Activities

You may find the following questions, comments and suggestions helpful when you think in detail about this piece.

Understanding

1. What do we learn about the author, Christopher Hope?
2. What do we learn about his audience?
3. What do we learn about his poetry?
4. What do we learn about his novel?
5. What does Christopher Hope learn about his audience's reaction to his novel?

Response

This experience gave the writer great pleasure and satisfaction, tinged with fear. Write an account of the experience which has given you most pleasure in the past few years. Plan your response.

Language

Words activity

In groups of four, each person select 10 unfamiliar words from the passage. Write them down, cut them out, and drop them face down on a desk. Pick up any five words from the pile and find them in the passage. Then explain to the other members of the group what these words mean. If you do not know, check the meanings in a dictionary.

Sentences

In the middle section of the passage (page 242) there are many short sentences:

'I get the point'
'Immediately I am challenged again'
'What do I mean, like home?'

The passage ends with a single, very long, sentence (over 100 words long!). What is the effect of these changes in sentence length? What pattern can you see to the sentence lengths?

Paragraphs

Do some paragraphs have more short sentences than others? If so, can you see why?

A changing world

Research

Christopher Hope refers to two places that are either changing or resisting change: East Germany and South Africa. Find out what is happening in these two places now, by watching the news and reading newspapers. Then find out something about the history of these two countries by consulting an encyclopaedia. Write an article of 400–500 words for the *TV Times* to go with a programme comparing the situation in the two countries. Your article should consider both the history of the countries and their current situation.

Talk

What is privacy and do we need it? Do we need:

Rooms which we can call our own? Walls or fences around our gardens? Borders between countries?

Assignment

Apart from political upheaval in Eastern Europe, the other great change predicted for the 1990s is the Green Revolution. What does the phrase mean?

Produce a booklet or information pack to display in your local public library. The materials should try to explain 'The Green Revolution' and give some local examples of 'Green' activities. The booklet or pack can include pictures, newspaper cuttings, your own writing, letters to organisations and the replies, questionnaires and their results, a tape with interviews and transcripts.

Further reading

Christopher Hope has written a number of books. You will probably find them in your local library. His short story 'Learning to Fly' is in *Contemporary Stories 2* edited by Nick Jones, published by OUP.

Many other writers have used South Africa as a setting for their writing, including H Rider Haggard, Olive Schreiner, Bessie Head, Beverley Naidoo, Nadine Gordimer and Andre Brink. You could read a range of South African writing; and try to find out if it has any distinctive features.

Here are the next two frames of the cartoon strip that began in Unit 2.1 (p 23). Did you expect the story to go on like this? The pictures come from an Evangelical Christian booklet. What do you now think will happen next?

Acknowledgements

The author and publishers wish to thank the following for permission to reproduce copyright material:

Edward Albee for extracts from *Who's Afraid of Virginia Woolf?* published by Jonathan Cape Ltd. W.H. Allen & Co plc for 'Dumb Insolence' by Adrian Mitchell; and for an extract from *The World is Full of Married Men* by Jackie Collins. Apple Computers for the 'Coca Cola' advertisement (p 50). Bantam Books for extracts from *Dancing in the Dark* by Carolyn Ross. BBC Enterprises Ltd for 'Frying Eggs' from *Delia Smith's Complete Cookery Course*, Part 1. Bella Magazine for *Neighbour in Distress* by D Ann Graham. Blackie and Son Ltd for 'Creation Story' from *Worlds of Difference* by M Palmer and E Bissett, published by Blackie and Son Ltd, Glasgow and London. BMP Davidson Pearce for photographs on p 5. Curtis Brown Ltd for 'Mother's Nerves' by X J Kennedy, from *One Winter Night in August*. BTA Studycards for 'Animal Welfare' © British Trades Alphabet, 1987. Cambridge University Press for an extract from the acting version of *Gregory's Girl* by A Bethell; for an extract from *Three Minute Heroes* by Leslie Stewart; and for 'Making a Film for Television' from *Flying Into the Wind* by David Leland. Camp America, American Institute for Foreign Study, for the Camp America application form. Jonathan Cape Ltd for 'A Nooligan' from *In the Glassroom* by Roger McGough; and for an extract from *Thunderball* by Ian Fleming. Centerprize Trust for 'Wha Happen Black Girl' by Angela Mars. Central Statistical Office for leisure activities information. Century Hutchinson Publishing Ltd for 'Beezley Street' from *Ten Years in an Open-Necked Shirt* by John Cooper Clark; and for an extract from *The Day of the Triffids* by John Wyndham. Chatto and Windus Ltd for 'Tiger' by Leslie Norris; and for an extract from *The Dark is Rising* by Susan Cooper. Chick Publications for cartoon frames from *The Sissy*? Rex Collings for 'Long Distance' from *Continuous* by T Harrison. Stanley Cook for 'Chips' from *Come Along: Poems for Younger Children* by Stanley Cook. André Deutsch Ltd for an extract from *My Mate Shofiq* by Jan Needle. *Exeter Express and Echo* for articles first published in 1987 and for 'Where the drinkers live'. Extracts from the Authorized King James Version of the Bible, the rights of which are vested in the Crown in perpetuity within the United Kingdom, are reproduced by permission of Eyre and Spottiswoode Publisher, Her Majesty's Printers, London. Faber and Faber Ltd for 'An Advancement of Learning' from *Death of a Naturalist* by Seamus Heaney; for 'Reading Scheme' from *Making Cocoa for Kingsley Amis* by Wendy Cope; for 'Roger the Dog' from *What is the truth*? by Ted Hughes; and for an extract from *Lord of the Flies* by William Golding. Roy Fuller for 'In the Bathroom' by Roy Fuller, from *A Second Poetry Book*, published by André Deutsch Ltd. Victor Gollancz Ltd for an extract from *The Chocolate War* by Robert Cormier; for 'Rythm' from *Love Poems and Elegies* by Iain Crichton Smith; for an extract from *Ruby* by Rosa Guy; for an extract from *Roll of Thunder Hear Me Cry* by Mildred Taylor; and for an extract from *Z for Zachariah* by Robert C O'Brien. Grafton Books for jacket material for *Brave New World* by Aldous Huxley, and *The Ragged-Trousered Philanthropists* by Robert Tressell. The *Guardian* for 'Coming to the end of a chapter' by Richard Bourne; for 'Dog Fight 1', first published 30.7.85; and for 'Pupils take pub and homework in moderation'. Gregory Harrison for 'Distracted the mother said to her boy' from *A Fourth Poetry Book*, published by Oxford University Press. Rupert Hart-Davis Ltd for 'Abersoch' by R S Thomas. Health Education Authority for 'The Drug Problem', 1987. Heinemann Ltd for an extract from *Brighton Rock* by Graham Greene. Her Majesty's Stationery Office for an extract from the Register of Electors, 1988; and for 'Your home' from *Practical Ways to Prevent Crime*. David Higham Associates Ltd for 'One Less Octopus at Paxos' by Russell Hoban, first published in *Granta 10* by Penguin Books Ltd; for 'One Flesh' and 'Poem Simply' from *Collected Poems* by Elizabeth Jennings, published by Macmillan Ltd; and for 'Orders of the Day' by John Cunliffe, from *A Second Poetry Book*, published by Oxford University Press; The Hogarth Press for an extract from *Cider with Rosie* by Laurie Lee. Island Music Ltd for 'The Harder they Come' by Jimmy Cliff. The *Independent* for 'Trouble up the Volga' by William Hartson, 11/2/89. P D James for extracts from a lecture given to the Royal Society of Arts. The *Listener* for 'The Old Couple' by F Pratt Green, first printed 27.4.64. Liz Lochhead for 'Poem for my Sister' from *Dreaming Frankenstein*, published by Polygon. Academic and Scientific Division, Longman Group plc for the cover of *Writing a Thesis* by George Watson. James MacGibbon for 'Not Waving but Drowning' by Stevie Smith, from *The Collected Poems of Stevie Smith*, published by Penguin Books. Wes Magee, the author, for 'Pig Farm Supreme'. Methuen Ltd for an extract from *A Taste of Honey* by Shelagh Delaney; Methuen Children's Books for 'The Birthday Present' by Marjorie Darke, from *The Methuen Book of Strange Tales*, ed Jean Russell; Methuen London for an extract from *Educating Rita* by Willy Russell. Mills and Boon Ltd for an extract from *Cage of Ice* by Sally Wentworth. The National Film Archive for stills from *The Big Sleep* and *Wuthering Heights*, used on the cover. The National Portrait Gallery for 'St George and the Dragon', Ucello. The News on Sunday for 'Little Phony Bashes the Beano'. The estate of the late Sonia Brownell Orwell and Martin Secker and Warburg for extracts from *1984* and from *Why I Write*, by George Orwell. Oval Projects Limited for extracts from the Cartoon *Macbeth*, published by Oval Projects in the UK and Greenhouse Publications in Australia. Oxfam for 'You can help along the road to survival'. Pan Books Ltd for the jacket of *The World is Full of Married Men* by Jackie Collins; and for an extract from *The Name is Zero*, by Lorna Reed. Penguin Books Ltd for 'Dream Interpretations' from the *Penguin Dictionary of Psychology*; for 'Kids Stuff', Bernard Ashley; and for 'The Song of the Whale' from *Hot Dog and Other Poems* by Kit Wright (Kestrel Books, 1981) © Kit Wright, 1981. Perkins/Carlin Music for *Blue Suede Shoes* by Carl Perkins. Peterloo Poets for 'Not my best side' by Ursula Fanthorpe, first published in *Side Effects* (Peterloo Poets, 1978) and reprinted in *Selected Poems* (Peterloo Poets, 1986). Peters, Fraser and Dunlop Group Ltd for an extract from *Unreliable Memoirs* by Clive James, published by Jonathan Cape Ltd; and for 'True Romance' by Jane Rogers, published in *Spare Rib*. The Post Office for 'Night Mail' by W H Auden. Alan Ross for 'Night Patrol' from *Night Patrol: poems 1942-1967* by Alan Ross, published by Eyre and Spottiswoode Ltd. Sackett and Marshall Ltd for 'How we see' from *The Doom Machine*. Schofield and Sims Ltd for an extract from *A Basic Dictionary*. Richard Scott Simon Ltd for an extract from *A Bit of Singing and Dancing* by Susan Hill. Rogers, Coleridge and White Ltd for 'Roots' from *Awapbopalopbop Alopbamboom* by Nik Cohn. Royal Society for the Prevention of Cruelty to Animals – photograph (p 5). See 4 Publications for 'No Pub in Brookside Close' by Stuart Doughty. Secker and Warburg Ltd for an extract from *White Boy Running* by Christopher Hope. The Society of Authors as the Literary Representative of the Estate of John Masefield for 'Sea Fever' by John Masefield. Star Books Ltd for an extract from *Gregory's Girl* by G Cole. Syndication International Ltd for 'Is Your Daughter Being Brainwashed?' *Daily Mirror*, 1986. Times Newspapers Ltd for 'An exhilarating view of teenage fantasy life' by David Robinson, from *The Times* 5.6.81. G Topping for book jacket photographs and for 'photostory' (p 205). Transworld Publishers Ltd for jacket material from *Catch 22* by Joseph Heller. Harvey Unna and Stephen Durbridge Ltd for 'Yosser's Story' from *Boys from the Blackstuff* by Alan Bleasdale. Unwin Hyman Ltd for 'The Projectionist's Nightmare' from *Little Johnny's Confession* by Brian Patten. Viking Penguin Inc for jacket material for *The Baby in the Icebox*. Virago Press for 'Still I rise' by Maya Angelou. Warner Chappell Music Ltd for 'Africa' by Peter Tosh. A P Watt Ltd on behalf of the Executors of the Estate of Robert Graves for 'Love Without Hope' from *Collected Poems, 1975* by Robert Graves, published by Cassell plc. The Women's Press Ltd for an extract from *French Letters* by Eileen Fairweather.

The publishers have made every effort to trace and contact copyright holders, but this has not always been possible. We apologise for any errors or omissions in the above list and would be grateful for notification of any corrections that should be incorporated in future editions of this book.